How to
Tell Stories
to Children

Sara Cone Bryant

How to Tell Stories to Children

SOPHIA INSTITUTE PRESS®
Manchester, New Hampshire

Sophia Institute Press®
Box 5284, Manchester, NH 03108
1-800-888-9344
www.sophiainstitute.com

Library of Congress Cataloging-in-Publication Data

Bryant, Sara Cone, 1873-
  How to tell stories to children / Sara Cone Bryant.
    p. cm.
  Originally published: London : George G. Harrap and Co., 1910.
  Includes bibliographical references.
  ISBN 978-1-933184-34-0 (pbk. : alk. paper)
  1. Storytelling. 2. Activity programs in education. I. Title.
  LB1042.B7 2008
  372.67′7 — dc22
                                                          2008002191

08 09 10 11 12   10 9 8 7 6 5 4 3 2 1

*To my mother,
the first, best storyteller*

Contents

⤚

Stories Selected and Adapted for Telling

Kindergarten and Grade 1

Poems

Preface

The stories that are given in the following pages are, for the most part, those I have found to be best liked by the children to whom I have told these and others. I have tried to reproduce the form in which I actually tell them — although that inevitably varies with every repetition — feeling that it would be of greater value to another storyteller than a more closely literary form.

For the same reason, I have confined my statements of theory as to method to those which reflect my own experience; my "rules" were drawn from introspection and retrospection, at the urging of others, long after the instinctive method they exemplify had become habitual.

These facts are the basis of my hope that this book may be of use to those who have much to do with children.

S.C.B.

Introduction

Not long ago, I chanced to open a magazine at a story of Italian life that dealt with a curious popular custom. It told of the love of the people for the performances of a strangely clad, periodically appearing old man who was a professional storyteller. This old man repeated whole cycles of myth and serials of popular history, holding his audience-chamber in whatever corner of the open court or square he happened upon, and always surrounded by an eager crowd of listeners. So great was the respect in which the storyteller was held, that any interruption was likely to be resented with violence.

As I read of the absorbed silence and the changing expressions of the crowd around the old man, I was suddenly reminded of a company of people I had recently seen. They were gathered in one of the parlors of a women's college, and their serious young faces had, habitually, none of the childlike responsiveness of the Italian populace; they were suggestive, rather, of a daily experience that precluded over-much surprise or curiosity about anything. In the midst of the group stood a frail-looking woman with bright eyes. She was telling a story, a children's story, about a good and a bad little mouse.

She had been asked to do that thing for a purpose, and she did it therefore. But it was easy to see from the expressions of the listeners how trivial a thing it seemed to them.

That was at first. But presently the room grew quieter, and yet quieter. The faces relaxed into amused smiles, sobered in unconscious sympathy, and finally broke in ripples of mirth. The storyteller had come to her own.

The memory of the college girls listening to the mouse story brought other memories with it. Many a swift composite view of faces passed before my mental vision, faces with the child's look on them, yet not the faces of children. And of the occasions to which the faces belonged, those were most vivid which were earliest in my experience. For it was those early experiences that first made me realize the modern possibilities of the old, old art of telling stories.

It had become a part of my work, some years ago, to give English lectures on German literature. Many of the members of my class were unable to read in the original the works with which I dealt, and as these were modern works, it was rarely possible to obtain translations. For this reason, I gradually formed the habit of telling the story of the drama or novel in question before passing to a detailed consideration of it. I enjoyed this part of the lesson exceedingly, but it was some time before I realized how much the larger part of the lesson it had become to the class. They were mature women, and they used to wait for the story as if it were a sugarplum and they, children; and to grieve openly if it were omitted. Substitution of reading from a translation was greeted with precisely the same abatement of eagerness that a child shows when he has asked you to tell a story, and you offer, instead, to "read one from the pretty book." And so general and constant were the tokens of enjoyment that there could ultimately be no doubt of the power that the mere storytelling exerted.

The attitude of the grown-up listeners did but illustrate the general difference between the effect of telling a story and of reading one. Everyone who knows children well has felt the difference.

With few exceptions, children listen twice as eagerly to a story told as to one read, and even a "recitation" or a so-called "reading" has not the charm for them that the person wields who can "tell a story." And there are sound reasons for their preference.

The great difference, including lesser ones, between telling and reading is that the teller is free; the reader is bound. The book in hand, or the wording of it in mind, binds the reader. The story-teller is bound by nothing; he stands or sits, free to watch his audience, free to follow or lead every changing mood, free to use body, eyes, and voice as aids in expression. Even his mind is unbound, because he lets the story come in the words of the moment, being so full of what he has to say. For this reason, a story told is more spontaneous than one read, however well read. And, consequently, the connection with the audience is closer, more electric, than is possible when the book or its wording intervenes.

Beyond this advantage is the added charm of the personal element in storytelling. When you make a story your own and tell it, the listener gets the story, *plus your appreciation of it*. It comes to him filtered through your own enjoyment. That is what makes the funny story thrice funnier on the lips of a jolly raconteur than in the pages of a memoir. It is the filter of personality. Everybody has something of the curiosity of the primitive man concerning his neighbor; what another has in his own person felt and done has an especial hold on each one of us. The most cultured of audiences will listen to the personal reminiscences of an explorer with a different tingle of interest from that which it feels for a scientific lecture on the results of the exploration. The longing for the personal in experience is a very human longing. And this instinct or longing is especially strong in children. It finds expression in their delight in tales of what Father or Mother did when they were little, of what happened to Grandmother when she went on a journey, and so on, but it also extends to stories that are not in themselves personal: that take their personal savor merely from the fact that they flow from the lips in spontaneous, homely phrases, with an appreciative gusto that suggests participation.

The greater ease in holding the attention of children is, for teachers, a sufficient practical reason for telling stories rather than reading them. It is incomparably easier to make the necessary exertion of "magnetism," or whatever it may be called, when nothing else distracts the attention. One's eyes meet the children's gaze naturally and constantly; one's expression responds to and initiates theirs without effort; the connection is immediate. For the ease of the teacher, then, no less than for the joy of the children, may the art of storytelling be urged as pre-eminent over the art of reading.

It is a very old, very beautiful art. Merely to think of it carries our imaginary vision to scenes of glorious and touching antiquity. The tellers of the stories of which Homer's *Iliad* was compounded; the transmitters of the legend and history that make up the *Gesta Romanorum*; the traveling raconteurs whose brief heroic tales are woven into our own national epic; the grannies of age-old tradition whose stories are parts of Celtic folklore, of Germanic myth, of Asiatic wonder-tales — these are but younger brothers and sisters to the generations of storytellers whose inventions are but vaguely outlined in resultant forms of ancient literatures, and the names of whose tribes are no longer even guessed.

There was a time when storytelling was the chief of the arts of entertainment; kings and warriors could ask for nothing better; serfs and children were satisfied with nothing less. In all times, there have been occasional revivals of this pastime, and in no time has the art died out in the simple human realms of which mothers are queens. But perhaps never, since the really old days, has storytelling so nearly reached a recognized level of dignity as a legitimate and general art of entertainment as now.

Its present popularity seems in a way to be an outgrowth of the recognition of its educational value, which was given impetus by the German pedagogues of Froebel's school. That recognition has, at all events, been a noticeable factor in educational conferences of late. The function of the story is no longer considered solely in the light of its place in the kindergarten; it is being sought in the first, the second, and indeed in every grade where the children are still children. Sometimes the demand for stories is made solely in the interests of literary culture, sometimes in far ampler and vaguer relations, ranging from inculcation of scientific fact to admonition of moral theory; but whatever the reason given, the conclusion is the same: tell the children stories.

Many a teacher cheerfully accepts the idea of instilling concepts and ideals in the pupil via the charming tale. But in deciding which concepts and ideals to present by which tale, and how, the average teacher sometimes finds her cheerfulness displaced by a sense of inadequacy to the situation.

People who have always told stories to children, who do not know when they began or how they do it; whose heads are stocked with the accretions of years of fairyland-dwelling and nonsense-sharing — these cannot understand the perplexity of one to whom the gift and the opportunity have not "come natural." But there are many who can understand it, personally and all too well. To these, the teachers who have not a knack for storytelling, who feel as shy as their own youngest scholar at the thought of it, who do not know where the good stories are, or which ones are easy to tell, it is my earnest hope that the following pages will bring something definite and practical in the way of suggestion and reference.

How to
Tell Stories
to Children

Chapter 1

The Purpose of Storytelling in Education

Let us first consider together the primary matter of the *aim* in educational storytelling. On our conception of this must depend very largely all decisions as to choice and method; and nothing in the whole field of discussion is more vital than a just and sensible notion of this first point. What shall we attempt to accomplish by stories in the schoolroom? What can we reasonably expect to accomplish? And what, of this, is best accomplished by this means and no other?

These are questions that become the more interesting and practical because the recent access of enthusiasm for stories in education has led many people to claim very wide and very vaguely outlined territory for their possession, and often to lay heaviest stress on their least essential functions. The most important instance of this is the fervor with which many compilers of stories for school use have directed their efforts solely toward illustration of natural phenomena. Geology, zoology, botany, and even physics are taught by means of more or less happily constructed narratives based on the simpler facts of these sciences. Kindergarten teachers are familiar with such narratives: the little stories of chrysalis-breaking, flower-growth, and the like. Now, this is a perfectly proper and practicable aim, but it is not a primary one. Others, to which, at best, this is but secondary, should have first place and receive greatest attention.

What is a story, essentially? Is it a textbook of science, an appendix to the geography, an introduction to the primer of history? Of course it is not. A story is essentially and primarily a work of art, and its chief function must be sought in the line of the uses of art. Just as the drama is capable of secondary uses, yet fails abjectly to realize its purpose when those are substituted for its real significance as a work of art, so does the story lend itself to subsidiary purposes, but claims first and most strongly to be recognized in its real significance as a work of art. Since the drama deals with life in all its parts, it can exemplify sociological theory, it can illustrate economic principle, it can even picture politics; but the drama that does only these things has no breath of its real life in its being and dies when the wind of popular tendency veers from its direction. So, you can teach a child interesting facts about bees and butterflies by telling him certain stories, and you can open his eyes to colors and processes in nature by telling certain others; but unless you do something more than that and before that, you are as one who should use the Venus of Milo for a demonstration in anatomy.

The message of the story is the message of beauty, as effective as that message in marble or paint. Its part in the economy of life is *to give joy*. And the purpose and working of the joy is found in that quickening of the spirit which answers every perception of the truly beautiful in the arts of man. To give joy; in and through the joy, to stir and feed the life of the spirit: is not this the legitimate function of the story in education?

Because I believe it to be such, not because I ignore the value of other uses, I venture to push aside all aims that seem secondary to this for later mention under specific heads. Here in the beginning of our consideration, I wish to emphasize this element alone. A story is a work of art. Its greatest use to the child is in the everlasting appeal of beauty by which the soul of man is constantly pricked to new hungers, quickened to new perceptions, and so given desire to grow.

The obvious practical bearing of this is that storytelling is first of all an art of entertainment; as with the stage, its immediate purpose is the pleasure of the hearer — his pleasure, not his instruction, first.

Now, the storyteller who has given the listening children such pleasure as I mean may or may not have added a fact to the content of their minds; she has inevitably added something to the vital powers of their souls. She has given a wholesome exercise to the emotional muscles of the spirit, has opened up new windows to the imagination, and has added some line or color to the ideal of life and art that is always taking form in the heart of a child. She has, in short, accomplished the one greatest aim of storytelling: to enlarge and enrich the child's spiritual experience, and stimulate healthy reaction upon it.

Of course, this result cannot be seen and proved as easily and early as can the apprehension of a fact. The most we can hope to recognize is its promise, and this is found in the tokens of that genuine pleasure which is itself the means of accomplishment. It is, then, the signs of right pleasure that the storyteller must look to for her guide, and which it must be her immediate aim to evoke. As for the recognition of the signs, no one who has ever seen the delight of a real child over a real story can fail to know the signals when given, or flatter himself into belief in them when absent.

Intimately connected with the enjoyment given are two very practically beneficial results the storyteller may hope to obtain, and at least one of which will be a kind of reward to her. The first is a relaxation of the tense schoolroom atmosphere, valuable for its refreshing recreative power. The second result, or aim, is not so obvious, but is even more desirable; it is this: storytelling is at once one of the simplest and quickest ways of establishing a happy relationship between teacher and children, and one of the most effective methods of forming the habit of fixed attention in the latter.

If you have never seen an indifferent child aroused or a hostile one conquered to affection by a beguiling tale, you can hardly appreciate the truth of the first statement; but nothing is more familiar in the storyteller's experience. An amusing, but (to me) touching experience recently reaffirmed in my mind this power of the story to establish friendly relations.

My three-year-old niece, who had not seen me since her babyhood, being told that Aunt Sara was coming to visit her, somehow confused the expected guest with a more familiar aunt, my sister. At the sight of me, her rush of welcome relapsed into a puzzled and hurt withdrawal, which yielded to no explanations or proffers of affection. All the first day, she followed me about at a wistful distance, watching me as if I might at any moment turn into the well-known and beloved relative I ought to have been. Even by undressing time, I had not progressed far enough to be allowed intimate approach to small sacred nightgowns and diminutive shirts. The next morning, when I opened the door of the nursery, where her maid was brushing her hair, the same dignity radiated from the little round figure perched on its high chair, the same almost hostile shyness gazed at me from the great expressive eyes. Obviously, it was time for something to be done.

Disregarding my lack of invitation, I drew up a stool and, seating myself opposite the small, unbending person, began in a conversational murmur: "M — , I guess those are tingly-tanglies up there in that curl Lottie's combing; did you ever hear about the tingly-tanglies? They live in little girls' hair, and they aren't any bigger than *that*, and when anybody tries to comb the hair, they curl both weeny legs round, *so*, and hold on tight with both weeny hands, *so*, and won't let go!" As I paused, my niece made an odd little sound indicative of query battling with reserve. I pursued the subject: "They like best to live right over a little girl's ear, or down in her neck, because it is easier to hang on there; tingly-tanglies are very smart indeed."

"What's ti-ly-ta-lies?" asked a curious, guttural little voice.

I explained the nature and genesis of tingly-tanglies, as revealed to me some decades before by my inventive mother and proceeded to develop their simple adventures. When next I paused, the small guttural voice demanded, "Say more," and I joyously obeyed.

When the curls were all curled and the last little button buttoned, my baby niece climbed hastily down from her chair, and deliberately up into my lap. With a caress rare to her habit, she spoke my name, slowly and tentatively, "An-ty Sai-ry?" Then, in an assured tone, "Anty Sairy, I love you so much I don't know what to do!" And, presently, tucking a confiding hand in mine to lead me to breakfast, she explained sweetly, "I didn' know you when you comed las' night, but now I know you all th' time!"

"Oh, blessed tale," thought I, "so easy a passport to a confidence so desired, so complete!" Never had the witchery of the story to the ear of a child come more closely home to me. But the fact of the witchery was no new experience. The surrender of the natural child to the storyteller is as absolute and invariable as that of a devotee to the priest of his own sect.

This power is especially valuable in the case of children whose natural shyness has been augmented by a rough environment or by the strangeness of foreign habit. And with such children, even more than with others, it is also true that the story is a simple and effective means of forming the habit of concentration, of fixed attention; any teacher who deals with this class of children knows the difficulty of doing this fundamental and indispensable thing, and the value of any practical aid in doing it.

How to Tell Stories to Children

More than one instance of the power of storytelling to develop attentiveness comes to my mind, but the most prominent in memory is a rather recent incident, in which the actors were boys and girls far past the child-stage of docility.

I had been asked to tell stories to about sixty boys and girls of a club; the president warned me in her invitation that the children were exceptionally undisciplined, but my previous experiences with similar gatherings led me to interpret her words with a moderation that left me totally unready for the reality. When I faced my audience, I saw a squirming jumble of faces, backs of heads, and the various members of many small bodies — not a person in the room was paying the slightest attention to me. The president's introduction could scarcely be said to succeed in interrupting the interchange of social amenities that was in progress, and which looked delusively like a free fight.

I came as near stage fright in the first minutes of that occasion as it is comfortable to be, and if it had not been impossible to run away, I think I should not have remained. But I began, with as funny a tale as I knew, following the safe plan of not speaking very loudly, and aiming my effort at the nearest children. As I went on, a very few faces held intelligently to mine; the majority answered only fitfully; and not a few of my hearers conversed with their neighbors as if I were nonexistent.

The sense of bafflement, the futile effort, forced the perspiration to my hands and face — yet something in the faces before me told me that it was no ill-will that fought against me; it was the apathy of minds without the power or habit of concentration, unable to follow a sequence of ideas any distance, and rendered more restless by bodies that were probably uncomfortable, certainly undisciplined.

The first story took ten minutes. When I began a second, a very short one, the initial work had to be done all over again, for the slight comparative quiet I had won had been totally lost in the resulting manifestation of approval.

At the end of the second story, the room was really orderly to the superficial view, but where I stood, I could see the small boy who deliberately made a hideous face at me each time my eyes met his, the two girls who talked with their backs turned, the squirms of a figure here and there.

It seemed so disheartening a record of failure that I hesitated much to yield to the uproarious request for a third story, but finally I did begin again, on a very long story that, for its own sake, I wanted them to hear.

This time, the little audience settled to attention almost at the opening words. After about five minutes, I was suddenly conscious of a sense of ease and relief, a familiar restful feeling in the atmosphere; and then, at last, I knew that my audience was "with me," that they and I were interacting without obstruction. Absolutely quiet, entirely unconscious of themselves, the boys and girls were responding to every turn of the narrative as easily and readily as any group of story-bred kindergarten children. From then on, we had a good time together.

The process that took place in that small audience was a condensed example of what one may expect in habitual storytelling to a group of children. Once having had the attention chained by crude force of interest, the children begin to expect something interesting from the teacher, and to wait for it. And having been led, step by step, from one grade of a logical sequence to another, their minds — at first beguiled by the fascination of the steps — glide into the habit of following any logical sequence.

My club formed its habit, as far as I was concerned, all in one session; the ordinary demands of school procedure lengthen the process, but the result is equally sure. By the end of a week in which the children have listened happily to a story every day, the habit of listening and deducing has been formed, and the expectation of pleasantness is connected with the opening of the teacher's lips.

These two benefits are well worth the trouble they cost, and for these two, at least, any teacher who tells a story well may confidently look: the quick gaining of a confidential relationship with the children, and the gradual development of concentration and interested attention in them.

These are direct and somewhat clearly discernible results, comfortably placed in a near future. There are other aims, reaching on into the far, slow modes of psychological growth, that must equally determine the choice of the storyteller's material and inform the spirit of her work. These other, less immediately attainable ends, I wish now to consider in relation to the different types of story by which they are severally best served.

The Fairytale

First, unbidden claimant of attention, comes the Fairytale. No one can think of a child and a story without thinking of the Fairytale. Is this, as some would have us believe, a bad habit of an ignorant old world? Or can the Fairytale justify her popularity with truly edifying and educational results? Is she a proper person to introduce here, and what are her titles to merit?

Oh dear, yes! Dame Fairytale comes bearing a magic wand in her wrinkled old fingers, with one wave of which she summons up that very spirit of joy which it is our chief effort to invoke. She raps smartly on the door, and *open sesames* echo to every imagination. Her red-heeled shoes twinkle down an endless lane of adventures, and every real child's footsteps quicken after. She is the natural, own great-grandmother of every child in the world, and her pocketfuls of treasures are his by right of inheritance. Shut her out, and you truly rob the children of something that is theirs; something marking their constant kinship with the children of the past, and adapted to their needs as it was to those of the generation of long ago! If there were no other criterion at all, it would be enough that the children love the fairytale; we give them fairy stories, first, because they like them. But that by no means lessens the importance of the fact that fairytales are also good for them.

How good? In various ways. First, perhaps, in their supreme power of presenting truth through the guise of images. This is the way the child took toward wisdom, and it is the way each child's individual instinct takes, after him. Elemental truths of moral law and general types of human experience are presented in the fairy-tale, in the poetry of their images, and although the child is aware only of the image at the time, the truth enters with it and becomes a part of his individual experience, to be recognized in its relations at a later stage. Every truth and type so given broadens and deepens the capacity of the child's inner life and adds an element to the store from which he draws his moral inferences.

The most familiar instance of a moral truth conveyed under a fairy-story image is probably the story of the pure-hearted and loving girl whose lips were touched with the wonderful power of dropping jewels with every spoken word, while her stepsister, whose heart was infested with malice and evil desires, let ugly toads fall from her mouth whenever she spoke. I mention the old tale because there is probably not one of my readers who has not heard it in childhood, and because there are undoubtedly many to whose mind it has often recurred in later life as a sadly perfect presentment of the fact that "out of the abundance of the heart the mouth speaketh."[1] That story has entered into the forming consciousness of many of us, with its implications of the inevitable

---

[1] Matt. 12:34.

result of visible evil from evil in the heart, and its revelation of the loathsomeness of evil itself.

And no less truly than this story has served to many as an embodiment of moral law has another household tale stood for a type of common experience. How much the poorer should we be, mentally, without our early prophecy of the "ugly ducklings" we are to meet later in life — those awkward offspring of our little human duckyard who are mostly well kicked and buffeted about, for that very length of limb and breadth of back which needs must be, to support swan's wings. The story of the ugly duckling is much truer than many a bald statement of fact. The English-speaking world bears witness to its verity in constant use of the title as an identifying phrase: "It is the old story of the ugly duckling," we say, or, "He has turned out a real ugly duckling." And we know that our hearers understand the whole situation.

The consideration of such familiar types and expressions as that of the ugly duckling suggests immediately another good reason for giving the child his due of fairy lore. The reason is that to omit it is to deprive him of one important element in the full appreciation of mature literature. If we think of it, we see that nearly all adult literature is made by people who, in their beginnings, were bred on the wonder tale. Whether he will or no, the grown-up author must incorporate into his work the tendencies, memories, and kinds of feeling that were his in childhood.

The literature of maturity is, naturally, permeated by the influence of the literature of childhood. Sometimes it is apparent merely in the use of a name, as suggestive of certain kinds of experience; such are the recurrences of reference to the Cinderella story. Sometimes it is an allusion that has its strength in long association of certain qualities with certain characters in fairydom — such as the slyness of Brother Fox and the cruelty of Brother Wolf. Sometimes the association of ideas lies below the surface, drawing from the hidden wells of poetic illusion that are sunk in childhood. The man or woman whose infancy was nourished exclusively on tales adapted from science-made-easy, or from biographies of good men and great, must remain blind to these beauties of literature. He may look up the allusion, or identify the reference, but when that is done, he is but richer by a fact or two; there is no remembered thrill in it for him, no savor in his memory, no suggestion to his imagination; and these are precisely the things that really count.

Leaving out the fairy element is a loss to literary culture much as would be the omission of the Bible or of Shakespeare. Just as all adult literature is permeated by the influence of these, familiar in youth, so in less degree is it transfused with the subtle reminiscences of childhood's commerce with the wonder world.

To turn now from the inner to the outer aspects of the old-time tale is to meet another cause of its value to children. This is the value of its style. Simplicity, directness, and virility characterize the classic fairytales and the most memorable relics of folklore. And these are three of the very qualities that are most seriously lacking in much of the new writing for children, and which are always necessary elements in the culture of taste. Fairy stories are not all well told, but the best fairy stories are supremely well told. And most folktales have a movement, a sweep, and an unaffectedness that make them splendid foundations for taste in style.

For this, and for poetic presentation of truths in easily assimilated form, and because it gives joyous stimulus to the imagination and is necessary to full appreciation of adult literature, we may freely use the wonder tale.

The Nonsense Tale
Closely related to, sometimes identical with, the fairytale is the old, old source of children's love and laughter, the nonsense tale.

How to Tell Stories to Children

Under this head I wish to include all the merely funny tales of childhood, embracing the cumulative stories such as that of the old woman and the pig that would not go over the stile. They all have a specific use and benefit, and are worth the repetition children demand for them. Their value lies, of course, in the tonic and relaxing properties of humor. Nowhere is that property more welcome or needed than in the schoolroom. It does us all good to laugh, if there is no sneer or smirch in the laugh. Fun sets the blood flowing more freely in the veins and loosens the strained cords of feeling and thought. The delicious shock of surprise at every "funny spot" is a kind of electric treatment for the nerves. But it especially does us good to laugh when we are children. Every little body is released from the conscious control school imposes on it, and huddles into restful comfort or responds gaily to the joke.

More than this, humor teaches children, as it does their grown-up brethren, some of the facts and proportions of life. What keener teacher is there than the kindly satire? What more penetrating and suggestive than the humor of exaggerated statement of familiar tendency? Is there one of us who has not laughed himself out of some absurd complexity of overanxiety with a sudden recollection of "clever Alice" and her fate? In our household, clever Alice is an old *habituée*, and her timely arrival has saved many a situation that was twining itself about more *ifs* than it could comfortably support. The wisdom that lies behind true humor is found in the nonsense tale of infancy as truly as in mature humor, but in its own kind and degree.

"Just for fun" is the first reason for the humorous story; the wisdom in the fun is the second.

The Nature Story
And now we come to the nature story. No other type of fiction is more familiar to the teacher, and probably no other kind is the

source of so much uncertainty of feeling. The nature story is much used, as I have noted, to illustrate or to teach the habits of animals and the laws of plant growth; to stimulate scientific interest as well as to increase culture in scientific fact. This is an entirely legitimate object. In view of its present preponderance, it is certainly a pity, however, that so few stories are available whose accuracy, from this point of view, can be vouched for. The carefully prepared book of today is refuted and scoffed at tomorrow.

The teacher who wishes to use storytelling chiefly as an element in nature study must at least limit herself to a small amount of absolutely unquestioned material, or else subject every new story to the judgment of an authority in the line dealt with. This is not easy for the teacher at a distance from the great libraries, and, for those who have access to well-equipped libraries, it is a matter of time and thought.

It does not so greatly trouble the teacher who uses the nature story as a story, rather than as a textbook, for she will not be so keenly attracted toward the books prepared with a didactic purpose. She will find a good gift for the child in nature stories that are stories, over and above any stimulus to his curiosity about fact. That good gift is a certain possession of all good fiction.

One of the best things good fiction does for any of us is to broaden our comprehension of other lots than our own. The average man or woman has little opportunity actually to live more than one kind of life. The chances of birth, occupation, and family ties determine for most of us a line of experience not very inclusive and but little varied; and this is a natural barrier to our complete understanding of others, whose lifeline is set at a different angle. It is not possible wholly to sympathize with emotions engendered by experience that one has never had. Yet we all long to be broad in sympathy and inclusive in appreciation; we long, greatly, to know the experience of others.

This yearning is probably one of the good but misconceived appetites so injudiciously fed by the gossip of the daily press. There is a hope, in the reader, of getting for the moment into the lives of people who move in wholly different sets of circumstances. But the relation of dry facts in newspapers, however tinged with journalistic color, helps very little to enter such other life. The entrance has to be by the door of the imagination, and the journalist is rarely able to open it for us. But there is a genius who can open it.

The author who can write fiction of the right sort can do it; his is the gift of seeing inner realities, and of showing them to those who cannot see them for themselves. Sharing the imaginative vision of the story writer, we can truly follow out many other roads of life than our own. The girl on a lone country farm is made to understand how a girl in a city sweatshop feels and lives; the London exquisite realizes the life of a Californian ranchman; royalty and tenement dwellers become acquainted, through the power of the imagination working on experience shown in the light of a human basis common to both. Fiction supplies an element of culture — that of the sympathies, which is invaluable. And the beginnings of this culture, this widening and clearing of the avenues of human sympathy, are especially easily made with children in the nature story.

When you begin, "There was once a little furry rabbit," the child's curiosity is awakened by the very fact that the rabbit is not a child, but something of a different species altogether. "Now for something new and adventuresome," says his expectation. "We are starting off into a foreign world." He listens wide-eyed, while you say, "And he lived in a warm, cozy nest, down under the long grass with his mother" — how delightful, to live in a place like that; so different from little boys' homes! "His name was Raggylug, and his mother's name was Molly Cottontail. And every morning, when Molly Cottontail went out to get their food, she said to Raggylug, 'Now, Raggylug, remember you are only a baby rabbit, and don't move from the nest. No matter what you hear, no matter what you see, don't you move!' "[2]

All this is different still, yet it is familiar, too; it appears that rabbits are rather like folks. So the tale proceeds, and the little furry rabbit passes through experiences strange to little boys, yet very like little boys' adventures in some respects; he is frightened by a snake, comforted by his mother, and taken to a new house, under the long grass a long way off. These are all situations to which the child has a key. There is just enough of strangeness to entice, just enough of the familiar to relieve any strain. When the child has lived through the day's happenings with Raggylug, the latter has begun to seem veritably a little brother of the grass to him. And because he has entered imaginatively into the feelings and fate of a creature different from himself, he has taken his first step out into the wide world of the lives of others.

It might be a recognition of this factor and its value that has led so many writers of nature stories into the error of overhumanizing their four-footed or feathered heroes and heroines. The exaggeration is unnecessary, for there is enough community of lot suggested in the sternest scientific record to constitute a natural basis for sympathy on the part of the human animal.

Without any falsity of presentation whatever, the nature story may be counted on as a help in the beginnings of culture of the sympathies. It is not, of course, a help confined to the powers of the nature story; all types of story share in some degree the powers of each. But each has some especial virtue in dominant degree, and the nature story is, on this ground, identified with the thought given.

[2] The full text of "Raggylug" can be found in the stories section, following chapter 6.

The Historical Story

The nature story shares its influence especially with the historical story. As the one widens the circle of connection with other kinds of life, the other deepens the sense of relation to past lives; it gives the sense of background, of the close and endless connection of generation with generation. A good historical story vitalizes the conception of past events and brings their characters into relation with the present.

This is especially true of stories of things and persons in the history of our own race. They foster race-consciousness, the feeling of kinship and community of blood. It is this property that makes the historical story so good an agent for furthering a proper national pride in children. Genuine patriotism, neither arrogant nor melodramatic, is so generally recognized as having its roots in early training that I need not dwell on this possibility, further than to note its connection with the instinct of hero-worship which is quick in the healthy child.

Let us feed that hunger for the heroic which gnaws at the imagination of every boy and of more girls than is generally admitted. There have been heroes in plenty in the world's records — heroes of action, of endurance, of decision, of faith. Biographical history is full of them. And the deeds of these heroes are every one a story. We tell these stories both to bring the great past into its due relation with the living present and to arouse that generous admiration and desire for emulation which is the source of so much inspiration in childhood. When these stories are tales of the doings and happenings of our own heroes, the strong men and women whose lives are a part of our own country's history, they serve the double demands of hero-worship and patriotism. Stories of wise and honest statesmanship, of struggle with primitive conditions, of generous love and sacrifice, and, in some measure, of physical courage form a subtle and powerful influence for pride in one's people, the intimate sense of kinship with one's own nation, and the desire to serve it in one's own time.

It is not particularly useful to tell batches of unrelated anecdote. It is much more profitable to take up the story of a period and connect it with a group of interesting persons whose lives affected it or were affected by it, telling the stories of their lives, or of the events in which they were concerned, as "true stories." These biographical stories must, usually, be adapted for use. But besides these, there is a certain number of pure stories — works of art — that already exist for us, and which illuminate facts and epochs almost without need of sidelights. Such may stand by themselves, or be used with only enough explanation to give background. Probably the best story of this kind known to lovers of modern literature is Daudet's famous *La Dernière Classe*.[3]

The historical story, to recapitulate, gives a sense of the reality and humanness of past events, is a valuable aid in patriotic training, and stirs the desire of emulating goodness and wisdom.

[3] The English translation, "The Last Lesson," can be found in the stories section of this book.

Chapter 2

How to Select Stories to Tell

There is one picture I can always review in my own collection of past scenes, although many a more highly colored one has been irrevocably curtained by the folds of forgetfulness. It is the picture of a little girl, standing by an old-fashioned marble-topped dressing-table in a pink, sunny room. I can never see the little girl's face, because, somehow, I am always looking down at her short skirts or twisting my head around against the hand that patiently combs her stubborn curls. But I can see the brushes and combs on the marble table quite plainly, and the pinker streaks of sun on the pink walls.

And I can hear. I can hear a low, wonder-working voice that goes smoothly on and on, as the fingers run up the little girl's locks or stroke the hair into place on her forehead. The voice says, "And little Goldilocks came to a little bit of a house. And she opened the door and went in. It was the house where three bears lived; there was a great bear, a little bear, and a middle-size bear; and they had gone out for a walk. Goldilocks went in, and she saw . . ."

The little girl is very still; she would not disturb that story by so much as a loud breath; but presently the comb comes to a tangle, pulls, and the girl begins to squirm. Instantly the voice becomes impressive, mysterious: "She went up to the table, and there were *three plates of porridge*. She tasted the first one" — the little girl swallows the breath she was going to whimper with, and waits — "and it was too hot! She tasted the next one, and *that* was too hot. Then she tasted the little bit of a plate, and that . . . was . . . just . . . right!"

How I remember the delightful sense of achievement that stole into the little girl's veins when the voice behind her said "just right." I think she always chuckled a little and hugged her stomach. So the story progressed, and the little girl got brushed and dressed without crying, owing to the wonderworking voice and its marvelous adaptation of climaxes to emergencies. Nine times out of ten, it was the story of "The Three Bears" she demanded when, with the appearance of brush and comb, the voice asked, "Which story shall Mother tell?"

It was a memory of the little girl in the pink room that made it easy for me to understand some other children's preferences when I recently had occasion to inquire about them. By asking many individual children which story of all they had heard they liked best, by taking votes on the best story of a series, after telling it, and by getting some obliging teachers to put similar questions to their pupils, I found three prime favorites common to a great many children of about the kindergarten age. They were "The Three Bears," "The Three Little Pigs," and "The Little Pig That Wouldn't Go Over the Stile."

Some of the teachers were genuinely disturbed because the few stories they had introduced merely for amusement had taken so pre-eminent a place in the children's affection over those that had been given seriously. It was of no use, however, to suggest substitutes. The children knew definitely what they liked, and although they accepted the recapitulation of scientific and moral stories with polite approbation, they returned to the original answer at a repetition of the question.

Inasmuch as the slightest of the things we hope to do for children by means of stories is quite impossible unless the children enjoy the stories, it may be worth our while to consider seriously these three which they surely do enjoy, to see what common qualities are in them, explanatory of their popularity, by which we may test the probable success of other stories we wish to tell.

Here they are — three prime favorites of proved standing.[4]

THE STORY OF THE THREE LITTLE PIGS

Once upon a time, there were three little pigs, who went from home to seek their fortune. The first that went off met a man with a bundle of straw, and said to him, "Good man, give me that straw to build me a house."

The man gave the straw, and the little pig built his house with it. Presently along came a wolf and knocked at the door and said, "Little pig, little pig, let me come in."

But the pig answered, "No, no, by the hair of my chinny-chin-chin."

So the wolf said, "Then I'll huff and I'll puff, and I'll blow your house in."

So he huffed and he puffed, and he blew his house in, and ate up the little pig.

The second little pig met a man with a bundle of sticks and said, "Good man, give me those sticks to build me a house."

The man gave the furze, and the pig built his house. Then once more came the wolf, and said, "Little pig, little pig, let me come in."

"No, no, by the hair of my chinny-chin-chin."

"Then I'll puff and I'll huff, and I'll blow your house in."

So he huffed and he puffed, and he puffed and he huffed, and at last he blew the house in and ate up the little pig.

[4] Adapted from Joseph Jacobs's *English Fairy Tales*.

The third little pig met a man with a load of bricks, and said, "Good man, give me those bricks to build me a house."

The man gave the bricks, and the pig built his house with them. Again the wolf came and said, "Little pig, little pig, let me come in."

"No, no, by the hair of my chinny-chin-chin."

"Then I'll huff and I'll puff, and I'll blow your house in."

So he huffed and he puffed, and he huffed and he puffed, and he puffed and he huffed, but he could not get the house down. Finding that he could not, with all his huffing and puffing, blow the house down, he said, "Little pig, I know where there is a nice field of turnips."

"Where?" said the little pig.

"Oh, in Mr. Smith's field, and if you will be ready tomorrow morning, we will go together, and get some for dinner."

"Very well," said the little pig. "What time do you mean to go?"

"Oh, at six o'clock."

So the little pig got up at five, and got the turnips before the wolf came crying, "Little pig, are you ready?"

The little pig said, "Ready! I have been and come back again, and got a nice potful for dinner."

The wolf felt very angry at this, but he thought that he would be a match for the little pig somehow or other, so he said, "Little pig, I know where there is a nice apple tree."

"Where?" said the pig.

"Down at Merry-garden," replied the wolf, "and if you will not deceive me, I will come for you at five o'clock tomorrow and get some apples."

The little pig got up the next morning at four o'clock, and went off for the apples, hoping to get back before the wolf came; but it took long to climb the tree, and just as he was coming down from it, he saw the wolf coming.

When the wolf came up, he said, "Little pig, what! Are you here before me? Are they nice apples?"

"Yes, very," said the little pig. "I will throw you down one."

And he threw it so far that, while the wolf was gone to pick it up, the little pig jumped down and ran home. The next day the wolf came again and said to the little pig, "Little pig, there is a fair in town this afternoon. Will you go?"

"Oh yes," said the pig. "I will go. What time?"

"At three," said the wolf. As usual, the little pig went off before the time, and got to the fair, and bought a butter-churn, which he was rolling home when he saw the wolf coming. So he got into the churn to hide, and in so doing, turned it round, and it rolled down the hill with the pig in it, which frightened the wolf so much that he ran home without going to the fair. He went to the little pig's house, and told him how frightened he had been by a great round thing that came past him down the hill.

Then the little pig said, "Ha, ha! I frightened you, then!"

Then the wolf was very angry indeed, and tried to get down the chimney in order to eat up the little pig. When the little pig saw what he was about to do, he put a pot full of water on the blazing fire, and, just as the wolf was coming down, he took off the cover, and in fell the wolf. Quickly the little pig clapped on the cover and, when the wolf was boiled, ate him for supper.

THE STORY OF THE THREE BEARS

Once upon a time, there were three bears who lived together in a house of their own, in a wood. One of them was a little small wee bear, and one was a middle-size bear, and the other was a great huge bear. They had each a pot for their porridge: a little pot for the little small wee bear, and a middle-size pot for the middle-size bear, and a great pot for the great huge bear. And they had each a chair to sit in: a little chair for the little small wee bear, and a middle-size chair for the middle-size bear, and a great chair for the great huge bear. And they had each a bed to sleep in: a little bed for the little small wee bear, and a middle-size bed for the middle-size bear, and a great bed for the great huge bear.

One day, after they had made the porridge for their breakfast, and poured it into their porridge-pots, they walked out into the wood while the porridge was cooling, so that they might not burn their mouths, by beginning too soon to eat it. And while they were walking, a little girl named Goldilocks came to the house. She had never seen the little house before, and it was such a strange little house that she forgot all the things her mother had told her about being polite: first she looked in at the window, and then she peeped in at the keyhole; and seeing nobody in the house, she lifted the latch. The door was not fastened, because the bears were good bears, who did nobody any harm, and never suspected that anybody would harm them.

So Goldilocks opened the door and went in; and well pleased she was when she saw the porridge on the table. If Goldilocks had remembered what her mother had told her, she would have waited until the bears came home, and then, perhaps, they would have asked her to breakfast; for they were good bears — a little rough, as the manner of bears is, but for all that, very good-natured and hospitable. But Goldilocks forgot, and set about helping herself.

So first, she tasted the porridge of the great huge bear, and that was too hot. And then she tasted the porridge of the middle-size bear, and that was too cold. And then she went to the porridge of the little small wee bear, and tasted that; and that was neither too hot nor too cold, but just right; and she liked it so well that she ate it all up.

Then Goldilocks sat in the chair of the great huge bear, and that was too hard for her. And she sat down in the chair of the middle-size bear, and that was too soft for her. Then she sat down in the chair of the little small wee bear, and that was neither too hard nor too soft, but just right. So there she sat until the bottom of the chair came out, and down she came, plump, upon the ground.

Then Goldilocks went upstairs into the bed-chamber in which the three bears slept. And first she lay down upon the bed of the great huge bear, but that was too high at the head for her. And next she lay down upon the bed of the middle-size bear, and that was too high at the foot for her. And then she lay down upon the bed of the little small wee bear, and that was neither too high at the head nor at the foot, but just right. So she covered herself up comfortably and lay there until she fell fast asleep.

By this time, the three bears thought their porridge would be cool enough; so they came home to breakfast. Now, Goldilocks had left the spoon of the great huge bear standing in his porridge.

"SOMEBODY HAS BEEN AT MY PORRIDGE!" said the great huge bear, in his great, rough, gruff voice.

And when the middle-size bear looked at hers, she saw that the spoon was standing in it too.

"Somebody has been at my porridge!" said the middle-size bear, in her middle-size voice.

Then the little small wee bear looked at his, and there was the spoon in the porridge-pot, but the porridge was all gone.

"Somebody has been at my porridge, and has eaten it all up!" said the little small wee bear, in his little small wee voice.

Upon this, the three bears, seeing that someone had entered their house, and eaten up the little small wee bear's breakfast, began to look around them. Now, Goldilocks had not put the hard cushion straight when she rose from the chair of the great huge bear.

"SOMEBODY HAS BEEN SITTING IN MY CHAIR!" said the great huge bear, in his great, rough, gruff voice.

And Goldilocks had crushed down the soft cushion of the middle-size bear.

"Somebody has been sitting in my chair!" said the middle-size bear, in her middle-size voice.

And you know what Goldilocks had done to the third chair.

"Somebody has been sitting in my chair and has sat the bottom out of it!" said the little small wee bear, in his little, small, wee voice.

Then the three bears thought it necessary that they should make further search; so they went upstairs into their bed-chamber. Now, Goldilocks had pulled the pillow of the great huge bear out of its place.

"SOMEBODY HAS BEEN LYING IN MY BED!" said the great huge bear, in his great, rough, gruff voice.

And Goldilocks had pulled the bolster of the middle-size bear out of its place.

"Somebody has been lying in my bed!" said the middle-size bear, in her middle-size voice.

And when the little small wee bear came to look at his bed, there was the bolster in its place, and the pillow in its place upon the bolster; and upon the pillow was the shining, yellow hair of little Goldilocks!

"Somebody has been lying in my bed — and here she is!" said the little small wee bear, in his little small wee voice.

Goldilocks had heard in her sleep the great, rough, gruff voice of the great huge bear; but she was so fast asleep that it was no more to her than the roaring of wind or the rumbling of thunder. And she had heard the middle-size voice of the middle-size bear, but it was only as if she had heard someone speaking in a dream. But when she heard the little, small, wee voice of the little small wee bear, it was so sharp, and so shrill, that it awakened her at once.

Up she started, and when she saw the three bears on one side of the bed, she tumbled herself out at the other and ran to the window. Now, the window was open, because the bears, like good, tidy bears as they were, always opened their bed-chamber window when they got up in the morning.

Out little Goldilocks jumped, and ran away home to her mother, as fast as ever she could.

THE OLD WOMAN AND HER PIG

It happened one day that as an old woman was sweeping her house, she found a little crooked sixpence. "What," said she, "shall I do with this little sixpence? I will go to market and buy a little pig."

On the way home, she came to a stile; but the piggy wouldn't go over the stile.

So she left the piggy and went on a little further, until she met a dog. She said to him, "Dog, dog, bite pig! Piggy won't go over the stile; and I shan't get home tonight." But the dog wouldn't bite piggy.

A little further on, she met a stick. So she said, "Stick, stick, beat dog! Dog won't bite pig; piggy won't go over the stile; and I shan't get home tonight." But the stick wouldn't beat the dog.

A little further on, she met a fire. So she said, "Fire, fire, burn stick! Stick won't beat dog; dog won't bite pig; piggy won't go over the stile; and I shan't get home tonight." But the fire wouldn't burn the stick.

A little further on, she met some water. So she said, "Water, water, quench fire. Fire won't burn stick; stick won't beat dog; dog won't bite pig; piggy won't go over the stile; and I shan't get home tonight." But the water wouldn't quench the fire.

A little further on, she met an ox. So she said, "Ox, ox, drink water! Water won't quench fire; fire won't burn stick; stick won't beat dog; dog won't bite pig; piggy won't go over the stile; and I shan't get home tonight." But the ox wouldn't drink the water.

A little further on, she met a butcher. So she said: "Butcher, butcher, kill ox! Ox won't drink water; water won't quench fire; fire won't burn stick; stick won't beat dog; dog won't bite pig; piggy won't go over the stile; and I shan't get home tonight." But the butcher wouldn't kill the ox.

A little further on, she met a rope. So she said, "Rope, rope, hang butcher! Butcher won't kill ox; ox won't drink water; water won't quench fire; fire won't burn stick; stick won't beat dog; dog won't bite pig; piggy won't go over the stile; and I shan't get home tonight." But the rope wouldn't hang the butcher.

A little further on, she met a rat. So she said, "Rat, rat, gnaw rope! Rope won't hang butcher; butcher won't kill ox; ox won't drink water; water won't quench fire; fire won't burn stick; stick won't beat dog; dog won't bite pig; piggy won't go over the stile; and I shan't get home tonight." But the rat wouldn't gnaw the rope.

A little further on, she met a cat. So she said, "Cat, cat, kill rat! Rat won't gnaw rope; rope won't hang butcher; butcher won't kill ox; ox won't drink water; water won't quench fire; fire won't burn stick; stick won't beat dog; dog won't bite pig; piggy won't go over the stile; and I shan't get home tonight." But the cat said to her, "If you will go to yonder cow, and fetch me a saucer of milk, I will kill the rat." So away went the old woman to the cow.

But the cow refused to give the milk unless the old woman first gave her a handful of hay. So away went the old woman to the haystack; and she brought the hay to the cow.

When the cow had eaten the hay, she gave the old woman the milk; and away she went with it in a saucer to the cat.

As soon as it had lapped up the milk, the cat began to kill the rat; the rat began to gnaw the rope; the rope began to hang the butcher; the butcher began to kill the ox; the ox began to drink the water; the water began to quench the fire; the fire began to burn the stick; the stick began to beat the dog; the dog began to bite the pig; the little pig, in a fright, jumped over the stile; and so the old woman did get home that night.

The briefest examination of these three stories reveals the fact that one attribute is beyond dispute in each. Something happens, all the time. Every step in each story is an event. There is no time spent in explanation, description, or telling how people felt; the stories tell what people did, and what they said. And the events are the links of a sequence of the closest kind; in point of time and of cause they follow as immediately as it is possible for events to follow. There are no gaps, and no complications of plot requiring a return on the road.

A second common characteristic appears on briefest examination. As you run over the little stories, you will see that each event presents a distinct picture to the imagination, and that these pictures are made out of very simple elements. The elements are either familiar to the child or analogous to familiar ones. Each object and happening is very like everyday, yet touched with a subtle difference, rich in mystery. For example, the details of the pictures in the Goldilocks story are parts of everyday life: house, chairs, beds, and so on; but they are the house, chairs, and beds of three bears; that is the touch of marvel which transforms the scene. The old woman who owned the obstinate pig is the center of a circle in which stand only familiar images: stick, fire, water, cow, and the rest; but the wonder enters with the fact that these usually inanimate or dumb objects of nature enter so humanly into the contest of wills. So it is, also, with the doings of the three little pigs. Every image is explicable to the youngest hearer, while none suggests actual familiarity, because the actors are not children, but pigs. Simplicity, with mystery, is the keynote of all the pictures, and these are clear and distinct.

A third characteristic common to the stories quoted is a certain amount of repetition. It is more definite, and of what has been called the "cumulative" kind, in the story of the old woman; but in all, it is a distinctive feature.

Here we have, then, three marked characteristics common to three stories almost invariably loved by children: action, in close sequence; familiar images, tinged with mystery; some degree of repetition.

It is not hard to see why these qualities appeal to a child. The first is the prime characteristic of all good stories — "stories as stories"; the child's demand for it but bears witness to the fact that his instinctive taste is often better than the taste he later develops under artificial culture. The second is a matter of common sense. How could the imagination create new worlds, save out of the material of the old? To offer strange images is to confuse the mind and dull the interest; to offer familiar ones "with a difference" is to pique the interest and engage the mind.

The charm of repetition, to children, is a more complex matter; there are undoubtedly a good many elements entering into it, hard to trace in analysis. But one or two of the more obvious may be seized and brought to view. The first is the subtle flattery of an unexpected sense of mastery. When the child-mind, following with toilful alertness a new train of thought, comes suddenly on a familiar epithet or expression, I fancy it is with much the same sense of satisfaction that we older people feel when, in the midst of a long program of new music, the orchestra strikes into something we have heard before — Handel, maybe, or one of the more familiar Beethoven sonatas. "I know that! I have heard that before!" we think, triumphant, and settle down to enjoyment without effort. So it is, probably, with the "middle-size" articles of the bears' house and the "and I shan't get home tonight" of the old woman. Each recurrence deepens the note of familiarity, tickles the primitive sense of humor, and eases the strain of attention.

When the repetition is cumulative, as in the extreme instance of "The House that Jack Built," I have a notion that the joy of the child is the pleasure of intellectual gymnastics, not too hard for fun, but not too easy for excitement. There is a deal of fun to be gotten out of purely intellectual processes, and childhood is not too soon for the rudiments of such fun to show. The delight the healthy adult mind takes in working out a neat problem in geometry, the pleasure a musician finds in following the involutions of a fugue, are of the same type of satisfaction as the liking of children for cumulative stories. Complexity and mass, arrived at by stages perfectly intelligible in themselves, mounting steadily from a starting point of simplicity; then the same complexity and mass resolving itself, as it were, miraculously back into simplicity — this is an intellectual joy. It does not differ materially, whether found in the study of counterpoint, at thirty, or in the story of the old woman and her pig, at five. It is perfectly natural and wholesome, and it may perhaps be a more powerful developing force for the budding intellect than we are aware.

For these reasons, let me urge you, when you are looking for stories to tell little children, to apply this threefold test as a kind of touchstone to their quality of fitness: Are they full of action, in close natural sequence? Are their images simple without being humdrum? Are they repetitive? The last quality is not an absolute requisite, but it is at least very often an attribute of a good child-story.

Having this touchstone in mind for general selection, we can now pass to the matter of specific choices for different ages of children. No one can speak with absolute conviction in this matter, so greatly do the taste and capacity of children of the same age vary. Any approach to an exact classification of juvenile books according to their suitability for different ages will be found impossible. The same book in the hands of a skillful narrator may be made to afford delight to children both of five and ten. The following are merely the inferences drawn from my own experience. They must be modified by each teacher according to the conditions of her small audience. In general, I believe it to be wise to plan the choice of stories much as indicated in the list beginning on page 36.

At a later stage, varying with the standard of capacity of different classes, we find the temper of mind that asks continually, "Is that true?" To meet this demand, one draws on historical and scientific anecdote, and on reminiscence. But the demand is never so exclusive that fictitious narrative need be cast aside. All that is necessary is to state frankly that the story you are telling is "just a story" or — if it be the case — that it is "part true and part story."

At all stages, I would urge the telling of Bible stories, as far as is allowed by the special circumstances of the school. These are stories from a source unsurpassed in our literature for purity of style and loftiness of subject. More especially, I urge the telling of the Christ-story, in such parts as seem likely to be within the grasp of the several classes. In all Bible stories, it is good to keep as near as possible to the original unimprovable text.[5] Some amplification can be made, but no excessive modernizing or simplifying is excusable in face of the austere grace and majestic simplicity of the original. Such adaptation as helps to cut the long narrative into separate units, making each an intelligible story, I have ventured to illustrate according to my own personal taste, in two stories given in the collection of stories in this book, following chapter 6. The object of the usual modernizing or enlarging of the text may be far better attained for the child listener by infusing into the text as it stands a strong realizing sense of its meaning and vitality, letting it give its own message through a fit medium of expression.

The stories given later in this book are grouped as illustrations of the types suitable for different stages. They are, however, very often interchangeable; and many stories can be told successfully to all classes. A vitally good story is little limited in its appeal. It is,

[5] *Stories from the Old Testament*, by Susan Platt, retells the Old Testament story as nearly as possible in the actual words of the Authorized Version.

nevertheless, a help to have certain plain results of experience as a basis for choice; that which is given is intended only for such a basis, not in the least as a final list.

Types of Story to Tell to Each Grade Level

KINDERGARTEN AND GRADE 1
>   Little rhymed stories (including the best
>   of the nursery rhymes and the more
>   poetic fragments of Mother Goose)
>   Stories with rhyme in parts
>   Nature stories (in which the element
>   of personification is strong)
>   Nonsense tales
>   Wonder tales

GRADES 2 AND 3
>   Nonsense tales
>   Wonder tales
>   Fairytales and folktales
>   Fables
>   Legends
>   Nature stories (especially stories
>   of animals)

GRADES 4 AND 5
>   Folktales
>   Fables
>   Myths and allegories
>   Developed animal stories
>   Legends: historic and heroic
>   Historical stories

Humorous adventure stories
"True stories"

The wonder tales most familiar and accessible to the teacher are probably those included in the collections of Andersen and the Brothers Grimm. So constant is the demand for these that the following list may be found useful, as indicating which of the stories are more easily and effectively adapted for telling, and commonly most successful.

It must be remembered that many of these standard tales need such adapting as has been suggested, cutting them down, and ridding them of vulgar or sophisticated detail.

BROTHERS GRIMM
    The Star Dollars
    The Cat and the Mouse
    The Nail
    The Hare and the Hedgehog
    Snow-White and Rose-Red
    Mother Holle
    Thumbling
    Three Brothers
    The Little Porridge Pot
    Little Snow-White
    The Wolf and the Seven Little Kids
    The Sea Mouse

HANS CHRISTIAN ANDERSEN
    Little Tiny
    The Lark and the Daisy
    The Ugly Duckling
    The Seven Stories of the Snow Queen

The Flax
The Little Match Girl
The Fir Tree
The Red Shoes
Olé Luköié
    Monday
    Saturday
    Sunday
The Elf of the Rose
Five Peas in a Pod
The Portuguese Duck
The Little Mermaid (much shortened)
The Nightingale (shortened)
The Girl Who Trod on a Loaf
The Emperor's New Clothes

Another familiar and easily attainable type of story is the classic myth, as retold in Kupfer's *Legends of Greece and Rome*.[6] Of these, again, certain tales are more successfully adapted to children than others. Among the best for telling are:

Arachne
Pandora
Midas
Apollo and Daphne
Apollo and Hyacinthus
Narcissus
Latona and the Rustics
Proserpine

[6] A well-nigh indispensable book for teachers is Guerber's *Myths of Greece and Rome*, which contains in brief form a complete collection of the classic myths.

Chapter 3

Adapting Stories for Telling

It soon becomes easy to pick out from a collection such stories as can be well told; but at no time is it easy to find a sufficient number of such stories. Stories simple, direct, and sufficiently full of incident for telling, yet having the beautiful or valuable motive we desire for children, do not lie hidden in every book. And even many of the stories that are most charming to read do not answer the double demand, for the appeal to the eye differs in many important respects from that to the ear. Unless we are able to change the form of a story to suit the needs of oral delivery, we are likely to suffer from poverty of material.

Perhaps the most common need of change is in the case of a story too long to tell, yet embodying one beautiful incident or lesson; or one including a series of such incidents. The story of *The Nurnberg Stove*, by Louisa de la Rame (Ouida), is a good example of the latter kind; John Ruskin's *King of the Golden River* will serve as an illustration of the former.[7]

The problem in one case is chiefly one of elimination; in the other, it is, in a large degree, one of rearrangement. In both cases, I have purposely chosen extreme instances, as furnishing plainer illustration. The usual story needs less adaptation than these, but

---

[7] The full text of both of these stories can be found in the appendix.

the same kind, in its own degree. Condensation and rearrangement are the commonest forms of change required.

Pure condensation is probably the easier for most persons. With *The Nurnberg Stove* in mind for reference, let us see what the process includes. The story as it stands is 2,400 words long, obviously too long to tell. What can be left out? Let us see what must be kept in.

The dramatic climax toward which we are working is the outcome of August's strange exploit: his discovery by the king and the opportunity for him to become an artist. The joy of this climax is twofold: August may stay with his beloved Hirschvogel, and he may learn to make beautiful things like it. To arrive at the twofold conclusion, we must start from a double premise: the love for the stove and the yearning to be an artist. It will, then, be necessary to include in the beginning of the story enough details of the family life to show plainly how precious and necessary Hirschvogel was to the children; and to state definitely how August had learned to admire and wish to emulate Hirschvogel's maker. We need no detail beyond what is necessary to make this clear.

The beginning and the end of a story decided upon, its body becomes the bridge from one to the other; in this case, it is August's strange journey, beginning with the catastrophe and his grief-dazed decision to follow the stove. The journey is long, and each stage of it is told in full. As this is impossible in oral reproduction, it becomes necessary to choose typical incidents that will give the same general effect as the whole. The incidents that answer this purpose are the beginning of the journey, the experience on the luggage train, the jolting while being carried on men's shoulders, and the final fright and suspense before the king opens the door.

The episode of the night in the *bric-a-brac* shop introduces a wholly new and confusing train of thought; therefore, charming as it is, it must be omitted. And the secondary thread of narrative interest, that of the prices for which the stove was sold, and the retribution visited on the cheating dealers, is also "another story" and must be ignored. Each of these destroys the clear sequence and the simplicity of plot, which must be kept for telling.

We are reduced, then, for the whole, to this: a brief preliminary statement of the place Hirschvogel held in the household affections, and the ambition aroused in August; the catastrophe of the sale; August's decision; his experiences on the train, on the shoulders of men, and just before the discovery; his discovery, and the *dénouement*. This not only reduces the story to tellable form, but it also leaves a suggestive interest that heightens later enjoyment of the original.

Ruskin's *King of the Golden River* is somewhat difficult to adapt. Not only is it long, but its style is mature, highly descriptive, and closely allegorical. Yet the tale is too beautiful and too suggestive to be lost to the storyteller. And it is also so recognized a part of the standard literary equipment of youth that teachers need to be able to introduce children to its charm. To make it available for telling, we must choose the most essential events of the series leading up to the climax, and present these so simply as to appeal to children's ears, and so briefly as not to tire them.

The printed story is eight thousand words in length. The first three thousand words depict the beauty and fertility of the Treasure Valley, and the cruel habits of Hans and Schwartz, its owners, and give the culminating incident that leads to their banishment by the Southwest Wind. This episode — the Southwest Wind's appearance in the shape of an aged traveler, his kind reception by the younger brother, little Gluck, and the subsequent wrath of Hans and Schwartz, with their resulting punishment — occupies about two thousand words. The rest of the story deals with the three brothers after the decree of Southwest Wind has turned Treasure Valley into a desert. In the little house where they are plying their trade as goldsmiths, the King of the Golden River appears to Gluck and tells him the magic secret of turning the river's waters to gold. Hans and Schwartz, in turn, attempt the miracle and, in turn, incur the penalty attached to failure. Gluck tries, and wins the treasure through self-sacrifice. The form of the treasure is a renewal of the fertility of Treasure Valley, and the moral of the whole story is summed up in Ruskin's words: "So the inheritance which was lost by cruelty was regained by love."

It is easy to see that the dramatic part of the story, and that which most pointedly illustrates the underlying idea, is the triple attempt to win the treasure: the two failures and the one success. But this is necessarily introduced by the episode of the King of the Golden River, which is also an incident sure to appeal to a child's imagination. And the regaining of the inheritance is meaningless without the fact of its previous loss, and the reason for the loss, as a contrast with the reason for its recovery. We need, then, the main facts recorded in the first three thousand words. But the West Wind episode must be avoided, not only for brevity, but because two supernatural appearances, so similar, yet of different personalities, would hopelessly confuse a told story.

Our oral story is now to be made out of a condensed statement of the character of the valley and of its owners, and the manner of its loss; the intervention of the King of the Golden River; the three attempts to turn the river to gold, and Gluck's success. Gluck is to be our hero, and our underlying idea is the power of love versus cruelty. Description is to be reduced to its lowest terms, and the language made simple and concrete.

With this outline in mind, it might be useful to compare the following adaptation with the original story. The adaptation is not intended in any sense as a substitute for the original, but merely as that form of it which can be *told*, while the original remains for reading.

THE GOLDEN RIVER

(adapted from Ruskin's "King of the Golden River")

There was once a beautiful little valley, where the sun was warm, and the rains fell softly; its apples were so red, its corn so yellow, its grapes so blue, that it was called the Treasure Valley. Not a river ran into it, but one great river flowed down the mountains on the other side, and because the setting sun always tinged its high cataract with gold after the rest of the world was dark, it was called the Golden River. The lovely valley belonged to three brothers. The youngest, little Gluck, was happy-hearted and kind, but he had a hard life with his brothers, for Hans and Schwartz were so cruel and so mean that they were known everywhere around as the "Black Brothers." They were hard to their farm hands, hard to their customers, hard to the poor, and hardest of all to Gluck.

At last, the Black Brothers became so bad that the Spirit of the West Wind took vengeance on them; he forbade any of the gentle winds, south and west, to bring rain to the valley. Then, since there were no rivers in it, it dried up, and instead of a treasure valley, it became a desert of dry, red sand. The Black Brothers could get nothing out of it, and they wandered out into the world on the other side of the mountain peaks; and little Gluck went with them.

Hans and Schwartz went out every day, wasting their time in wickedness, but they left Gluck in the house to work. And they lived on the gold and silver they had saved in Treasure Valley, until at last it was all gone. The only precious thing left was Gluck's gold mug. This the Black Brothers decided to melt into spoons, to sell; and in spite of Gluck's tears, they put it in the melting pot, and went out, leaving him to watch it.

Poor little Gluck sat at the window, trying not to cry for his dear golden mug, and as the sun began to go down, he saw the beautiful cataract of the Golden River turn red, and yellow, and then pure gold.

"Oh, dear!" he said to himself. "How fine it would be if the river were really golden! I needn't be poor then."

"It wouldn't be fine at all!" said a thin, metallic little voice, in his ear.

"Mercy, what's that!" said Gluck, looking all about. But nobody was there.

Suddenly the sharp little voice came again.

"Pour me out," it said. "I am too hot!"

It seemed to come right from the oven, and as Gluck stood, staring in fright, it came again: "Pour me out; I'm too hot!"

Gluck was very much frightened, but he went and looked in the melting pot. When he touched it, the little voice said, "Pour me out, I say!" And Gluck took the handle and began to pour the gold out.

First came out a tiny pair of yellow legs; then a pair of yellow coattails; then a strange little yellow body; and, last, a wee yellow face, with long curls of gold hair. And the whole put itself together as it fell, and stood up on the floor — the strangest little yellow dwarf, about a foot high!

"Dear, me!" said Gluck.

But the little yellow man said, "Gluck, do you know who I am? I am the King of the Golden River."

Gluck did not know what to say, so he said nothing; and, indeed, the little man gave him no chance. He said, "Gluck, I have been watching you, and what I have seen of you I like. Listen, and I will tell you something for your good. Whoever shall climb to the top of the mountain from

44

which the Golden River falls, and shall cast into its waters three drops of holy water, for him and him only shall its waters turn to gold. But no one can succeed except at the first trial, and anyone who casts unholy water in the river will be turned into a black stone."

And then, before Gluck could draw his breath, the king walked straight into the hottest flame of the fire, and vanished up the chimney!

When Gluck's brothers came home, they beat him black and blue, because the mug was gone. But when he told them about the King of the Golden River, they quarreled all night, as to which should go to get the gold. At last, Hans, who was the stronger, got the better of Schwartz and started off. The priest would not give such a bad man any holy water, so he stole a bottleful. Then he took a basket of bread and wine, and began to climb the mountain.

He climbed fast, and soon came to the end of the first hill. But there he found a great glacier, a hill of ice, which he had never seen before. It was horrible to cross; the ice was slippery, great gulfs yawned before him, and noises like groans and shrieks came from under his feet. He lost his basket of bread and wine, and was quite faint with fear and exhaustion when his feet touched firm ground again.

Next he came to a hill of hot, red rock, without a bit of grass to ease the feet, or a particle of shade. After an hour's climb, he was so thirsty that he felt that he must drink. He looked at the flask of water. "Three drops are enough," he thought. "I will just cool my lips."

He was lifting the flask to his lips when he saw something beside him in the path. It was a small dog, and it seemed to be dying of thirst. Its tongue was out, its legs were lifeless, and a swarm of black ants were crawling about its lips. It looked piteously at the bottle that Hans held. Hans raised the bottle to his lips, drank, kicked at the animal, and passed on.

A strange black shadow came across the blue sky.

Another hour Hans climbed; the rocks grew hotter and the way steeper every moment. At last, he could bear it no longer; he must drink. The bottle was half-empty, but he decided to drink half of what was left. As he lifted it, something moved in the path beside him. It was a child, lying nearly dead of thirst on the rock, his eyes closed, his lips burning, his breath coming in gasps. Hans looked at him, drank, and passed on.

A dark cloud came over the sun, and long shadows crept up the mountainside.

It grew very steep now, and the air weighed like lead on Hans's forehead, but the Golden River was very near. Hans stopped a moment to breathe, and then started to climb the last height.

As he clambered on, he saw an old, old man lying in the path. His eyes were sunken, and his face deadly pale.

"Water!" he said. "Water!"

"I have none for you," said Hans. "You have had your share of life." He strode over the old man's body and climbed on.

A flash of blue lightning dazzled him for an instant, and then the heavens were dark.

At last, Hans stood on the brink of the cataract of the Golden River. The sound of its roaring filled the air. He drew the flask from his side and hurled it into the torrent. As he did so, an icy chill shot through him; he shrieked and fell. And the river rose and flowed over

the black stone.

When Hans did not come back, Gluck grieved, but Schwartz was glad. He decided to go and get the gold for himself. He thought it might not do to steal the holy water, as Hans had done, so he took the money little Gluck had earned and bought holy water from a bad priest. Then he took a basket of bread and wine and started off.

He came to the great hill of ice and was as surprised as Hans had been, and found it as hard to cross. Many times he slipped, and he was much frightened at the noises and was very glad to get across, although he had lost his basket of bread and wine.

Then he came to the same hill of sharp, red stone, without grass or shade, that Hans had climbed. And like Hans, he became very thirsty. Like Hans, too, he decided to drink a little of the water. As he raised it to his lips, he suddenly saw the same fair child Hans had seen.

"Water!" said the child. "Water! I am dying."

"I have not enough for myself," said Schwartz, and he passed on.

A low bank of black cloud rose out of the west.

When he had climbed for another hour, the thirst overcame him again, and again he lifted the flask to his lips. As he did so, he saw an old man who begged for water.

"I have not enough for myself," said Schwartz, and he passed on.

A mist, of the color of blood, came over the sun.

Then Schwartz climbed for another hour, and once more he had to drink. This time, as he lifted the flask, he thought he saw his brother Hans before him. The figure stretched its arms to him, and cried out for water.

"Ha, ha," laughed Schwartz, "do you suppose I brought the water up here for you?" And he strode over the figure.

But when he had gone a few yards farther, he looked back, and the figure was not there.

Then he stood at the brink of the Golden River, and its waves were black, and the roaring of the waters filled all the air. He cast the flask into the stream. And as he did so, the lightning glared in his eyes, the earth gave way beneath him, and the river flowed over

the two black stones.

When Gluck found himself alone, he at last decided to try his luck with the King of the Golden River. The priest gave him some holy water as soon as he asked for it, and with this and a basket of bread, he started off.

The hill of ice was much harder for Gluck to climb, because he was not so strong as his brothers. He lost his bread, fell often, and was exhausted when he got on firm ground. He began to climb the hill in the hottest part of the day. When he had climbed for an hour, he was very thirsty and lifted the bottle to drink a little water. As he did so, he saw a feeble old man coming down the path toward him.

"I am faint with thirst," said the old man. "Will you give me some of that water?"

Gluck saw that he was pale and tired, so he gave him the water, saying, "Please don't drink it all." But the old man drank a great deal and gave back the bottle two-thirds emptied. Then he bade Gluck good speed, and Gluck went on merrily.

Some grass appeared on the path, and the grasshoppers began to sing.

At the end of another hour, Gluck felt that he must drink again. But, as he raised the flask, he saw a little child lying by the roadside, and the child cried out pitifully for water. After a struggle with himself, Gluck decided to bear the thirst a little longer. He put the bottle to the child's lips, and he drank all but a few drops. Then the child got up and ran down the hill.

All kinds of sweet flowers began to grow on the rocks, and crimson and purple butterflies flitted about in the air.

At the end of another hour, Gluck's thirst was almost unbearable. He saw that there were only five or six drops of water in the bottle, however, and he did not dare to drink. So he was putting the flask away again when he saw a little dog on the rocks, gasping for breath. He looked at it, and then at the Golden River, and he remembered the dwarf's words, "No one can succeed except at the first trial"; and he tried to pass the dog. But it whined piteously, and Gluck stopped. He could not bear to pass it. "Confound the King and his gold, too!" he said, and he poured the few drops of water into the dog's mouth.

The dog sprang up; its tail disappeared, its nose grew red, and its eyes twinkled. The next minute, the dog was gone, and the King of the Golden River stood there. He stooped and plucked a lily that grew beside Gluck's feet. Three drops of dew were on its white leaves. These the dwarf shook into the flask that Gluck held in his hand.

"Cast these into the river," he said, "and go down the other side of the mountains into the Treasure Valley." Then he disappeared.

Gluck stood on the brink of the river, and cast the three drops of dew into the stream. Where they fell, a little whirl-pool opened; but the water did not turn to gold. Indeed, the water seemed to vanish altogether. Gluck was disappointed not to see gold, but he obeyed the King of the Golden River, and went down the other side of the mountains.

When he came out into the Treasure Valley, a river, like the Golden River, was springing from a new cleft in the rocks above, and flowing among the heaps of dry sand. And then fresh grass sprang beside the river, flowers opened along its sides, and vines began to cover the whole valley. The Treasure Valley was becoming a garden again.

Gluck lived in the valley, and his grapes were blue, and his apples were red, and his corn was yellow; and the poor were never driven from his door. For him, as the King had promised, the river was really a river of gold.

It will probably be clear to anyone who has followed these attempts, that the first step in adaptation is analysis, careful analysis of the story as it stands: What is the story? Which events are necessary links in the chain? How much of the text is pure description?

Having this essential body of the story in mind, we then decide which of the steps toward the climax are needed for safe arrival there, and keep these. When two or more steps can be covered in a single stride, we make the stride. When a necessary explanation is unduly long, or is woven into the story in too many strands, we dispose of it in an introductory statement, or perhaps in a side remark. If there are two or more threads of narrative, we choose among them and hold strictly to the one chosen, eliminating details that concern the others.

In order to hold the simplicity of plot so attained, it is also desirable to have but few personages in the story, and to narrate the action from the point of view of one of them — usually the hero. To shift the point of view of the action is confusing to the child's mind.

When the analysis and condensation have been accomplished, the whole must be cast in simple language, keeping, if possible, the same kind of speech as that used in the original, but changing difficult or technical terms to plain ones, and complex images to simple and familiar ones.

Adapting Anecdotes

All types of adaptation share in this need of simple language; stories that are too short, as well as those that are too long, have this feature in their changed form. The change in a short story is applied most often where it becomes desirable to amplify a single anecdote, or perhaps a fable, which is told in very condensed form. Such an instance is the following anecdote of heroism, which, in the original, is quoted in one of F. W. Robertson's lectures on poetry.

> A detachment of troops was marching along a valley whose overhanging cliffs were crested by the enemy. A sergeant, with eleven men, chanced to become separated from the rest by taking the wrong side of a ravine, which they ex-pected soon to terminate, but which suddenly deepened into an impassable chasm. The officer in command signaled to the party an order to return. They mistook the signal for a command to charge; the brave fellows answered with a cheer, and charged. At the summit of the steep mountain was a triangular platform, defended by a breastwork, behind which were seventy of the foe. On they went, charging up one of those fearful paths, eleven against seventy. The con-test could not long be doubtful with such odds. One after another, they fell; six upon the spot, the remainder hurled backward; but not until they had slain nearly twice their own number.
>
> There is a custom, we are told, among the hillsmen, that when a great chieftain of their own falls in battle, his wrist is bound with a thread either of red or green — the

red denoting the highest rank. According to custom, they stripped the dead, and threw their bodies over the precipice. When their comrades came, they found their corpses stark and gashed; but round both wrists of every British hero was twined the red thread!

This anecdote serves its purpose of illustration perfectly well, but considered as a separate story, it is somewhat too explanatory in diction, and too condensed in form. Just as the long story is analyzed for reduction of given details, so this must be analyzed — to find the details implied. We have to read into it again all that has been left between the lines.

Moreover, the order must be slightly changed, if we are to end with the proper "snap," the final sting of surprise and admiration given by the point of the story; the point must be prepared for. The purpose of the original is equally well served by the explanation at the end, but we must never forget that the place for the climax, or the effective point in a story told, is the last thing said. That is what makes a story "go off" well.

Imagining vividly the situation suggested, and keeping the logical sequence of facts in mind, shall we not find the storytelling itself to boys and girls in somewhat this form?

THE RED THREAD OF COURAGE

This story I am going to tell you is a true one. It happened while the English troops in India were fighting against some of the native tribes. The natives who were making trouble were people from the hill country, called Hillsmen, and they were strong enemies. The English knew very little about them, except their courage, but they had noticed one peculiar custom, after certain battles: the Hillsmen had a way of marking the bodies of their greatest chiefs who were killed in battle by binding a red thread around the wrist; this was the highest tribute they could pay a hero. The English, however, found the common men of them quite enough to handle, for they had proved themselves good fighters and clever at ambushes.

One day, a small body of the English had marched a long way into the hill country, after the enemy, and in the afternoon, they found themselves in a part of the country strange even to the guides. The men moved forward very slowly and cautiously, for fear of an ambush. The trail led into a narrow valley with very steep, high, rocky sides, topped with woods in which the enemy might easily hide.

Here the soldiers were ordered to advance more quickly, although with caution, to get out of the dangerous place.

After a little, they came suddenly to a place where the passage was divided in two by a big three-cornered boulder that seemed to rise from the midst of the valley. The main line of men kept to the right; to save crowding the path, a sergeant and eleven men took the left, meaning to go around the rock and meet the rest beyond it.

They had been in the path only a few minutes when they saw that the rock was not a single boulder at all, but an arm of the left wall of the valley, and that they were marching into a deep ravine with no outlet except the way they came.

Both sides were sheer rock, almost perpendicular, with thick trees at the top; in front of them, the ground rose in a steep hill, bare of woods. As they looked up, they saw that the top was barricaded by the trunks of trees and guarded by a strong body of Hillsmen. As the English hesitated, looking at this, a shower of spears fell from the wood's edge, aimed by hidden foes. The place was a death trap.

At this moment, their danger was seen by the officer in command of the main body, and he signaled to the sergeant to retreat.

By some terrible mischance, the signal was misunderstood. The men took it for the signal to charge. Without a moment's pause, straight up the slope they charged on the run, cheering as they ran.

Some were killed by the spears that were thrown from the cliffs, before they had gone halfway; some were stabbed as they reached the crest, and hurled backward from the precipice; two or three got to the top, and fought hand to hand with the Hillsmen. They were outnumbered, seven to one; but when the last of the English soldiers lay dead, twice their number of Hillsmen lay dead around them!

When the relief party reached the spot, later in the day, they found the bodies of their comrades, full of wounds, huddled over and in the barricade, or crushed on the rocks below. They were mutilated and battered, and bore every sign of the terrible struggle. *But around both wrists of every British soldier was bound the red thread!*

The Hillsmen had paid greater honor to their heroic foes than to the bravest of their own brave dead.

Adapting Poems

Another instance is the short poem, which, while being perfectly simple, is rich in suggestion of more than the young child will see for himself. The following example shows the working out of details in order to provide a satisfactorily rounded story.

THE ELF AND THE DORMOUSE

Once upon a time, a dormouse lived in the wood with his mother. She had made a snug little nest, but Sleepyhead, as she called her little mousie, loved to roam about among the grass and fallen leaves, and it was a hard task to keep him at home.

One day, the mother went off as usual to look for food, leaving Sleepyhead curled up comfortably in a corner of the nest. "He will lie there safely until I come back," she thought.

Presently, however, Sleepyhead opened his eyes and thought he would like to take a walk out in the fresh air. So he crept out of the nest and through the long grass that nodded over the hole in the bank. He ran here and he ran there, stopping again and again to cock his little ears for sound of any creeping thing that might be close at hand. His little fur coat was soft and silky as velvet. Mother had licked it clean before starting her day's work, you may be sure. As Sleepyhead moved from place to place, his long tail swayed from side to side and tickled the daisies so that they could not hold themselves still for laughing.

Presently something very cold fell on Sleepyhead's nose. What could it be? He put up his little paw and dabbed at the place. Then the same thing happened to his tail. He whisked it quickly around to the front. Ah, it was raining!

Now, Sleepyhead couldn't bear rain, and he had gotten a long way from home. What would Mother say if his nice furry coat got wet and draggled? He crept under a bush, but soon the rain found him out. Then he ran to a tree, but this was poor shelter. He began to think that he was in for a soaking when what should he spy, a little distance off, but a fine toadstool that stood bolt upright just like an umbrella.

The next moment, Sleepyhead was crawling underneath the friendly shelter. He fixed himself up as snugly as he could, with his little nose upon his paws and his little tail curled around all, and before you could count six, eight, ten, twenty, he was fast asleep.

Now it happened that Sleepyhead was not the only creature that was caught by the rain that morning in the wood. A little elf had been flitting about in search of fun or mischief, and he, too, had gotten far from home when the raindrops began to come pattering through the leafy roof of the beautiful wood. It would never do to get his pretty wings wet, for he hated to walk; it was such slow work and, besides, he might meet some big wretched animal that could run faster than he. However, he was beginning to think that there was no help for it, when, on a sudden, there before him was the toadstool, with Sleepyhead snug and dry underneath! There was room for another little fellow, thought the elf, and ere long, he had safely bestowed himself under the other half of the toadstool, which was just like an umbrella.

Sleepyhead slept on, warm and comfortable in his furry coat, and the elf began to feel annoyed with him for being so happy. He was always a great mischief, and he could not bear to sit still for long at a time. Presently he laughed an odd little laugh. He had got an idea! Putting his two small arms around the stem of the toadstool, he tugged and he pulled until, all of a sudden, *snap!* He had broken the stem and, a moment later, was soaring in air safely sheltered under the toadstool, which he held upright by its stem as he flew.

Sleepyhead had been dreaming, oh, so cozy a dream! It seemed to him that he had discovered a storehouse filled with golden grain and soft, juicy nuts with little bunches of sweet-smelling hay, where tired mousies might sleep dull hours away. He thought that he was settled in the sweetest bunch of all, with nothing in the world to disturb his nap, when gradually he became aware that something had happened. He shook himself in his sleep and settled down again, but the dream had altered. He opened his eyes. Rain was falling, *pit-a-pat*, and he was without cover on a wet patch of grass. What could be the matter?

Sleepyhead was now wide awake. Said he, "DEAR ME, WHERE IS MY TOADSTOOL?"

From these four instances, we may, perhaps, deduce certain general principles of adaptation that have at least proved valuable to those using them.

These are suggestions that the practiced storyteller will find trite. But to others, they may prove a fair foundation on which to build a personal method to be developed by experience:

The preliminary step in all cases is *analysis of the story*. The aim, then, is to *reduce* a long story or to *amplify* a short one.

For reducing a long story, the need is *elimination* of secondary threads of narrative, extra personages, description, and irrelevant events.

For amplifying a short story, the great need is of *realizing imagination*.

For both, it is desirable to keep *close logical sequence, a single point of view, simple language*, and *the point at the end*.

Chapter 4

How to Tell a Story

Selection, and, if necessary, adaptation are the preliminaries to the act of telling. That, after all, is the real test of one's power. That is the real joy, when achieved; the real bugbear, when dreaded. And that is the subject of this chapter.

How to tell a story: it is a short question that demands a long answer. The right beginning of the answer depends on a right conception of the thing the question is about; and that naturally reverts to an earlier discussion of the real nature of a story. In that discussion, it was stated that a story is a work of art — a message, as all works of art are.

To tell a story, then, is to pass on the message, to share the work of art. The message may be merely one of humor — of nonsense, even; works of art range all the way from the "Victory" to a "Dresden Shepherdess," from an "Assumption" to a "Broken Pitcher," and farther. Each has its own place. But whatever its quality, the storyteller is the passer-on, the interpreter, the transmitter. He comes bringing a gift. Always he gives; always he bears a message.

Choose a Story You Appreciate

This granted, the first demand of the storyteller is not far to seek. No one can repeat a message he has not heard, or interpret what he does not understand. You cannot give unless you first possess. The first demand of the storyteller is that he possess. He must *feel* the story. Whatever the particular quality and appeal of the work of art, from the lightest to the grandest emotion or thought, he must have responded to it, grasped it, felt it intimately, before he can give it out again. Listen, humbly, for the message.

I realize that this has an incongruous sound, when applied to such stories as that of the little pig at the stile or of the greedy cat who ate up man and beast. But, believe me, it does apply even to those. For the transmittable thing in a story is the identifying essence, the characterizing savor, the peculiar quality and point of view of the humor, pathos, or interest. Every tale that claims a place in good fiction has this identifying savor and quality, each different from every other. The laugh that echoes one of Seumas McManus's rigmaroles is not the chuckle that follows one of Joel Chandler Harris's anecdotes; the gentle sadness of an Andersen allegory is not the heart-searching tragedy of a tale from the Greek; nor is any one story of an author just like any other of the same making. Each has its personal likeness, its facial expression, as it were.

And the mind must be sensitized to these differences. No one can tell stories well who has not a keen and just feeling of such emotional values. A positive and a negative injunction depend on this premise — the positive: cultivate your feeling, striving toward increasingly just appreciation; the negative: never tell a story you do not feel.

Fortunately, the number and range of stories one can appreciate grow with cultivation; but it is the part of wisdom not to step outside the range at any stage of its growth.

I feel the more inclined to emphasize this caution because I once had a rather embarrassing and pointed proof of its desirability. There is a certain nonsense tale that a friend used to tell with such effect that her hearers became helpless with laughter, but which, for some reason, never seemed funny to me. I could not laugh at it. But my friend constantly urged me to use it, quoting her own success. At last, with much curiosity and some trepidation, I included it in a program before people with whom I was so closely in sympathy that no chill was likely to emanate from their side. I told the story as well as I knew how, putting into it more genuine effort than most stories can claim. The audience smiled politely, laughed gently once or twice, and relapsed into the mildest of amusement. The most one could say was that the story was not a hopeless failure. I tried it again, after study, and yet again; but the audiences were all alike. And in my heart, I would have been startled if they had behaved otherwise, for all the time I was telling it, I was conscious in my soul that it was a stupid story! At last, I owned my defeat to myself and put the thing out of mind.

Some time afterward, I happened to take out the notes of the story, and idly looked them over; and suddenly — I do not know how — I got the point of view! The salt of the humor was all at once on my lips; I felt the tickle of the pure folly of it; it *was* funny.

The next afternoon I told the story to a hundred or so children and as many mothers — and the battle was won. Chuckles punctuated my periods; helpless laughter ran like an undercurrent below my narrative; it was a struggle for me to keep sober myself. The nonsense tale had found its own atmosphere.

Now, of course, I had known all along that the humor of the story emanated from its very exaggeration, its absurdly illogical smoothness. But I had not *felt* it. I did not really "see the joke." And that was why I could not tell the story. I undoubtedly impressed my own sense of its fatuity on every audience to which I gave it. The case is very clear.

Equally clear have been some happy instances where I have found audiences responding to a story I myself greatly liked, but which common appreciation usually ignored. This is an experience even more persuasive than the other, certainly more to be desired.

Every storyteller has lines of limitation; certain types of story will always remain his or her best effort. There is no reason why any type of story should be told really ill, and of course, the number of kinds one tells well increases with the growth of the appreciative capacity. But nonetheless, it is wise to recognize the limits at each stage, and not try to tell any story to which the honest inner consciousness says, "I do not like you."

Let us, then, set down as a prerequisite for good storytelling *a genuine appreciation of the story.*

Get a Feel for Your Audience

Now, we may suppose this genuine appreciation to be your portion. You have chosen a story, have felt its charm, and identified the quality of its appeal.

You are now to tell it in such wise that your hearers will get the same kind of impression you yourself received from it. How?

I believe the inner secret of success is the measure of force with which the teller wills the conveyance of his impression to the hearer.

Anyone who has watched, or has himself been, the teller of a story that held an audience knows that there is something approaching hypnotic suggestion in the close connection of effort and effect, and in the elimination of self-consciousness from speaker and listeners alike.

I would not for a moment lend the atmosphere of charlatanry, or of the ultra-psychic, to the wholesome and vivid art of storytelling. But I would, if possible, help the teacher to realize how largely success in that art is a subjective and psychological matter, dependent on her control of her own mood and her sense of direct, intimate communion with the minds attending her. The "feel" of an audience — that indescribable sense of the composite human soul waiting on the initiative of your own, the emotional currents interplaying along a medium so delicate that it takes the baffling torture of an obstruction to reveal its existence — cannot be taught. But it can and does develop with use. And a realization of the immense latent power of strong desire and resolution vitalizes and disembarrasses the beginner.

That is, undoubtedly, rather an intangible beginning; it sets the root of the matter somewhat in the realm of "spirits and influences." There are, however, outward and visible means of arriving at results. Every art has its technique. The art of storytelling, intensely personal and subjective as it is, yet comes under the law sufficiently not to be a matter of sheer "knack." It has its technique. The following suggestions are an attempt to state what seem the foundation principles of that technique. The general statements are deduced from many consecutive experiences; partly, too, they are the results of introspective analysis, confirmed by observation. They do not make up an exclusive body of rules, wholly adequate to produce good work, of themselves; they do include, so far as my observation and experience allow, the fundamental requisites of good work — being the qualities uniformly present in the successful work of many storytellers.

Know the Story

First of all, most fundamental of all, is a rule without which any other would be but folly: *Know your story.*

One would think so obvious a preliminary might be taken for granted. But alas, even slight acquaintance with the average storyteller proves the dire necessity of the admonition. The halting tongue, the slip in name or incident, the turning back to forge an omitted link in the chain, the repetition, the general weakness of statement consequent on imperfect grasp: these are common features of the stories we hear told. And they are features that will deface the best story ever told.

The teller must know the story absolutely; it must have been so assimilated that it partakes of the nature of personal experience; its essence must be so clearly in mind that the teller does not have to think of it at all in the act of telling, but rather lets it flow from his lips with the unconscious freedom of a vivid reminiscence.

Such knowledge does not mean memorizing. Memorizing utterly destroys the freedom of reminiscence, takes away the spontaneity, and substitutes a mastery of form for a mastery of essence. It means, rather, a perfect grasp of the gist of the story, with sufficient familiarity with its form to determine the manner of its telling.

The easiest way to obtain this mastery is, I think, to analyze the story into its simplest elements of plot. Strip it bare of style, description, interpolation, and find out simply *what happened*. Personally, I find that I get first an especially vivid conception of the climax; this then has to be rounded out by a clear perception of the successive steps that lead up to the climax. One has, thus, the framework of the story.

Practice Telling the Story Aloud

The next process is the filling in.

There must be many ways of going about this filling in. Doubtless many of my readers, in the days when it was their pet ambition to make a good recitation in school, evolved personally effective ways of doing it; for it is, after all, the same thing as preparing a bit of history or a recitation in literature. But for the consideration of those who find it hard to gain mastery of fact without mastery of its stated form, I give my own way.

I have always used the childlike plan of talking it out. Sometimes inaudibly, sometimes in loud and penetrating tones that arouse the sympathetic curiosity of my family, I tell it over and over, to an imaginary hearer. That hearer is as present to me, always has been, as Stevenson's "friend of the children" who takes

64

the part of the enemy in their solitary games of war. His criticism (although he is a most composite double-sexed creature who should not have a designating personal pronoun) is all-revealing. For talking it out instantly brings to light the weak spots in one's recollection. "What was it the little crocodile said?" "Just how did the little pig get into his house?" "What was that link in the chain of circumstances which brought the wily fox to confusion?" The slightest cloud of uncertainty becomes obvious in a moment. And as obvious becomes one's paucity of expression, one's week-kneed imagination, one's imperfect assimilation of the spirit of the story. It is not a flattering process.

But when these faults have been corrected by several attempts, the method gives a confidence, a sense of sureness, which makes the real telling to a real audience ready and spontaneously smooth. Scarcely an epithet or a sentence comes out as it was in the preliminary telling; but epithets and sentences in sufficiency do come; the beauty of this method is that it brings freedom instead of bondage.

Avoid Memorizing

A valuable exception to the rule against memorizing must be noted here. Especially beautiful and indicative phrases of the original should be retained, and even whole passages, where they are identified with the beauty of the tale. And in stories such as "The Three Bears" or "Red Riding Hood," the exact phraseology of the conversation as given in familiar versions should be preserved; it is in a way sacred, a classic, and not to be altered. But beyond this, the language should be the teller's own, and probably never twice the same.

Sureness, ease, freedom, and the effect of personal reminiscence come only from complete mastery. I repeat, with emphasis: Know your story.

Get Your Listeners' Attention

The next suggestion is a purely practical one concerning the preparation of physical conditions. See that the children are seated in close and direct range of your eye; the familiar half-circle is the best arrangement for small groups of children, but the story-teller should be at a point *opposite* the center of the arc, *not in* its center: it is important also not to have the ends too far at the side, and to have no child directly behind another, or in such a position that he has not an easy view of the teller's full face. Little children have to be physically close in order to be mentally close.

It is, of course, desirable to obtain a hushed quiet before beginning; but it is not so important as to preserve your own mood of holiday, and theirs. If the fates and the atmosphere of the day are against you, it is wiser to trust to the drawing power of the tale itself, and abate the irritation of didactic methods.

And never break into that magic tale, once begun, with an admonition to Ethel or Tommy to stop squirming, or a rebuke to "that little girl over there who is not listening." Make her listen! It is probably your fault if she is not. If you are telling a good story, and telling it well, she can't help listening — unless she is an abnormal child; and if she is abnormal, you ought not to spoil the mood of the others to attend to her.

I say "never" interrupt your story; perhaps it is only fair to amend that, after the fashion of dear little Marjorie Fleming, and say "never — if you can help it." For, of course, there are exceptional occasions, and exceptional children; some latitude must be left for the decisions of good common sense acting on the issue of the moment.

Create the Mood

The children ready, your own mood must be ready. It is desirable that the spirit of the story should be imposed upon the room from the beginning, and this result hangs on the clearness and intensity of the teller's initiatory mood. An act of memory and of will is the requisite. The storyteller must call up — it comes with the swiftness of thought — the essential emotion of the story as he felt it first. A single volition puts him in touch with the characters and the movement of the tale. This is scarcely more than a brief and condensed reminiscence; it is the stepping back into a mood once experienced.

Let us say, for example, that the story to be told is the immortal fable "The Ugly Duckling." Before you open your lips, the whole pathetic series of the little swan's mishaps should flash across your mind — not accurately and in detail, but blended to a composite of undeserved ignominy, of baffled innocent wonderment, and of delicious underlying satire on average views. With this is mingled the feeling of Andersen's delicate whimsicality of style. The dear little Ugly Duckling waddles, bodily, into your consciousness, and you pity his sorrows and anticipate his triumph, before you begin.

This preliminary recognition of mood is what brings the delicious quizzical twitch to the mouth of a good raconteur who begins an anecdote the hearers know will be side-splitting. It is what makes grandmother sigh gently and look far over your heads, when her soft voice commences the story of "the little girl who lived long, long ago." It is a natural and instinctive thing with the born storyteller; a necessary thing for anyone who will become a storyteller.

From the very start, the mood of the tale should be definite and authoritative, beginning with the mood of the teller and emanating therefrom in proportion as the physique of the teller is a responsive medium.

Tell the Story
Now we are off. Knowing your story, having your hearers well arranged, and being as thoroughly as you are able in the right

mood, you begin to tell it. Tell it, then, simply, directly, dramatically, with zest.

• *Simplicity* here applies both to manner and matter. As to manner, I mean without affectation, without any form of pretense — in short, without posing. It is a pity to "talk down" to the children, to assume a honeyed voice, to think of the edifying or educational value of the work one is doing. Naturalness, being oneself, is the desideratum. I wonder why we so often use a preposterous voice, a super-sweetened whine, in talking to children? Is it that the effort to realize an ideal of gentleness and affectionateness overreaches itself in this form of the grotesque? Some good intention must be the root of it. But the thing is nonetheless pernicious. A "cant" voice is as abominable as a cant phraseology. Both are of the very substance of evil.

"But it is easier to *say*, 'Be natural' than to *be* it," said one teacher to me desperately.

Beyond dispute. To those of us who are cursed with an overabundant measure of self-consciousness, nothing is harder than simple naturalness. The remedy is to lose oneself in one's art. Think of the story so absorbingly and vividly that you have no room to think of yourself. Live it. Sink yourself in that mood you have summoned up, and let it carry you.

If you do this, simplicity of matter will come easily. Your choice of words and images will naturally become simple.

It is, I think, a familiar precept to educators that children should not have their literature too much simplified for them. We are told that they like something beyond them, and that it is good for them to have a sense of mystery and power beyond the sense they grasp. That may be true; but if so, it does not apply to storytelling as it does to reading. We have constantly to remember that the movement of a story told is very swift. A concept not grasped in passing is irrevocably lost; there is no possibility of turning back, or lingering over the page. Also, since the art of storytelling is primarily an art of entertainment, its very object is sacrificed if the ideas and images do not slip into the child's consciousness smoothly enough to avoid the sense of strain. For this reason short, familiar, vivid words are best.

Simplicity of manner and of matter are both essential to the right appeal to children.

• *Directness* in telling a story is a most important quality. The story listened to is like the drama beheld. Its movement must be unimpeded, increasingly swift, winding up "with a snap." Long-windedness, or talking around the story, utterly destroys this movement. The incidents should be told, one after another, without explanation or description beyond what is absolutely necessary; and *they should be told in logical sequence.* Nothing is more distressing than the cart-before-the-horse method — nothing more quickly destroys interest than the failure to get a clue in the right place.

Sometimes, to be sure, a side remark adds piquancy and a personal savor. But the general rule is great discretion in this respect.

Every epithet or adjective beyond what is needed to give the image is a five-barred gate in the path of the eager mind traveling to a climax.

Explanations and moralizing are usually sheer clatter. Some few stories necessarily include a little explanation, and stories of the fable order may quaintly end with an obvious moral. But here again, the rule is — great discretion.

It is well to remember that you have one great advantage over the writer of stories. The writer must present a clear image and make a vivid impression — all with words. The teller has face, voice, and body to do it with. The teller needs, consequently, but one swiftly incisive verb to the writer's two; but one expressive adjective to his three. Often, indeed, a pause and an expressive gesture do the whole thing.

It may be said here that it is a good trick of description to repeat an epithet or phrase once used, when referring again to the same thing. The recurrent adjectives of Homer were the device of one who entertained a childlike audience. His trick is unconscious and instinctive with people who have a natural gift for children's stories. Of course this matter also demands common sense in the degree of its use; in moderation, it is a most successful device.

Brevity, close logical sequence, exclusion of foreign matter, unhesitant speech — to use these is to tell a story directly.

• *Drama:* After simplicity and directness comes that quality which to advise is to become a rock of offense to many. It is the suggestion, "Tell the story *dramatically.*" Yet when we quite understand each other as to the meaning of *dramatically,* I think you will agree with me that a good storyteller includes this in his qualities of manner. It means, not in the manner of the elocutionist, not excitably, not any of the things that are incompatible with simplicity and sincerity; but with a wholehearted throwing of ourselves into the game, which identifies us in a manner with the character or situation of the moment. It means responsively, vividly, without interposing a blank wall of solid self between the drama of the tale and the mind's eye of the audience.

It is such fun, pure and simple, so to throw ourselves into it, and to see the answering expressions mimic our own, that it seems superfluous to urge it. Yet many persons do find it difficult. The instant, slight but suggestive change of voice, the use of onomatopoetic words, the response of eyes and hands, which are all immediate and spontaneous with some temperaments, are to others a matter of shamefacedness and labor. To those, to all who are not by nature bodily expressive, I would reiterate the injunction already given — not to pretend. Do nothing you cannot do naturally and happily. But lay your stress on the inner and spiritual effort to appreciate, to feel, to imagine out the tale; and let the expressiveness of your body grow gradually with the increasing freedom from crippling self-consciousness. The physique will become more mobile as the emotion does.

The expression must, however, always *remain suggestive rather than illustrative*. This is the side of the case which those who are overdramatic must not forget. The storyteller is not playing the parts of his stories; he is merely arousing the imagination of his hearers to picture the scenes for themselves. One element of the dual consciousness of the tale-teller remains always the observer, the reporter, the quiet outsider.

I like to think of the storyteller as a good fellow standing at a great window overlooking a busy street or a picturesque square, and reporting with gusto to the comrade in the rear of the room what of mirth or sadness he sees; he hints at the policeman's strut, the organ-grinder's shrug, the schoolgirl's gaiety, with a gesture that is born of an irresistible impulse to imitate; but he never leaves his fascinating post to carry the imitation further than a hint.

The verity of this figure lies in the fact that the dramatic quality of storytelling depends closely upon the *clearness and power with which the storyteller visualizes the events and characters he describes*. You must hold the image before your mind's eye, using your imagination to embody to yourself every act, incident, and appearance. You must, indeed, stand at the window of your consciousness and watch what happens.

This is a point so vital that I am tempted to put it in ornate type. You must *see* what you *say*!

It is not too much even to say *you must see more than you say*. True vividness is lent by a background of picture realized by the listener beyond what you tell him. Children see, as a rule, no image you do not see; they see most clearly what you see most largely. Draw, then, from a full well, not from a supply so low that the pumps wheeze at every pull.

Dramatic power of the reasonably quiet and suggestive type demanded for telling a story will come pretty surely in the train of effort along these lines; it follows the clear concept and sincerity in imparting it and is a natural consequence of the visualizing imagination.

• *Zest:* It is inextricably bound up, also, with the causes and results of the quality that finds place in my final injunction, to tell your story *with zest*. It might almost be assumed that the final suggestion renders the preceding one superfluous, so direct is the effect of a lively interest on the dramatic quality of a narration; but it would not of itself be adequate; the necessity of visualizing imagination is paramount. Zest is, however, a close second to this clearness of mental vision.

It is entirely necessary to be interested in your own story, to enjoy it as you tell it. If you are bored and tired, the children will soon be bored and tired, too. If you are not interested, your manner cannot get that vitalized spontaneity which makes dramatic power possible. Nothing else will give that relish on the lips, that gusto, which communicates its joy to the audience and makes it receptive to every impression.

I used to say to teachers, "Tell your story with all your might," but I found that this, by a natural misconception, was often interpreted to mean "laboriously." And of course nothing is more injurious to the enjoyment of an audience than obvious effort on the part of the entertainer.

True zest can be — often is — extremely quiet, but it gives a savor nothing else can impart.

"But how, at the end of a hard morning's work, can I be interested in a story I have told twenty times before?" asks the kindergarten or primary teacher, not without reason.

There are two things to be said. The first is a reminder of the wisdom of choosing stories in which you originally have interest; and of having a store large enough to permit variety. The second applies to those inevitable times of weariness which attack the most interested and well-stocked storyteller. You are, perhaps, tired out physically. You have told a certain story until it seems as if a repetition of it must produce bodily effects dire to contemplate, yet that happens to be the very story you must tell. What can you do? I answer, "Make believe." The device seems incongruous with the repeated warnings against pretense; but it is necessary, and it is wise. Pretend as hard as ever you can to be interested. And the result will be — before you know it — that you will *be* interested. That is the chief cause of the recommendation; it brings about the result it simulates. Make believe, as well as you know how, and the probability is that you will not even know when the transition from pretended to real interest comes.

And fortunately, the children never know the difference. They have not that psychological infallibility which is often attributed to them. They might, indeed, detect a pretense that continued through a whole tale; but that is so seldom necessary that it needs little consideration.

So then: enjoy your story; be interested in it — if you possibly can; and if you cannot, pretend to be, until the very pretense brings about the virtue you have assumed.

Speak in a Clear, Easy Voice

There is much else that might be said and urged regarding the method of storytelling, even without encroaching on the domain of personal variations. A whole chapter might, for example, be devoted to voice and enunciation, and then leave the subject fertile. But voice and enunciation are, after all, merely single manifestations of degree and quality of culture, of taste, and of natural gift. No set rules can bring charm of voice and speech to a person whose feeling and habitual point of view are fundamentally wrong; the person whose habitual feeling and mental attitude are fundamentally right needs few or no rules. As the whole matter of storytelling is in the first instance an expression of the complex personal product, so will this feature of it vary in perfection according to the beauty and culture of the human mechanism manifesting it.

A few generally applicable suggestions may, however, be useful — always assuming the storyteller to have the fundamental qualifications of fine and wholesome habit. These are not rules for the art of speaking; they are merely some practical considerations regarding speaking to an audience.

First, I would reiterate my earlier advice, be simple. Affectation is the worst enemy of voice and enunciation alike. Slovenly enunciation is certainly very dreadful, but the unregenerate may be pardoned if they prefer it to the affected mouthing which some overly nice people without due sense of values expend on every syllable that is so unlucky as to fall between their teeth.

Next, I would urge avoidance of a fault very common with those who speak much in large rooms: the mistaken effort at loudness. This results in tightening and straining the throat, finally producing nasal head-tones or a voice of metallic harshness. And it is entirely unnecessary. There is no need to speak loudly. The ordinary schoolroom needs no vocal effort. A hall seating three or four hundred persons demands no effort whatever beyond a certain clearness and definiteness of speech. A hall seating from five to eight hundred needs more skill in aiming the voice, but still demands no shouting.

It is indeed largely the psychological quality of a tone that makes it reach in through the ear to the comprehension. The quiet, clear, restful, persuasive tone of a speaker who knows his power goes straight home; but loud speech confuses. Never speak loudly. In a small room, speak as gently and easily as in conversation; in a large room, think of the people farthest away, and speak clearly, with a slight separation between words, and with definite phrasing — aiming your *mind* toward the distant listeners.

If one is conscious of nasality or throatiness of voice, it certainly pays to study the subject seriously with an intelligent teacher. But a good, natural speaking-voice, free from extraordinary vices, will fill all the requirements of storytelling to small audiences, without other attention than comes indirectly from following the general principles of the art.

To sum it all up, then, let us say of the method likely to bring success in telling stories, that it includes sympathy, grasp, and spontaneity: one must appreciate the story, and know it; and then, using the realizing imagination as a constant vivifying force, and dominated by the mood of the story, one must tell it with all one's might — simply, vitally, joyously.

Chapter 5

Storytelling in the Classroom

In chapter 2, I tried to give my conception of the general aim of storytelling in school. From that conception, it is not difficult to deduce certain specific uses. The one most plainly intimated is that of a brief recreation period, a feature that has proved valuable in many classes. Less definitely implied, but not to be ignored, was the use of the story during, or accessory to, the lesson in science or history.

But more distinctive and valuable than these, I think, is a specific use I have recently had the pleasure of seeing exemplified. Tersely stated, the object of the general plan is the freeing and developing of the power of expression in the pupils. I think there can be no need of dwelling on the desirability of this result. The apathy and "woodenness" of children under average modes of pedagogy is apparent to anyone who is interested enough to observe. In elementary work, the most noticeable lack of natural expression is probably in the reading classes; the same drawback appears at a later stage in English composition. But all along the line, every thoughtful teacher knows how difficult it is to obtain spontaneous, creative reaction on material given.

Storytelling has a real mission to perform in setting free the natural creative expression of children, and in vitalizing the general atmosphere of the school. The method in use for this purpose is a threefold *giving back* of the story by the children. Two of the forms of reproduction are familiar to many teachers; the first is the obvious one of telling the story back again.

Listeners Retell the Story

It is such fun to listen to a good story that children remember it without effort, and later, when asked if they can tell the story of "The Red-Headed Woodpecker" or "The Little Red Hen," they are as eager to try it as if it were a personal experience they were burning to impart.

Each pupil is given a chance to try each story at some time. Then, the story that each child has told especially well is allotted to him for his own particular story, on which he has an especial claim thereafter.

It is surprising to note how comparatively individual and distinctive the expression of voice and manner becomes, after a short time. The child instinctively emphasizes the points that appeal to him, and the element of fun in it all helps to bring forgetfulness of self. The main inflections and the general tenor of the language, however, remain imitative, as is natural with children. But this is a gain rather than otherwise, for it is useful in forming good habits. In no other part of her work, probably, has a teacher so good a chance to foster in her pupils pleasant habits of enunciation and voice.

They told us their stories, and there was truly not one told poorly or inexpressively; all the children had learned something of the joy of creative effort. But one little fellow stands out in my memory beyond all the rest, yet as a type of all the rest.

Rudolph was very small, and square, and merry of eye; life was all eagerness and expectancy to him. Having come from another country, he knew no English beyond that of one school year. But he stood staunchly in his place and told me the story of "The Little Half-Chick" with an abandon and bodily emphasis that left no doubt of his sympathetic understanding of every word. The depth of moral reproach in his tone was quite beyond description when he said, "Little Half-Chick, little Half-Chick, when *I* was in trubbul, you wouldn't help *me!*" He heartily relished that repetition, and became more dramatic each time.

Throughout the telling, in the tones of the tender little voice, the sideways pose of the neat dark head, and the occasional use of a chubby pointing finger, one could trace a vague reflection of the teacher's manner. It was not strong enough to dominate at all over the child's personality, but it was strong enough to suggest possibilities.

In different rooms, I was told "The Little Half-Chick," "The Little Red Hen," "The Three Bears," "The Red-Headed Woodpecker," "The Fox and the Grapes," and many other simple stories, and in every instance, there was a noticeable degree of spontaneity and command of expression.

When the reading classes were held, the influence of this work was very visible. It had crept into the teachers' method, as well as the children's attitude. The story interest was still paramount. In the discussion, in the teachers' remarks, and in the actual reading, there was a joyousness and an interest in the subject-matter that totally precluded that preoccupation with sounds and syllables so deadly to any real progress in reading. There was less of the mechanical in the reading than in any I had heard in my visits to schools; but it was exceptionally accurate.

Listeners Illustrate the Story

The second form of giving back that has proved a keen pleasure and a stimulus to growth is a kind of seat work. The children are allowed to make original illustrations of the stories by cutting silhouette pictures.

It will be readily seen that no child can do this without visualizing each image very perfectly. In the simplest and most unconscious

way possible, the small artists are developing the power of con-
ceiving and holding the concrete image of an idea given, the
power that is at the bottom of all arts of expression.

Listeners Play the Story

The pictures and the retelling are both popular with children,
but neither is as dear to them as the third form of reproduction of
which I wish to speak. This third kind is taken entirely on the
ground of play, and no visibly didactic element enters into it. It
consists simply of *playing the story.*

When a good story with a simple sequence has been told, and
while the children are still athrill with the delight of it, they are
told they may play it.

"Who would like to be Red Riding Hood?" says the teacher; up
go the little girls' hands, and Mary or Hannah or Gertrude is
chosen.

"Who will be the wolf?" Johnny or Marcus becomes the wolf.
The kind woodchopper and the mother are also happily distrib-
uted, for in these little dramatic companies, it is an all-star cast,
and no one realizes any indignity in a subordinate role.

"Now, where shall we have little Red Riding Hood's house?
Over in that corner, Katie? Very well, Riding Hood shall live over
there. And where shall the Grandmother's cottage be?"

The children decide that it must be a long distance through the
wood — halfway around the schoolroom, in fact. The wolf selects
the spot where he will meet Red Riding Hood, and the woodchopper chooses a position from which he can rush in at the criti-
cal moment, to save Red Riding Hood's life.

Then, with gusto good to see, they play the game. The teacher
makes no suggestions; each actor creates his part. Some children
prove extremely expressive and facile, while others are limited by
nature. But each is left to his spontaneous action.

In the course of several days, several sets of children have been allowed to try; then, if any of them are notably good in the several roles, they are given an especial privilege in that story, as was done with the retelling. When a child expresses a part badly, the teacher sometimes asks if anyone thinks of another way to do it; from different examples offered, the children then choose the one they prefer; this is adopted. At no point is the teacher apparently teaching. She lets the audience teach itself and its actors.

The children played a good many stories for me during my visit. Of them all, "Red Riding Hood," "The Fox and the Grapes," and "The Lion and the Mouse" were most vividly done.

It will be long before the chief of the Little Red Riding Hoods fades from my memory. She had a dark, foreign little face, with a good deal of darker hair tied back from it, and brown, expressive hands. Her eyes were so full of dancing lights that when they met mine unexpectedly, it was as if a chance reflection had dazzled me. When she was told that she might play, she came up for her riding hood like an embodied delight, almost dancing as she moved. (Her teacher used a few simple elements of stage-setting for her stories, such as bowls for the Bears, a cape for Riding Hood, and so on.)

The game began at once. Riding Hood started from the rear corner of the room, basket on arm; her mother gave her strict injunctions as to lingering on the way, and she returned a respectful "Yes, Mother." Then she trotted around the aisle, greeting the woodchopper on the way to the deep wood that lay close by the teacher's desk. There Master Wolf was waiting, and there the two held converse — Master Wolf very crafty indeed, Red Riding Hood extremely polite. The wolf then darted on ahead and crouched down in the corner, which represented grandmother's bed. Riding Hood tripped sedately to the imaginary door, and knocked. The familiar dialogue followed, and with the words "the better to eat you with, my dear!" the wolf clutched Red Riding Hood, to eat her up. But we were not forced to undergo the threatened scene of horrid carnage, as the woodchopper opportunely arrived, and stated calmly, "I will not let you kill Little Red Riding Hood."

All was now happily culminated, and with the chopper's grave injunction as to future conduct in her ears, the rescued heroine tiptoed out of the woods, to her seat.

I wanted to applaud, but I realized in the nick of time that we were all playing, and held my peace.

"The Fox and the Grapes" was more dramatically done, but was given by a single child. He was the chosen "fox" of another primary room, and had the fair coloring and sturdy frame that matched his Swedish name. He was naturally dramatic. It was easy to see that he instinctively visualized everything, and this he did so strongly that he suggested to the onlooker every detail of the scene.

He chose for his grape-trellis the rear wall of the room.

Standing there, he looked longingly up at the invisible bunch of grapes. "My gracious," he said, "what fine grapes! I will have some."

Then he jumped for them.

"Didn't get them," he muttered. "I'll try again," and he jumped higher.

"Didn't get them this time," he said disgustedly and hopped up once more. Then he stood still, looked up, shrugged his shoulders, and remarked in an absurdly worldly-wise tone, "Those grapes are sour!" After that he walked away.

Of course, the whole thing was infantile, and without a touch of grace; but it is no exaggeration to say that the child did what many grown-up actors fail to do: he preserved the illusion.

It was in still another room that I saw "The Lion and the Mouse" fable played.

The lion lay flat on the floor for his nap, but started up when he found his paw laid on the little mouse, who crouched as small as she could beside him. (The mouse was by nature rather larger than the lion, but she called what art she might to her assistance.) The mouse persuaded the lion to lift his paw, and ran away.

Presently a most horrific groaning emanated from the lion. The mouse ran up, looked him over, and soliloquized in precise language — evidently remembered — "What is the matter with the lion? Oh, I see; he is caught in a trap." And then she gnawed with her teeth at the imaginary rope that bound him.

"What makes you so kind to me, little mouse?" said the rescued lion.

"You let me go, when I asked you," said the mouse demurely.

"Thank you, little mouse," answered the lion; and therewith, *finis*.

It is not impossible that all this play atmosphere may seem incongruous and unnecessary to teachers used to more conventional methods, but I feel sure that an actual experience of it would modify that point of view conclusively. The children of the schools where storytelling and "dramatizing" were practiced were startlingly better in reading, in attentiveness, and in general power of expression than the pupils of like social conditions in the same grades of other cities I visited soon after, and in which the more conventional methods were exclusively used. The teachers, also, were stronger in power of expression.

But the most noticeable, although the least tangible, difference was in the moral atmosphere of the schoolroom. There had been a great gain in vitality in all the rooms where stories were a part of the work. It had acted and reacted on pupils and teachers alike. The telling of a story well so depends on being thoroughly vitalized that, naturally, habitual telling had resulted in habitual vitalization.

This result was not, of course, wholly due to the practice of storytelling, but it was in some measure due to that. And it was a result worth the effort.

I beg to urge these specific uses of stories, as both recreative and developing, and as especially tending toward enlarged power of expression: retelling the story; illustrating the story in seat work; dramatization.

Chapter 6

The Child-Mind and How to Satisfy It

"It is the grown people who make the nursery stories," wrote Stevenson. "All the children do is jealously preserve the text." And the grown person, whether he makes his stories with pen or with tongue, should bring two qualities at least to the work: simplicity of language and a serious sincerity. The reason for the simplicity is obvious, for no one, child or otherwise, can thoroughly enjoy a story clouded by words that convey no meaning to him.

The second quality is less obvious but equally necessary. No absence of fun is intended by the words "serious sincerity," but they mean that the storyteller should bring to the child an equal interest in what is about to be told; an honest acceptance, for the time being, of the fairies, or the heroes, or the children, or the animals who talk, with which the tale is concerned. The child deserves this equality of standpoint, and without it, there can be no entire success.

As for the stories themselves, the difficulty lies with the material, not with the *child*. Styles may be varied generously, but the matter must be quarried for. Out of a hundred children's books, it is more than likely that ninety-nine will be useless; yet perhaps out of one autobiography may be gleaned an anecdote, or a reminiscence that can be amplified into an absorbing tale. Almost every storyteller will find that the open eye and ear will serve him better than much arduous searching. No one book will yield him the increase to his repertoire that will come to him by listening, by browsing in chance volumes and magazines, and even newspapers, by observing everyday life, and in all, remembering his own youth, and his youthful, waiting audience.

And that youthful audience? A rather too common mistake is made in allowing overmuch for the creative imagination of the normal child. It is not creative imagination that the normal child possesses so much as an enormous credulity and no limitations. If we consider for a moment, we see that there has been little or nothing to limit things for him; therefore anything is possible. It is the years of our life as they come that narrow our fancies and set a bound to our beliefs; for experience has taught us that, for the most part, a certain cause will produce a certain effect.

The child, on the contrary, has but little knowledge of causes, and as yet but an imperfect realization of effects. If we, for instance, go into the midst of a savage country, we know that there is the chance of our meeting a savage. But to the young child, it is quite as possible to meet a Red Indian coming around the bend of the brook at the bottom of the orchard, as it is to meet him in his own wigwam.

The child is an adept at make-believe, but his make-believes are, as a rule, practical and serious. It is credulity rather than imagination that helps him. He takes the tales he has been *told*, the facts he has observed, and, for the most part, reproduces them to the best of his ability. And "nothing," as Stevenson says, "can stagger a child's faith; he accepts the clumsiest substitutes and can swallow the most staring incongruities. The chair he has just been besieging as a castle is taken away for the accommodation of a morning visitor, and he is nothing abashed; he can skirmish by the hour with a stationary coal-scuttle; in the midst of the enchanted pleasuance he can see, without sensible shock, the gardener soberly digging potatoes for the day's dinner."

The child, in fact, is neither undeveloped "grown-up" nor un-spoiled angel. Perhaps he has a dash of both, but most of all, he is akin to the grown person who dreams. With the dreamer and with the child, there is that unquestioning acceptance of circumstances as they arise, however unusual and disconcerting they may be. In dreams, the wildest, most improbable, and fantastic things happen, but they are not so to the dreamer. The veriest cynic among us must take his dreams seriously and without a sneer, whether he is forced to leap from the edge of a precipice, whether he finds himself utterly incapable of packing his trunk in time for the train, whether, in spite of his distress at the impropriety, he finds himself at a dinner party minus his collar, or whether the riches of El Dorado are laid at his feet. For him at the time, it is all quite real and harassingly or splendidly important.

To the child and to the dreamer, all things are possible; frogs may talk, bears may be turned into princes, gallant tailors may overcome giants, fir-trees may be filled with ambitions. A chair may become a horse, a chest of drawers a coach and six, a hearth-rug a battlefield, a newspaper a crown of gold. And these are facts that the storyteller must realize, and choose and shape the stories accordingly.

Many an old book, which to a modern grown person may seem prim and over-rigid, will be to the child a delight; for him the primness and the severity slip away, and the story remains. Such a book as Mary Martha Sherwood's *Fairchild Family* is an example of this. To a grown person reading it for the first time, the loafing propensities of the immaculate Mrs. Fairchild, who never does a hand's turn of good work for anyone from cover to cover, the hard piety, the snobbishness, the brutality of taking the children to the old gallows and seating them before the dangling remains of a murderer, while the lesson of brotherly love is impressed are shocking when they are not amusing; but to the child, the doings of the naughty and repentant little Fairchilds are engrossing; and experience proves to us that the twentieth-century child is as eager for the book as were ever his nineteenth-century grandfather and grandmother.

Sarah Trimmer's *History of the Robins*, too, is a continuous delight; and from its pompous and high-sounding dialogue, a skillful adapter may glean not only one story, but one story with two versions; for the infant of eighteen months can follow the narrative of the joys and troubles, errors and kindnesses of Robin, Dicky, Flopsy, and Pecksy; while the child of five or ten or even more will be keenly interested in a fuller account of the birds' adventures and the development of their several characters and those of their human friends and enemies.

From these two books, from Maria Edgeworth's wonderful *Moral Tales*; from Elizabeth Wetherell's delightful volume *Mr. Rutherford's Children*; from Jane and Ann Taylor's *Original Poems*; from Thomas Day's *Sandford and Merton*; from Bunyan's *Pilgrim's Progress* and Lamb's *Tales from Shakespeare*, and from many another old friend, stories may be gathered, but the storyteller will find that, in almost all cases, adaptation is a necessity. The joy of the hunt, however, is a real joy, and with a field that stretches from the myths of Greece to Uncle Remus, from *Le Morte d'Arthur* to the *Jungle Books*, there need be no more lack of pleasure for the seeker than for the receiver of the spoil.

⁒

The following is a list of valuable sources for the storyteller, all yielding either good original material for adaptation, or stories that need only a slight alteration in the telling:[8]

[8] Readers may be interested in Arthur Ransome's *A History of Storytelling*.

The Bible
Mother Goose's Melody
The Story Hour, by Kate Douglas Wiggin
Stories for Kindergarten
St. Nicholas Magazine, bound volumes
Little Folks, bound volumes
Fables and Nursery Tales, edited by Prof. Charles Eliot Norton
Stories to Tell the Littlest Ones, by Sara Cone Bryant
Mother Stories, by Maud Lindsay
More Mother Stories, by Maud Lindsay
Aesop's Fables
Stories to Tell to Children, by Sara Cone Bryant
The Book of Stories for the Storyteller, by Fanny Coe
Songs and Stories for the Little Ones, by Gordon Browne
Character Training, by E. L. Cabot and E. Eyles
Stories for the Story Hour, by Ada M. Marzials
Stories for the History Hour, by Nannie Niemeyer
Stories for the Bible Hour, by R. Brimley Johnson
Nature Stories to Tell to Children, by H. Waddingham Seers
Old Time Tales, by Florence Dugdale
The Mabinogion
Percy's Reliques

TOLD THROUGH THE AGES SERIES
  Legends of Greece and Rome, by G. H. Kupfer, M.A.
  Favorite Greek Myths, by L. S. Hyde
  Stories of Robin Hood, by J. W. McSpadden
  Stories of King Arthur, by U. W. Cutler
  Stories from Greek History, by H. L. Havell, B.A.
  Stories from Wagner, by J. W. McSpadden
  Britain Long Ago (stories from Old English and Celtic sources),
      by E. M. Wilmot-Buxton, F.R.Hist.S.

Stories from Scottish History (selected from *"Tales of a Grand-father"*), by Madalen Edgar, M.A.
Stories from Greek Tragedy, by H. L. Havell, B.A.
Stories from the Earthly Paradise, by Madalen Edgar, M.A.
Stories from Chaucer, by J. W. McSpadden
Stories from the Old Testament, by Susan Platt
Told by the Northmen (stories from the Norse Eddas and Sagas), by E. M. Wilmot-Buxton, F.R.Hist.S.
Stories from Don Quixote, by H. L. Havell, B.A.
The Story of Roland and the Peers of Charlemagne, by James Baldwin

Stories of the English
Old Greek Folk Stories, by Josephine Peabody
Red Cap Tales, by S. R. Crockett
A Child's Book of Saints, by William Canton
Cuchulain, the Hound of Ulster, by Eleanor Hull
The High Deeds of Finn, by T. W. Rolleston, M.A.
The Book of the Epic, by H. A. Guerber
The Myths of Greece and Rome, by H. A. Guerber
Myths of the Norsemen, by H. A. Guerber
Myths and Legends of the Middle Ages, by H. A. Guerber
Hero-Myths and Legends of the British Race, by M. I. Ebbutt, M.A.
The Minstrelsy of the Scottish Border
Gleanings in Buddha-Fields, by Lafcadio Hearn
The Golden Windows, by Laura E. Richards
Hans Andersen's Fairy Tales
Grimms' Fairy Tales
English Fairy Tales, by Joseph Jacobs
Folk-Tales from Many Lands, by Lilian Gask
Celtic Fairy Tales, by Joseph Jacobs
Indian Fairy Tales, by Joseph Jacobs

West African Folk-Tales, by W. H. Barker and C. Sinclair
Russian Fairy Tales, by R. Nisbet Bain
Cossack Fairy Tales, by R. Nisbet Bain
The Happy Prince, by Oscar Wilde
Donegal Fairy Tales, by Seumas McManus
In Chimney Corners, by Seumas McManus
The Arabian Nights
The Blue Fairy Book (and others), by Andrew Lang
Fairy Stories, by John Finnemore
The Japanese Fairy Book
Fairy Tales from Far Japan, translated by Susan Bollard
In The Child's World
Legends from Fairyland, by Holme Lee
The King of the Golden River, by John Ruskin
The Welsh Fairy Book, by Jenkyn Thomas
At the Back of the North Wind, by George MacDonald
Tell-Me-Why Stories about Animals, by C. H. Claudy
Tell-Me-Why Stories about Great Discoveries, by C. H. Claudy
Uncle Remus, by Joel Chandler Harris
Macaulay's Lays of Ancient Rome
Le Morte d'Arthur, by Sir Thomas Malory
The Boy's Froissart, by Henry Newbolt
Stories from Dante, by Susan Cunnington
The Jungle Books, by Rudyard Kipling
Just So Stories, by Rudyard Kipling
Wood Magic, by Richard Jefferies
Among the Farmyard People, by Clara D. Pierson
Among the Night People, by Clara D. Pierson
Among the Meadow People, by Clara D. Pierson
The Animal Story Book, by Andrew Lang
Wild Animals I Have Known, by Ernest Thompson Seton
A Book of Nature Myths, by Florence Holbrook

More Nature Myths, by F. V. Farmer

Parables from Nature, by Margaret Gatty

Northern Trails, by W. J. Long

The Kindred of the Wild, by Charles G. D. Roberts

Rab and His Friends, by John Brown

A Child's Garden of Verses, by Robert Louis Stevenson

A Treasury of Verse for Little Children, compiled by Madalen
Edgar, M.A.

A Treasury of Verse for Boys and Girls, compiled by Madalen
Edgar, M.A.

A Treasury of Ballads, compiled by Madalen Edgar, M.A.

Bimbi, by Louisa de la Rame (Ouida)

Stories from Shakespeare, by Thomas Carter

Stories from the Faerie Queene, by Laurence H. Dawson

Moral Tales, by Maria Edgeworth

Stories Selected
and Adapted for Telling

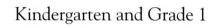

Kindergarten and Grade 1

Wee Willie Winkie runs through the town,
Upstairs and downstairs in his nightgown,
Rapping at the window, crying through the
    lock,
"Are the children in their beds, for now it's
    eight o'clock?"

There was a crooked man, and he went
    a crooked mile,
He found a crooked sixpence against
    a crooked stile;
He bought a crooked cat, which caught
    a crooked mouse,
And they all lived together in a little
    crooked house.

Cushy cow bonny, let down thy milk,
And I will give thee a gown of silk;
A gown of silk and a silver tee,
If thou wilt let down thy milk to me.

"Little girl, little girl, where have you been?"
"Gathering roses to give to the queen."
"Little girl, little girl, what gave she you?"
"She gave me a diamond as big as my shoe."

Little Bo-Peep has lost her sheep,
And can't tell where to find them.
Leave them alone, and they'll come home,
And bring their tails behind them.

Little Bo-Peep fell fast asleep,
And dreamt she heard them bleating.
But when she awoke, she found it a joke,
For still they all were fleeting.

Then up she took her little crook,
Determined for to find them.
She found them indeed, but it made her
    heart bleed,
For they'd left their tails behind them.

Five Little White Heads[9]

by Walter Learned

Five little white heads peeped out of the mold,
When the dew was damp and the night was cold;
And they crowded their way through the soil
   with pride;
"Hurrah! We are going to be mushrooms!"
   they cried.

But the sun came up, and the sun shone down,
And the little white heads were withered and
   brown;
Long were their faces, their pride had a fall —
They were nothing but toadstools, after all.

[9] From Charlotte Brewster Jordan's *Mother-Song and Child-Song*.

Bird Thoughts[10]

I lived first in a little house,
And lived there very well;
I thought the world was small and round,
And made of pale blue shell.

I lived next in a little nest,
Nor needed any other;
I thought the world was made of straw,
And brooded by my mother.

One day I fluttered from the nest
To see what I could find.
I said, "The world is made of leaves;
I have been very blind."

At length I flew beyond the tree,
Quite fit for grown-up labors.
I don't know how the world is made,
And neither do my neighbors!

---

[10] From Charlotte Brewster Jordan's *Mother-Song and Child-Song*.

How We Came to Have Pink Roses

Once, ever and ever so long ago, we didn't have any pink roses. All the roses in the world were white. There weren't any red ones at all, any yellow ones, or any pink ones — only white roses.

And one morning, very early, a little white rosebud woke up, and saw the sun looking at her. He stared so hard that the little white rosebud did not know what to do; so she looked up at him and said, "Why are you looking at me so hard?"

"Because you are so pretty!" said the big round sun. And the little white rosebud blushed! She blushed pink. And all her children after her were little pink roses!

Raggylug[11]

Once there was a little furry rabbit, who lived with his mother deep down in a nest under the long grass. His name was Raggylug, and his mother's name was Molly Cottontail.

Every morning, when Molly Cottontail went out to hunt for food, she said to Raggylug, "Now, Raggylug, lie still, and make no noise. No matter what you hear, no matter what you see, don't you move. Remember you are only a baby rabbit, and lie low." And Raggylug always said he would.

One day, after his mother had gone, he was lying very still in the nest, looking up through the feathery grass. By just cocking his eye so, he could see what was going on up in the world. Once, a big blue jay perched on a twig above him, and scolded someone very loudly; he kept saying, "Thief! Thief!" But Raggylug never moved his nose or his paws; he lay

---

[11] Adapted from Ernest Thompson Seton's *Wild Animals I Have Known*.

still. Once a ladybird took a walk down a blade of grass, over his head; she was so top-heavy that pretty soon she tumbled off and fell to the bottom, and had to begin all over again. But Raggylug never moved his nose or his paws; he lay still.

The sun was warm, and it was very still.

Suddenly Raggylug heard a little sound, far off. It sounded like *swish, swish*, very soft and far away. He listened. It was an odd little sound, low down in the grass, *rustle-rustle-rustle*; Raggylug was interested. But he never moved his nose or his paws; he lay still. Then the sound came nearer — *rustle-rustle-rustle*. Then it grew fainter, then came nearer — in and out, nearer and nearer, like something coming. Only, when Raggylug heard anything coming, he always heard its feet, stepping ever so softly. What could it be that came so smoothly — *rustle-rustle* — without any feet?

He forgot his mother's warning and sat up on his hind paws; the sound stopped then.

"Pooh," thought Raggylug. "I'm not a baby rabbit. I am three weeks old. I'll find out what this is." He stuck his head over the top of the nest, and looked — straight into the wicked eyes of a great big snake.

"Mammy, Mammy!" screamed Raggylug. "Oh, Mammy, Mam—" But he couldn't scream anymore, for the big snake had his ear in his mouth and was winding about the soft little body, squeezing Raggylug's life out. He tried to call "Mammy!" again, but he could not breathe.

Ah, but Mammy had heard the first cry. Straight over the fields she flew, leaping the stones and hummocks, fast as the wind, to save her baby. She wasn't a timid little cottontail rabbit then; she was a mother whose child was in danger. And when she came to Raggylug and the big snake, she took one look, and then *hop! hop!* she went over the snake's back; and as she jumped, she struck at the snake with her strong hind claws so that they tore his skin. He hissed with rage, but he did not let go.

Hop! hop! she went again, and this time she hurt him so that he twisted and turned; but he held on to Raggylug.

Once more the mother rabbit hopped, and once more she struck and tore the snake's back with her sharp claws. *Zzz!* How she hurt! The snake dropped Raggylug to strike at her, and Raggylug rolled onto his feet and ran.

"Run, Raggylug, run!" said his mother, keeping the snake busy with her jumps; and you may believe Raggylug ran! Just as soon as he was out of the way, his mother came, too, and showed him where to go. When she ran, there was a little white patch that showed under her tail; that was for Raggylug to follow. He followed it now.

Far, far away she led him, through the long grass, to a place where the big snake could not find him, and there she made a new nest. And this time, when she told Raggylug to lie low, you'd better believe he minded!

The Golden Cobwebs[12]

A Story to Tell by the Christmas Tree

I am going to tell you a story about something wonderful that happened to a Christmas tree like this, ever and ever so long ago, when it was once upon a time.

It was before Christmas, and the tree was trimmed with bright spangled threads and many-colored candles and [name the trimmings of the tree before you], and it stood safely out of sight in a room where the doors were locked, so that the children should not see it before the proper time. But ever so many other little house-people had seen it. The big black pussycat saw it with her great green eyes; the little gray kitty saw it with her little blue eyes; the kind

---

[12] This story was told me in the mother-tongue of a German friend, at the kindly request of a common friend of both; the narrator had heard it at home from the lips of a father of story-loving children for whom he often invented such little tales. The present adaptation has passed by hearsay through so many minds that it is perhaps little like the original, but I venture to hope it has a touch of the original fancy, at least.

house-dog saw it with his steady brown eyes; the yellow canary saw it with his wise, bright eyes. Even the wee, wee mice that were so afraid of the cat had peeped one peep when no one was by.

But there was someone who had not seen the Christmas tree. It was the little gray spider!

You see, the spiders lived in the corners — the warm corners of the sunny attic and the dark corners of the nice cellar. And they were expecting to see the Christmas tree as much as anybody. But just before Christmas, a great cleaning-up began in the house. The house-mother came sweeping and dusting and wiping and scrubbing, to make everything grand and clean for the Christ-Child's birthday. Her broom went into all the corners, *poke, poke* — and of course, the spiders had to run. Dear, dear, *how* the spiders had to run! Not one could stay in the house while the Christmas cleanness lasted. So, you see, they couldn't see the Christmas tree.

Spiders like to know all about everything, and to see all there is to see, and these were very sad. So at last they went to the Christ-Child and told Him about it.

"All the others see the Christmas tree, dear Christ-child," they said, "but we, who are so domestic and so fond of beautiful things, we are *cleaned up*! We cannot see it at all."

The Christ-Child was sorry for the little spiders when He heard this, and He said they should see the Christmas tree.

The day before Christmas, when nobody was noticing, He let them all go in, to look as long as ever they liked.

They came *creepy, creepy*, down the attic stairs, *creepy, creepy*, up the cellar stairs, *creepy, creepy*, along the halls — and into the beautiful room. The fat mother spiders and the old papa spiders were there, and all the little teeny, tiny, curly spiders, the baby ones. And then they looked! 'Round and 'round the tree they crawled, and looked and looked and looked. Oh, what a good time they had! They thought it was perfectly beautiful. And when they had looked at everything they could see from the floor, they started up the tree to see more. All over the tree they ran, *creepy, crawly*, looking at every single thing. Up and down, in and out, over every branch and twig, the little spiders ran, and saw every one of the pretty things right up close.

They stayed until they had seen all there was to see, you may be sure, and then they went away at last, *quite* happy.

Then, in the still, dark night before Christmas Day, the dear Christ-Child came, to bless the tree for the children. But when He looked at it — *what* do you suppose? — it was covered with cobwebs! Everywhere the little spiders had been, they had left a spider web; and you know they had been everywhere. So the tree was covered from its trunk to its tip with spider webs, all hanging from the branches and looped 'round the twigs; it was a strange sight.

What could the Christ-Child do? He knew that house-mothers do not like cobwebs; it would never, never do to have a Christmas tree covered with those. No, indeed.

So the dear Christ-Child touched the spiders' webs and turned them all to gold! Wasn't that a lovely trimming? They shone and shone, all over the beautiful tree. And that is the way the Christmas tree came to have golden cobwebs on it.

Why the Morning Glory Climbs

Once the morning glory was flat on the ground. She grew that way, and she had never climbed at all. Up in the top of a tree near her lived Mrs. Jennie Wren and her little baby wren. The little wren was lame; he had a broken wing and couldn't fly. He stayed in the nest all day. But the mother wren told him all about what she saw in the world, when she came flying home at night. She used to tell him about the beautiful morning glory she saw on the ground. She told him about the morning glory every day, until the little wren was filled with a desire to see her for himself.

"How I wish I could see the morning glory!" he said.

The morning glory heard this, and she longed to let the little wren see her face. She pulled herself along the ground, a little at a time, until she was at the foot of the tree where the little wren lived. But she could not get any farther, because she did not know how to climb. At last she wanted to go up so much, that she caught hold of the bark of the tree, and pulled herself up a little. And little by little, before she knew it, she was climbing.

And she climbed right up the tree to the little wren's nest, and put her sweet face over the edge of the nest, where the little wren could see.

That was how the morning glory came to climb.

The Story of Little Tavwots[13]

This is the story an Indian woman told a little white boy who lived with his father and mother near the Indians' country; and Tavwots is the name of the little rabbit.

But once, long ago, Tavwots was not little: he was the largest of all four-footed things, and a mighty hunter. He used to hunt every day; as soon as it was day, and light enough to see, he used to get up and go to his hunting. But every day, he saw the track of a great foot on the trail, before him. This troubled him, for his pride was as big as his body.

"Who is this," he cried, "that goes before me to the hunting, and makes so great a stride? Does he think to put me to shame?"

"T'sst!" said his mother. "There is none greater than thou."

"Still, there are the footprints in the trail," said Tavwots.

[13] Adapted from Mary Austin's *The Basket Woman*.

And the next morning, he got up earlier; but still the great footprints and the mighty stride were before him. The next morning, he got up still earlier; but there were the mighty foot-tracks and the long, long stride.

"Now I will set me a trap for this impudent fellow," said Tavwots, for he was very cunning. So he made a snare of his bowstring and set it in the trail overnight.

And when in the morning he went to look, behold, he had caught the sun in his snare! All that part of the earth was beginning to smoke with the heat of it.

"Is it you who made the tracks in my trail?" cried Tavwots.

"It is I," said the sun. "Come and set me free, before the whole earth is afire."

Then Tavwots saw what he had to do, and he drew his sharp hunting-knife and ran to cut the bowstring. But the heat was so great that he ran back before he had done it; and when he ran back, he was melted down to half his size! Then the earth began to burn, and the smoke curled up against the sky.

"Come again, Tavwots," cried the sun.

And Tavwots ran again to cut the bowstring. But the heat was so great that he ran back before he had done it, and he was melted down to a quarter of his size!

"Come again, Tavwots, and quickly," cried the sun, "or all the world will be burned up."

And Tavwots ran again; this time he cut the bow-string and set the sun free. But when he got back, he was melted down to the size he is now! Only one thing is left of all his greatness: you may still see by the print of his feet as he leaps in the trail, how great his stride was when he caught the sun in his snare.

The Pig Brother[14]

There was once a child who was untidy. He left his books on the floor, and his muddy shoes on the table; he put his fingers in the jam-pots, and spilled ink on his best clothes; there was really no end to his untidiness.

One day the Tidy Angel came into his nursery.

"This will never do!" said the angel. "This is really shocking. You must go out and stay with your brother while I set things to rights here."

"I have no brother!" said the child.

"Yes, you have," said the angel. "You may not know him, but he will know you. Go out in the garden and watch for him, and he will soon come."

"I don't know what you mean!" said the child; but he went out into the garden and waited.

Presently a squirrel came along, whisking his tail.

"Are you my brother?" asked the child.

The squirrel looked him over carefully.

[14] From Laura E. Richards's *The Golden Windows*.

"Well, I should hope not!" he said. "My fur is neat and smooth, my nest is handsomely made and in perfect order, and my young ones are properly brought up. Why do you insult me by asking me such a question?"

He whisked off, and the child waited.

Presently a wren came hopping by.

"Are you my brother?" asked the child.

"No, indeed!" said the wren. "What impertinence! You will find no tidier person than I in the whole garden. Not a feather is out of place, and my eggs are the wonder of all for smoothness and beauty. Brother, indeed!" He hopped off, ruffling his feathers, and the child waited.

By and by, a large tomcat came along.

"Are you my brother?" asked the child.

"Go and look at yourself in the glass," said the tomcat haughtily, "and you will have your answer. I have been washing myself in the sun all morning, while it is clear that no water has come near you for a long time. There are no such creatures as you in my family, I am humbly thankful to say."

He walked on, waving his tail, and the child waited.

Presently a pig came trotting along.

The child did not wish to ask the pig if he were his brother, but the pig did not wait to be asked.

"Hallo, brother!" he grunted.

"I am not your brother!" said the child.

"Oh yes, you are!" said the pig. "I confess I am not proud of you, but there is no mistaking the members of our family. Come along, and have a good roll in the barnyard! There is some lovely black mud there."

"I don't like to roll in mud!" said the child.

"Tell that to the hens!" said the pig-brother. "Look at your hands and your shoes, and your clothes! Come along, I say! You may have some of the pig-slop for supper, if there is more than I want."

"I don't want pig-slop!" said the child, and he began to cry.

Just then the Tidy Angel came out.

"I have set everything to rights," she said, "and so it must stay. Now, will you go with the pig-brother, or will you come back with me, and be a tidy child?"

"With you, with you!" cried the child; and he clung to the angel's dress.

The pig-brother grunted.

"Small loss!" he said. "There will be all the more slop for me!" And he trotted off.

The Cake[15]

A child quarreled with his brother one day about a cake.

"It is my cake!" said the child.

"No, it is mine!" said his brother.

"You shall not have it!" said the child. "Give it to me this minute!" And he fell upon his brother and beat him.

Just then came by an angel who knew the child.

"Who is this that you are beating?" asked the angel.

"It is my brother," said the child.

"No, but truly," said the angel, "who is it?"

"It is my brother, I tell you!" said the child.

"Oh no," said the angel. "That cannot be; and it seems a pity for you to tell an untruth, because that makes spots on your soul. If it were your brother, you would not beat him."

"But he has my cake!" said the child.

[15] From Laura E. Richards's *The Golden Windows*.

"Oh," said the angel, "now I see my mistake. You mean that the cake is your brother; and that seems a pity, too, for it does not look like a very good cake — and, besides, it is all crumbled to pieces."

The Pied Piper of Hamelin Town[16]

Once I made a pleasure trip to a country called Germany; and I went to a funny little town, where all the streets ran uphill. At the top was a big mountain, steep like the roof of a house, and at the bottom was a big river, broad and slow. And the funniest thing about the little town was that all the shops had the same thing in them; bakers' shops, grocers' shops, everywhere we went, we saw the same thing: big chocolate rats, rats and mice, made out of chocolate. We were so surprised that after a while, we asked, "Why do you have rats in your shops?"

"Don't you know this is Hamelin town?" they said.

"What of that?" said we.

"Why, Hamelin town is where the Pied Piper came," they told us. "Surely you know about the Pied Piper?"

---

[16] From traditions, with rhymes from Robert Browning's "The Pied Piper of Hamelin."

"What about the Pied Piper?" we said. And this is what they told us about him.

It seems that once, long, long ago, that little town was dreadfully troubled with rats. The houses were full of them, the shops were full of them; the churches were full of them; they were everywhere. The people were all but eaten out of house and home.

Those rats,
They fought the dogs and killed the cats,
And bit the babies in the cradles,
And ate the cheeses out of the vats,
And licked the soup from the cooks' own ladles,
Split open the kegs of salted sprats,
Made nests inside men's Sunday hats,
And even spoiled the women's chats
By drowning their speaking
With shrieking and squeaking
In fifty different sharps and flats!

At last it got so bad that the people simply couldn't stand it any longer. So they all came together and went to the town hall, and they said to the mayor (you know what a mayor is?), "See here, what do we pay you your salary for? What are you good for, if you can't do a little thing like getting rid of these rats? You must go to work and clear the town of them;

find the remedy that's lacking, or we'll send you packing!"

Well, the poor mayor was in a terrible way. What to do he didn't know. He sat with his head in his hands, and thought and thought and thought.

Suddenly there came a little *rat-tat* at the door. Oh, how the mayor jumped! His poor old heart went *pit-a-pat* at anything like the sound of a rat. But it was only the scraping of shoes on the mat. So the mayor sat up, and said, "Come in!"

And in came the strangest figure! It was a man, very tall and very thin, with a sharp chin and a mouth where the smiles went out and in, and two blue eyes, each like a pin; and he was dressed half in red and half in yellow — he really was the strangest fellow! — and 'round his neck he had a long red and yellow ribbon, and on it was hung a thing something like a flute, and his fingers went straying up and down it as if he wanted to be playing.

He came up to the mayor and said, "I hear you are troubled with rats in this town."

"I should say we were," groaned the mayor.

"Would you like to get rid of them? I can do it for you."

"You can?" cried the mayor. "How? Who are you?"

"Men call me the Pied Piper," said the man, "and I know a way to draw after me everything that walks, or flies, or swims. What will you give me if I rid your town of rats?"

"Anything, anything," said the mayor. "I don't believe you can do it, but if you can, I'll give you a thousand guineas."

"All right," said the piper. "It is a bargain."

And then he went to the door and stepped out into the street and stood, and put the long flute-like thing to his lips, and began to play a little tune. A strange, high, little tune.

And before three shrill notes the pipe uttered,
You heard as if an army muttered;
And the muttering grew to a grumbling;
And the grumbling grew to a mighty rumbling;
And out of the houses the rats came tumbling!
Great rats, small rats, lean rats, brawny rats,
Brown rats, black rats, gray rats, tawny rats,
Grave old plodders, gay young friskers,
Fathers, mothers, uncles, cousins,
Cocking tails and pricking whiskers,
Families by tens and dozens,
Brothers, sisters, husbands, wives —
Followed the piper for their lives!

From street to street he piped, advancing; from street to street they followed, dancing. Up one street and down another, until they came to the edge of the big river, and there the piper turned sharply about and stepped aside, and all those rats tumbled *hurry-scurry*, head over heels, down the bank into the river *and were drowned*. Every single one. No, there was one big old fat rat; he was so fat he didn't sink, and he swam across and ran away to tell the tale.

Then the piper came back to the town hall. And all the people were waving their hats and shouting for joy. The mayor said they would have a big celebration and build a tremendous bonfire in the middle of the town. He asked the piper to stay and see the bonfire — very politely.

"Yes," said the piper. "That will be very nice; but first, if you please, I would like my thousand guineas."

"H'm — er — ahem!" said the mayor. "You mean that little joke of mine; of course, that was a joke." (You see it is always harder to pay for a thing when you no longer need it.)

"I do not joke," said the piper very quietly. "My thousand guineas, if you please."

"Oh, come, now," said the mayor. "You know very well it wasn't worth sixpence to play a little tune like that. Call it one guinea, and let it go at that."

"A bargain is a bargain," said the piper. "For the last time, will you give me my thousand guineas?"

"I'll give you a pipe of tobacco, something good to eat, and call you lucky at that!" said the mayor, tossing his head.

Then the piper's mouth grew strange and thin, and sharp blue and green lights began dancing in his eyes, and he said to the mayor very softly, "I know another tune than the one I played. I play it to those who play me false."

"Play what you please! You can't frighten me! Do your worst!" said the mayor, making himself big.

Then the piper stood high up on the steps of the town hall, and put the pipe to his lips, and began to play a little tune. It was quite a different little tune, this time, very soft and sweet, and very, very strange.

And before he had played three notes, you heard
a rustling, that seemed like a bustling
Of merry crowds justling at pitching and hustling;
Small feet were pattering, wooden shoes clattering,
Little hands clapping and little tongues chattering,
And like fowls in a farmyard when barley is
    scattering,
Out came the children running.
All the little boys and girls,
With rosy cheeks and flaxen curls,
And sparkling eyes and teeth like pearls,
Tripping and skipping, ran merrily after
The wonderful music with shouting and laughter.

"Stop, stop!" cried the people. "He is taking our children! Stop him, Mister Mayor!"

"I will give you your money, I will!" cried the mayor and tried to run after the piper.

But the very same music that made the children dance made the grown-up people stand stock-still; it was as if their feet had been tied to the ground; they could not move a muscle. There they stood and saw the piper move slowly down the street, playing his little tune, with the children at his heels. On and on he went; on and on the children danced; until he came to the bank of the river.

"Oh, oh! He will drown our children in the river!" cried the people.

But the piper turned and went along by the bank, and all the children followed after. Up, and up, and up the hill they went, straight toward the mountain which is like the roof of a house. And just as they got to it, the mountain *opened* — like two great doors, and the piper went in through the opening, playing the little tune, and the children danced after him. And just as they got through, the great doors slid together again and shut them all in! Every single one. No, there was one little lame child, who couldn't keep up with the rest and didn't get there in time. But none of his little companions ever came back anymore, not one.

But years and years afterward, when the fat old rat who had swum across the river was a grandfather, his children used to ask him, "What made you follow the music, Grandfather?" and he used to tell them, "My dears, when I heard that tune, I thought I heard the moving aside of pickle-tub boards, and the leaving ajar of preserve cupboards, and I smelled the most delicious old cheese in the world, and I saw sugar barrels ahead of me; and then, just as a great yellow cheese seemed to be saying, 'Come, bore me' — I felt the river rolling o'er me!"

And in the same way, the people asked the little lame child, "What made you follow the music?"

"I do not know what the others heard," he said, "but I, when the piper began to play, I heard a voice that told of a wonderful country hard by, where the bees had no stings and the horses had wings, and the trees bore wonderful fruits, where no one was tired or lame, and children played all day; and just as the beautiful country was but one step away — the mountain closed on my playmates, and I was left alone."

That was all the people ever knew. The children never came back. All that was left of the piper and the rats was just the big street that led to the river; so they called it the Street of the Pied Piper.

And that is the end of the story.

Why Evergreen Trees Keep Their Leaves in Winter

One day, a long, long time ago, it was very cold; winter was coming. And all the birds flew away to the warm south, to wait for the spring.

But one little bird had a broken wing and could not fly. He did not know what to do. He looked all around, to see whether there was any place where he could keep warm. And he saw the trees of the great forest.

"Perhaps the trees will keep me warm through the winter," he said.

So he went to the edge of the forest, hopping and fluttering with his broken wing. The first tree he came to was a slim silver birch.

"Beautiful birch tree," he said, "will you let me live in your warm branches until the springtime comes?"

"Dear me!" said the birch tree, "what a thing to ask! I have to take care of my own leaves through the winter; that is enough for me. Go away."

The little bird hopped and fluttered with his broken wing until he came to the next tree. It was a great big oak tree.

"O big oak tree," said the little bird, "will you let me live in your warm branches until the springtime comes?"

"Dear me," said the oak tree, "what a thing to ask! If you stay in my branches all winter, you will be eating my acorns. Go away."

So the little bird hopped and fluttered with his broken wing until he came to the willow tree by the edge of the brook.

"O beautiful willow tree," said the little bird, "will you let me live in your warm branches until the springtime comes?"

"No, indeed," said the willow tree; "I never speak to strangers. Go away."

The poor little bird did not know where to go, but he hopped and fluttered along with his broken wing. Presently the spruce tree saw him and said, "Where are you going, little bird?"

"I do not know," said the bird. "The trees will not let me live with them, and my wing is broken so that I cannot fly."

"You may live on one of my branches," said the spruce. "Here is the warmest one of all."

"But may I stay all winter?"

"Yes," said the spruce. "I shall like to have you."

The pine tree stood beside the spruce, and when he saw the little bird hopping and fluttering with his broken wing, he said, "My branches are not very warm, but I can keep the wind off because I am big and strong."

So the little bird fluttered up into the warm branch of the spruce, and the pine tree kept the wind off his house. Then the juniper tree saw what was going on, and said that she would give the little bird his dinner all the winter, from her branches. Juniper berries are very good for little birds.

The little bird was very comfortable in his warm nest sheltered from the wind, with juniper berries to eat.

The trees at the edge of the forest remarked upon it to each other:

"I wouldn't take care of a strange bird," said the birch.

"I wouldn't risk my acorns," said the oak.

"I would not speak to strangers," said the willow. And the three trees stood up very tall and proud.

That night the North Wind came to the woods to play. He puffed at the leaves with his icy breath, and every leaf he touched fell to the ground. He wanted to touch every leaf in the forest, for he loved to see the trees bare.

"May I touch every leaf?" he said to his father, the Frost King.

"No," said the Frost King. "The trees that were kind to the bird with the broken wing may keep their leaves."

So the North Wind had to leave them alone, and the spruce, the pine, and the juniper tree kept their leaves through all the winter. And they have done so ever since.

The Star Dollars

There was once a little girl who was very, very poor. Her father and mother had died, and at last she had no little room to stay in, and no little bed to sleep in, and nothing more to eat except one piece of bread. So she said a prayer, put on her little jacket and her hood, took her piece of bread in her hand, and went out into the world.

When she had walked a little way, she met an old man, bent and thin. He looked at the piece of bread in her hand and said, "Will you give me your bread, little girl? I am very hungry." The little girl said, "Yes" and gave him her piece of bread.

When she had walked a little farther, she came upon a child, sitting by the path, crying. "I am so cold!" said the child. "Won't you give me your little hood, to keep my head warm?" The little girl took off her hood and tied it on the child's head. Then she went on her way.

After a time, as she went, she met another child. This one shivered with the cold, and she said to the little girl, "Won't you give me your jacket, little girl?" And the little girl gave her her jacket. Then she went on again.

By and by, she saw another child, crouching almost naked by the wayside. "O little girl," said the child, "won't you give me your dress? I have nothing to keep me warm." So the little girl took off her dress and gave it to the other child. And now she had nothing left but her little shirt. It grew dark, and the wind was cold, and the little girl crept into the woods, to sleep for the night. But in the woods a child stood, weeping and naked. "I am cold," she said. "Give me your little shirt!" And the little girl thought, "It is dark, and the woods will shelter me; I will give her my little shirt." So she did, and now she had nothing left in all the world.

She stood looking up at the sky, to say her nighttime prayer. As she looked up, the whole skyful of stars fell in a shower 'round her feet. There they were, on the ground, shining bright, and round. The little girl saw that they were silver dollars. And in the midst of them was the finest little shirt, all woven out of silk! The little girl put on the little silk shirt, and gathered the star dollars, and she was rich all the days of her life.

The Lion and the Gnat

Far away in Central Africa, that vast land where dense forests and wild beasts abound, the shades of night were once more descending, warning all creatures that it was time to seek repose.

All day long, the sun had been like a great burning eye, but now, after painting the western sky with crimson and scarlet and gold, he had disappeared into his fleecy bed; the various creatures of the forest had sought their holes and resting-places; the last sound had rumbled its rumble, the last bee had mumbled his mumble, and the last bear had grumbled his grumble; even the grasshoppers that had been *chirruping, chirruping* through all the long hours without a pause, at length had ceased their shrill music, tucked up their long legs, and given themselves to slumber.

There on a nodding grass blade, a tiny gnat had made a swinging couch, and he, too, had folded his wings, closed his tiny eyes, and was fast asleep. Darker, darker, darker became the night until the darkness could almost be felt, and over all was a solemn stillness as though some powerful finger had been raised, and some potent voice had whispered, "Hush!"

Just when all was perfectly still, there came suddenly from the faraway depths of the forest, like the roll of thunder, a mighty *ROAR-R-R-R!*

In a moment, all the beasts and birds were wide awake, and the poor little gnat was nearly frightened out of his little senses, and his little heart went *pit-a-pat.* He rubbed his little eyes with his feelers, and then peered all around trying to penetrate the deep gloom as he whispered in terror, "What — was — that?"

What do *you* think it was? . . . Yes, a LION! A great, big lion who, while most other denizens of the forest slept, was out hunting for prey. He came rushing and crashing through the thick undergrowth of the forest, swirling his long tail and opening wide his great jaws, and as he rushed, he ROARED!

Presently he reached the spot where the little gnat hung panting at the tip of the waving grass blade. Now, the little gnat was not afraid of lions, so when he saw it was only a lion, he cried out, "Hi, stop, stop! What are you making that horrible noise about?"

The lion stopped short, then backed slowly and regarded the gnat with scorn.

"Why, you tiny, little, mean, insignificant creature you, how DARE you speak to ME?" he raged.

"How dare I speak to you?" repeated the gnat quietly. "By the virtue of *right*, which is always greater than *might*. Why don't you keep to your own part of the forest? What right have you to be here, disturbing folks at this time of night?"

By a mighty effort, the lion restrained his anger. He knew that to obtain mastery over others, one must be master over oneself.

"What *right*?" he repeated in dignified tones. "*Because I'm king of the forest.* That's why. I can do no wrong, for all the other creatures of the forest are afraid of me. I DO what I please, I SAY what I please, I EAT whom I please, I GO where I please — simply because I'm king of the forest."

"But who told you you were king?" demanded the gnat. "Just answer me that!"

"Who told ME?" roared the lion. "Why, everyone acknowledges it. Didn't I tell you that everyone is afraid of me?"

"Indeed!" cried the gnat disdainfully. "Pray, don't say *all*, for I'm not afraid of you. And further, I deny your right to be king."

This was too much for the lion. He now worked himself into a perfect fury.

"You — you — YOU deny my right as king?"

"I *do*, and, what is more, you shall never be king until you have fought and conquered me."

The lion laughed a great lion laugh, and a lion laugh cannot be laughed at like a cat laugh, as everyone ought to know. "Fight — did you say *fight?*" he asked. "Who ever heard of a lion fighting a gnat? Here, out of my way, you atom of nothing! I'll blow you to the other end of the world."

But although the lion puffed his cheeks until they were like great bellows, and then blew with all his might, he could not disturb the little gnat's hold on the swaying grass blade.

"You'll blow all your whiskers away if you are not careful," he said, with a laugh, "but you won't move me. And if you dare leave this spot without fighting me, I'll tell all the beasts of the forest that you are afraid of me, and they'll make me king."

"Ho, ho!" roared the lion. "Very well. Since you will fight, let it be so."

"You agree to the conditions, then? The one who conquers shall be king?"

"Oh, certainly," laughed the lion, for he expected an easy victory. "Are you ready?"

"Quite ready."

"Then — GO!" roared the lion.

And with that he sprang forward with open jaws, thinking he could easily swallow a million gnats.

But just as the great jaws were about to close upon the blade of grass to which the gnat clung, what should happen but that the gnat suddenly spread his wings and nimbly flew — where do you think? — right into one of the lion's nostrils! And there he began to sting, sting, sting. The lion wondered, and thundered, and blundered, but the gnat went on stinging. The lion foamed, and he moaned, and he groaned; still the gnat went on stinging. The lion rubbed his head on the ground in agony, he swirled his tail in furious passion, he roared, he spluttered, he sniffed, he snuffed; and still the gnat went on stinging.

"Oh, my poor nose, my nose, my nose!" the lion began to moan. "Come down, come DOWN, come DOWN! My nose, my NOSE, my NOSE!! You're king of the forest, you're king, you're king — only come down. My nose, my NOSE, my NOSE!"

So at last the gnat flew out of the lion's nostril and went back to his waving grass blade, while the lion slunk away into the depths of the forest with his tail between his legs — *beaten*, and by a tiny gnat!

"What a fine fellow am I, to be sure!" exclaimed the gnat, as he proudly plumed his wings. "I have beaten a lion — a lion! Dear me, I ought to have been king long ago! I'm so clever, so big, so strong — oh!"

The gnat's frightened cry was caused by finding himself entangled in some silky sort of threads. While gloating over his victory, the wind had risen, and his grass blade had swayed violently to and fro, unnoticed by him. A stronger gust than usual had bent the blade downward close to the ground, and then something caught it and held it fast and, with it, the victorious gnat.

Oh, the desperate struggles he made to get free! Alas! He became more entangled than ever. You can guess what it was: a spider's web, hung out from the overhanging branch of a tree. Then — *flipperty-flopperty, flipperty-flopperty, flop, flip, flop* — down his stairs came cunning Father Spider and quickly gobbled up the little gnat for his supper, and that was the end of him.

A strong lion — and what overcame him? A *gnat*.

A clever gnat — and what overcame him? A *spider's web!* He who had beaten the strong lion had been overcome by the subtle snare of a spider's thread.

Grades 2 and 3

The Cat and the Parrot

Once there was a cat and a parrot. And they had agreed to ask each other to dinner, turn and turn about: first, the cat should ask the parrot, then the parrot should invite the cat, and so on.

It was the cat's turn first. Now, the cat was very mean. He provided nothing at all for dinner except a pint of milk, a little slice of fish, and a biscuit. The parrot was too polite to complain, but he did not have a very good time.

When it was his turn to invite the cat, he cooked a fine dinner. He had a roast of meat, a pot of tea, a basket of fruit, and, best of all, he baked a whole clothes-basketful of little cakes — little brown, crispy, spicy cakes! Oh, I should say as many as 500. And he put 498 of the cakes before the cat, keeping only two for himself.

Well, the cat ate the roast, drank the tea, sucked the fruit, and then began on the pile of cakes. He ate all the 498 cakes, and then he looked 'round and said, "I'm hungry. Haven't you anything to eat?"

"Why," said the parrot, "here are my two cakes, if you want them."

The cat ate up the two cakes, and then he licked his chops and said, "I am beginning to get an appetite. Have you anything to eat?"

"Well, really," said the parrot, who was now rather angry, "I don't see anything more, unless you wish to eat me!" He thought the cat would be ashamed when he heard that, but the cat just looked at him and licked his chops again — and *slip! slop! gobble!* down his throat went the parrot!

Then the cat started down the street. An old woman was standing by, and she had seen the whole thing, and she was shocked that the cat should eat his friend. "Why, cat!" she said. "How dreadful of you to eat your friend the parrot!"

"Parrot, indeed!" said the cat. "What's a parrot to me? I've a great mind to eat you, too."

And before you could say "Jack Robinson" — *slip! slop! gobble!* down went the old woman!

Then the cat started down the road again, walking like this, because he felt so fine. Pretty soon he met a man driving a donkey.

The man was beating the donkey, to hurry him up, and when he saw the cat, he said, "Get out of my way, cat. I'm in a hurry, and my donkey might tread on you."

"Donkey, indeed!" said the cat. "Much I care for a donkey! I have eaten five hundred cakes, I've eaten my friend the parrot, I've eaten an old woman — what's to hinder my eating a miserable man and a donkey?"

And *slip! slop! gobble!* down went the old man and the donkey.

Then the cat walked on down the road, jauntily, like this. After a little, he met a procession, coming that way. The king was at the head, walking proudly with his newly married bride, and behind him were his soldiers, marching, and behind them were ever and ever so many elephants, walking two by two. The king felt very kind to everybody, because he had just been married, and he said to the cat, "Get out of my way, pussycat, get out of my way; my elephants might hurt you."

"Hurt me!" said the cat, shaking his fat sides. "Ho, ho! I've eaten five hundred cakes, I've eaten my friend the parrot, I've eaten an old woman, I've eaten a man and a donkey. What's to hinder my eating a beggarly king?"

And *slip! slop! gobble!* down went the king; down went the queen; down went the soldiers — and down went all the elephants!

Then the cat went on, more slowly; he had really had enough to eat now. But a little farther on, he met two land crabs, scuttling along in the dust. "Get out of our way, cat," they squeaked.

"Ho, ho, ho!" cried the cat in a terrible voice. "I've eaten five hundred cakes, I've eaten my friend the parrot, I've eaten an old woman, a man with a donkey, a king, a queen, his men-at-arms, and all his elephants; and now I'll eat you too."

And *slip! slop! gobble!* down went the two land crabs.

When the land crabs had gotten down inside, they began to look around. It was very dark, but they could see the poor king sitting in a corner with his bride on his arm; she had fainted. Near them were the men-at-arms, treading on one another's toes, and the elephants, still trying to form in twos, but they couldn't, because there was not room. In the opposite corner sat the old woman, and near her stood the man and his donkey. But in the other corner was a great pile of cakes, and by them perched the parrot, his feathers all drooping.

"Let's get to work!" said the land crabs. And, *snip, snap,* they began to make a little hole in the side, with their sharp claws. *Snip, snap, snip, snap* — until it was big enough to get through.

Then out they scuttled. Then out walked the king, carrying his bride; out marched the men-at-arms; out tramped the elephants, two by two; out came the old man, beating his donkey; out walked the old woman, scolding the cat; and last of all, out hopped the parrot, holding a cake in each claw. (You remember, two cakes were all he wanted.)

But the poor cat had to spend the whole day sewing up the hole in his coat!

The Rat Princess

Once upon a time, there was a rat princess, who lived with her father, the rat king, and her mother, the rat queen, in a rice field in faraway Japan. The rat princess was so pretty that her father and mother were quite foolishly proud of her and thought no one good enough to play with her. When she grew up, they would not let any of the rat princes come to visit her, and they decided at last that no one should marry her until they had found the most powerful person in the whole world; no one else was good enough.

And the rat king started out to find the most powerful person in the whole world.

The wisest and oldest rat in the rice field said that the sun must be the most powerful person, because he made the rice grow and ripen; so the rat king went to find the sun. He climbed up the highest mountain, ran up the path of a rainbow, and traveled and traveled across the sky until he came to the sun's house.

"What do you want, little brother?" the sun said, when he saw him.

"I come," said the rat king, very importantly, "to offer you the hand of my daughter, the princess, because you are the most powerful person in the world; no one else is good enough."

"Ha, ha!" laughed the jolly round sun, and winked his eye. "You are very kind, little brother, but if that is the case, the princess is not for me; the cloud is more powerful than I am; when he passes over me, I cannot shine."

"Oh, indeed," said the rat king, "then you are not my man at all." And he left the sun without more words. The sun laughed and winked to himself. And the rat king traveled and traveled across the sky until he came to the cloud's house.

"What do you want, little brother?" sighed the cloud when he saw him.

"I come to offer you the hand of my daughter, the princess," said the rat king, "because you are the most powerful person in the world; the sun said so, and no one else is good enough."

The cloud sighed again. "I am not the most powerful person," he said. "The wind is stronger than I. When he blows, I have to go wherever he sends me."

"Then you are not the person for my daughter," said the rat king proudly. And he started at once to find the wind. He traveled and traveled across the sky until he came at last to the wind's house, at the very edge of the world.

When the wind saw the rat king coming, he laughed a big, gusty laugh, "Ho, ho!" and asked him what he wanted; and when the rat king told him that he had come to offer him the rat princess's hand because he was the most powerful person in the world, the wind shouted a great gusty shout, and said, "No, no, I am not the strongest. The wall that man has made is stronger than I; I cannot make him move, with all my blowing. Go to the wall, little brother!"

And the rat king climbed down the sky-path again, and traveled and traveled across the earth until he came to the wall. It was quite near his own rice field.

"What do you want, little brother?" grumbled the wall when he saw him.

"I come to offer you the hand of the princess, my daughter, because you are the most powerful person in the world, and no one else is good enough."

"Ugh, ugh," grumbled the wall. "I am not the strongest. The big gray rat who lives in the cellar is stronger than I. When he gnaws and gnaws at me, I crumble and crumble, and at last I fall. Go to the rat, little brother."

And so, after going all over the world to find the strongest person, the rat king had to marry his daughter to a rat, after all; but the princess was very glad of it, for she had wanted to marry the gray rat all the time.

The Frog and the Ox

Once a little frog sat by a big frog, by the side of a pool. "Oh, Father," said he, "I have just seen the biggest animal in the world; it was as big as a mountain, and it had horns on its head, and it had hoofs divided in two."

"Pooh, child," said the old frog, "that was only Farmer White's ox. He is not so very big. I could easily make myself as big as he." And he blew, and he blew, and he blew, and swelled himself out.

"Was he as big as that?" he asked the little frog.

"Oh, much bigger," said the little frog.

The old frog blew, and blew, and blew again, and swelled himself out, more than ever.

"Was he bigger than that?" he said.

"Much, much bigger," said the little frog.

"I can make myself as big," said the old frog. And once more he blew, and blew, and blew, and swelled himself out — and he burst!

Moral: *Self-conceit leads to self-destruction.*

The Fire-Bringer[17]

This is the Indian story of how fire was brought to the tribes. It was long, long ago, when men and beasts talked together with understanding, and the gray coyote was friend and counselor of man.

There was a boy of the tribe who was swift of foot and keen of eye, and he and the coyote ranged the wood together. They saw the men catching fish in the creeks with their hands, and the women digging roots with sharp stones. This was in summer.

But when winter came on, they saw the people running naked in the snow, or huddled in caves of the rocks, and most miserable. The boy noticed this and was very unhappy for the misery of his people.

"I do not feel it," said the coyote.

"You have a coat of good fur," said the boy, "and my people have not."

"Come to the hunt," said the coyote.

[17] Adapted from Mary Austin's *The Basket Woman*.

"I will hunt no more, until I have found a way to help my people against the cold," said the boy. "Help me, O counselor!"

Then the coyote ran away and came back after a long time; he said he had found a way, but it was a hard way.

"No way is too hard," said the boy. So the coyote told him that they must go to the Burning Mountain and bring fire to the people.

"What is fire?" said the boy. And the coyote told him that fire was red like a flower, yet not a flower; swift to run in the grass and to destroy, like a beast, yet no beast; fierce and hurtful, yet a good servant to keep one warm, if kept among stones and fed with small sticks.

"We will get this fire," said the boy.

First the boy had to persuade the people to give him 100 swift runners. Then he and they and the coyote started at a good pace for the faraway Burning Mountain. At the end of the first day's trail, they left the weakest of the runners, to wait; at the end of the second, the next stronger; at the end of the third, the next; and so for each of the hundred days of the journey; and the boy was the strongest runner and went to the last trail with the counselor.

High mountains they crossed, and great plains, and giant woods, and at last they came to the Big

Water, quaking along the sand at the foot of the Burning Mountain.

It stood up in a high peaked cone, and smoke rolled out of it endlessly along the sky. At night, the Fire Spirits danced, and the glare reddened the Big Water far out.

There the counselor said to the boy, "Stay here until I bring you a brand from the burning; be ready and right for running, for I shall be far spent when I come again, and the Fire Spirits will pursue me."

Then he went up to the mountain; and the Fire Spirits only laughed when they saw him, for he looked so slinking, inconsiderable, and mean that none of them thought harm from him. And in the night, when they were at their dance about the mountain, the coyote stole the fire, and ran with it down the slope of the burning mountain. When the Fire Spirits saw what he had done, they streamed out after him, red and angry, with a humming sound like a swarm of bees. But the coyote was still ahead; the sparks of the brand streamed out along his flanks, as he carried it in his mouth; and he stretched his body to the trail.

The boy saw him coming, like a falling star against the mountain; he heard the singing sound of the Fire Spirits close behind, and the laboring breath of the counselor. And when the good beast panted down beside him, the boy caught the brand from his jaws and was off, like an arrow from a bent bow. Out he shot on the homeward path, and the Fire Spirits snapped and sang behind him. But fast as they pursued, he fled faster, until he saw the next runner standing in his place, his body bent for the running. To him he passed it, and it was off and away, with the Fire Spirits raging in chase.

So it passed from hand to hand, and the Fire Spirits tore after it through the scrub, until they came to the mountains of the snows; these they could not pass. Then the dark, sleek runners with the backward streaming brand bore it forward, shining starlike in the night, glowing red in sultry noons, violet pale in twilight glooms, until they came in safety to their own land.

And there they kept it among stones and fed it with small sticks, as the counselor had advised; and it kept the people warm.

Ever after, the boy was called the Fire-Bringer; and ever after, the coyote bore the sign of the bringing, for the fur along his flanks was singed and yellow from the flames that streamed backward from the brand.

The Burning of the Rice Fields[18]

Once there was a good old man who lived up on a mountain, far away in Japan. All around his little house, the mountain was flat, and the ground was rich; and there were the rice fields of all the people who lived in the village at the mountain's foot. Mornings and evenings, the old man and his little grandson, who lived with him, used to look far down on the people at work in the village, and watch the blue sea that lay all around the land, so close that there was no room for fields below, only for houses. The little boy loved the rice fields, dearly, for he knew that all the good food for all the people came from them; and he often helped his grandfather to watch over them.

One day, the grandfather was standing alone before his house, looking far down at the people, and out at the sea, when suddenly he saw something very strange far off where the sea and the sky meet.

[18] Adapted from Lafcadio Hearn's *Gleanings in Buddha-Fields*.

Something like a great cloud was rising there, as if the sea were lifting itself high into the sky. The old man put his hands to his eyes and looked again, as hard as his old sight could. Then he turned and ran to the house. "Yone, Yone!" he cried. "Bring a brand from the hearth!"

The little grandson could not imagine what his grandfather wanted with fire, but he always obeyed, so he ran quickly and brought the brand. The old man already had one and was running for the rice fields. Yone ran after. But to his horror, he saw his grandfather thrust his burning brand into the ripe, dry rice, where it stood.

"Oh, Grandfather, Grandfather!" screamed the little boy. "What are you doing?"

"Quick, set fire! Thrust your brand in!" said the grandfather.

Yone thought his dear grandfather had lost his mind, and he began to sob; but a little Japanese boy always obeys, so although he sobbed, he thrust his torch in, and the sharp flame ran up the dry stalks, red and yellow. In an instant, the field was ablaze, and thick black smoke began to pour up on the mountainside. It rose like a cloud, black and fierce, and in no time, the people below saw that their precious rice fields were on fire. Ah, how they ran! Men, women, and children climbed the mountain, running as fast as they could to save the rice; not one soul stayed behind.

And when they came to the mountaintop, and saw the beautiful rice-crop all in flames, beyond help, they cried bitterly, "Who has done this thing? How did it happen?"

"I set fire," said the old man, very solemnly; and the little grandson sobbed, "Grandfather set fire."

But when they came fiercely around the old man, with "Why? Why?" he only turned and pointed to the sea. "Look!" he said.

They all turned and looked. And there, where the blue sea had lain so calm, a mighty wall of water, reaching from earth to sky, was rolling in. No one could scream, so terrible was the sight. The wall of water rolled in on the land, passed quite over the place where the village had been, and broke, with an awful sound, on the mountainside. One wave more, and still one more, came; and then all below was water, as far as they could see; the village where they had been was under the sea.

But the people were all safe. And when they saw what the old man had done, they honored him above all men for the quick wit that had saved them all from the tidal wave.

The Story of Wylie[19]

This is a story about a dog — not the kind of dog you often see in the street here; not a fat, wrinkly pugdog, nor a smooth-skinned bulldog, or even a big shaggy fellow, but a slim, silky-haired, sharp-eared little dog, the prettiest thing you can imagine. Her name was Wylie, and she lived in Scotland, far up on the hills, and helped her master take care of his sheep.

You can't think how clever she was! She watched over the sheep and the little lambs like a soldier, and never let anything hurt them. She drove them out to pasture when it was time and brought them safely home when it was time for that. When the silly sheep got frightened and ran this way and that, hurting themselves and getting lost, Wylie knew exactly what to do: around on one side she would run, barking and scolding, driving them back; then around on the other, barking and scolding, driving

[19] Adapted from John Brown's *Rab and His Friends*.

them back, until they were all bunched together in front of the right gate. Then she drove them through as neatly as any person. She loved her work and was a wonderfully fine sheepdog.

At last her master grew too old to stay alone on the hills, and so he went away to live. Before he went, he gave Wylie to two kind young men who lived in the nearest town; he knew they would be good to her. They grew very fond of her, and so did their old grandmother and the little children: she was so gentle and handsome and well-behaved.

So now Wylie lived in the city where there were no sheep farms, only streets and houses, and she did not have to do any work at all; she was just a pet dog. She seemed very happy, and she was always good.

But after a while, the family noticed something odd, something very strange indeed, about their pet. Every single Tuesday night, about nine o'clock, Wylie *disappeared*. They would look for her, call her — no, she was gone. And she would be gone all night. But every Wednesday morning, there she was at the door, waiting to be let in. Her silky coat was all sweaty and muddy and her feet heavy with weariness, but her bright eyes looked up at her masters as if she were trying to explain where she had been.

Week after week the same thing happened. Nobody could imagine where Wylie went every Tuesday night. They tried to follow her to find out, but she always slipped away; they tried to shut her in, but she always found a way out. It grew to be a real mystery. Where in the world did Wylie go?

You could never guess, so I am going to tell you.

In the city near the town where the kind young men lived was a big market like [name a local one]. Every sort of thing was sold there, even live cows and sheep and hens. On Tuesday nights, the farmers used to come down from the hills with their sheep to sell, and drive them through the city streets into the pens, ready to sell on Wednesday morning; that was the day they sold them.

The sheep weren't used to the city noises and sights, and they always grew afraid and wild, and gave the farmers and the sheepdogs a great deal of trouble. They broke away and ran about, in everybody's way.

But just as the trouble was worst, about sunrise, the farmers would see a little silky, sharp-eared dog come trotting all alone down the road, into the midst of them.

And then!

In and out the little dog ran like the wind, around and about, always in the right place, driving, coaxing, pushing, making the sheep mind like a good schoolteacher, and never frightening them, until they were all safely in! All the other dogs together could not do as much as the little strange dog. She was a perfect wonder. And no one knew whose dog she was or where she came from. The farmers grew to watch for her, every week, and they called her the *wee fell yin*, which is Scottish for "the little terror"; they used to say when they saw her coming, "There's the *wee fell yin!* Now we'll get them in."

Every farmer would have liked to keep her, but she let no one catch her. As soon as her work was done, she was off and away like a fairy dog, no one knew where. Week after week this happened, and nobody knew who the little strange dog was.

But one day Wylie went to walk with her two masters, and they happened to meet some sheep farmers. The sheep farmers stopped short and stared at Wylie, and then they cried out, "Why, *that's* the *dog!* That's the *wee fell yin!*" And so it was. The little strange dog who helped with the sheep was Wylie.

Her masters, of course, didn't know what the farmers meant, until they were told all about what I have been telling you. But when they heard about the pretty strange dog that came to market all alone, they knew at last where Wylie went every Tuesday night. And they loved her better than ever.

Wasn't it wise of the dear little dog to go and work for other people when her own work was taken away? I fancy she knew that the best people and the best dogs always work hard at something. Anyway, she did that same thing as long as she lived, and she was always just as gentle, and silky-haired, and loving as at first.

Little Daylight

Once there was a beautiful palace that had a great wood at one side. The king and his courtiers hunted in the wood near the palace, and there it was kept open, free from underbrush. But farther away it grew wilder and wilder, until at last it was so thick that nobody knew what was there. It was a very great wood indeed.

In the wood lived eight fairies. Seven of them were good fairies, who had lived there always; the eighth was a bad fairy, who had just come. And the worst of it was that nobody but the other fairies knew she was a fairy; people thought she was just an ugly old witch.

The good fairies lived in the dearest little houses. One lived in a hollow silver birch, one in a little moss cottage, and so on. But the bad fairy lived in a horrid mud house in the middle of a dark swamp.

Now, when the first baby was born to the king and queen, her father and mother decided to name her Daylight, because she was so bright and sweet.

And of course they had a christening party. And of course they invited the fairies, because the good fairies had always been at the christening party when a princess was born in the palace, and everybody knew that they brought good gifts.

But, alas, no one knew about the swamp fairy, and she was not invited, which really pleased her, because it gave her an excuse for doing something mean.

The good fairies came to the christening party, and, one after another, five of them gave little Daylight good gifts. The other two stood among the guests, so that no one noticed them. The swamp fairy thought there were no more of them; so she stepped forward, just as the archbishop was handing the baby back to the lady-in-waiting.

"I am just a little deaf," she said, mumbling a laugh with her toothless gums. "Will your reverence tell me the baby's name again?"

"Certainly, my good woman," said the bishop. "The infant is little Daylight."

"And little Daylight it shall be, forsooth," cried the bad fairy. "I decree that she shall sleep all day." Then she laughed a horrid shrieking laugh, "*He, he, hi, hi!*"

Everyone looked at everyone else in despair, but out stepped the sixth good fairy, who, by arrangement with her sisters, had remained in the background to undo what she could of any evil that the swamp fairy might decree.

"Then at least she shall wake all night," she said, sadly.

"Ah!" screamed the swamp fairy, "you spoke before I had finished, which is against the law, and gives me another chance." All the fairies started at once to say, "I beg your pardon!" But the bad fairy said, "I had only laughed *he, he!* and *hi, hi!* I had still *ho, ho!* and *hu, hu!* to laugh."

The fairies could not gainsay this, and the bad fairy had her other chance. She said, "Since she is to wake all night, I decree that she shall wax and wane with the moon! *Ho, ho, hu, hu!*"

Out stepped the seventh good fairy. "Until a prince shall kiss her without knowing who she is," she said quickly.

The swamp fairy had been prepared for the trick of keeping back one good fairy, but she had not suspected it of two, and she could not say a word, for she had laughed *ho, ho!* and *hu, hu!*

The poor king and queen looked sad enough. "We don't know what you mean," they said to the good fairy who had spoken last. But the good fairy smiled. "The meaning of the thing will come with the thing," she said.

That was the end of the party, but it was only the beginning of the trouble. Can you imagine what a strange household it would be where the baby laughed and crowed all night, and slept all day? Little Daylight was as merry and bright all night as any baby in the world, but with the first sign of dawn, she fell asleep, and slept like a little dormouse until dark. Nothing could waken her while day lasted.

Still, the royal family got used to this. But the rest of the bad fairy's gift was a great deal worse — that about waxing and waning with the moon. You know how the moon grows bigger and brighter each night, from the time it is a curly silver thread low in the sky until it is round and golden, flooding the whole sky with light? That is the waxing moon. Then, you know, it wanes; it grows smaller and paler again, night by night, until at last it disappears for a while altogether.

Well, poor little Daylight waxed and waned with it. She was the rosiest, plumpest, merriest baby in the world when the moon was at the full; but as it began to wane, her little cheeks grew paler, her tiny hands thinner, with every night, until she lay in her cradle like a shadow-baby, without sound or motion. At first they thought she was dead when the moon disappeared, but after some months, they got used to this, too, and only waited eagerly for the new moon, to see her revive. When it shone again, faint and silver, on the horizon, the baby stirred weakly, and then they fed her gently; each night she grew a little better, and when the moon was near the full again, she was again a lively, rosy, lovely child.

So it went on until she grew up. She grew to be the most beautiful maiden the moon ever shone on, and everyone loved her so much, for her sweet ways and her merry heart, that someone was always planning to stay up at night, to be near her. But she did not like to be watched, especially when she felt the bad time of waning coming on; so her ladies-in-waiting had to be very careful. When the moon waned, she became shrunken and pale and bent, like an old, old woman, worn out with sorrow. Only her golden hair and her blue eyes remained un-changed, and this gave her a terribly strange look. At last, as the moon disappeared, she faded away to a little, bowed, old creature, asleep and helpless.

No wonder she liked best to be alone! She got in the way of wandering by herself in the beautiful wood, playing in the moonlight when she was well, stealing away in the shadows when she was fading with the moon. Her father had a lovely little house of roses and vines built for her there. It stood at the edge of a most beautiful open glade, inside the wood, where the moon shone best. There the princess lived with her ladies. And there she danced when the moon was full. But when the moon waned, her ladies often lost her altogether, so far did she wander; and sometimes they found her sleeping under a great tree, and brought her home in their arms.

When the princess was about seventeen years old, there was a rebellion in a kingdom not far from her father's. Wicked nobles murdered the king of the country and stole his throne, and would have murdered the young prince, too, if he had not escaped, dressed in peasant's clothes.

Dressed in his poor rags, the prince wandered about a long time, until one day he got into a great wood and lost his way. It was the wood where the princess Daylight lived, but of course he did not know anything about that or about her. He wandered until night, and then he came to a strange little house. One of the good fairies lived there, and the minute she saw him, she knew all about everything; but to him she looked only like a kind old woman. She gave him a good supper and a bed for the night, and told him to come back to her if he found no better place for the next night. But the prince said he must get out of the wood at once; so in the morning he took leave of the fairy.

All day long he walked, and walked; but at nightfall he had not found his way out of the wood, so he lay down to rest until the moon should rise and light his path.

When he woke, the moon was glorious; it was three days from the full and bright as silver. By its light he saw what he thought to be the edge of the wood, and he hastened toward it. But when he came to it, it was only an open space, surrounded with trees. It was so very lovely, in the white moonlight, that the prince stood a minute to look. And as he looked, something white moved out of the trees on the far side of the open space. It was something slim and white, which swayed in the dim light like a young birch.

"It must be a moon fairy," thought the prince; and he stepped into the shadow.

The moon fairy came nearer and nearer, dancing and swaying in the moonlight. And as she came, she began to sing a soft, sweet little song.

But when she was quite close, the prince saw that she was not a fairy after all, but a real human maiden — the loveliest maiden he had ever seen. Her hair was like yellow corn, and her smile made all the place merry. Her white gown fluttered as she danced, and her little song sounded like a bird note.

The prince watched her until she danced out of sight, and then until she once more came toward him; and she seemed so like a moonbeam herself, as she lifted her face to the sky, that he was almost afraid to breathe. He had never seen anything so lovely. By the time she had danced twice around the circle, he could think of nothing in the world except the hope of finding out who she was and staying near her.

But while he was waiting for her to appear the third time, his weariness overcame him, and he fell asleep. And when he awoke, it was broad day, and the beautiful maiden had vanished.

He hunted about, hoping to find where she lived, and on the other side of the glade he came upon a lovely little house, covered with moss and climbing roses. He thought she must live there, so he went around to the kitchen door and asked the kind cook for a drink of water, and while he was drinking it, he asked who lived there. She told him it was the house of the princess Daylight, but she told him nothing else about her, because she was not allowed to talk about her mistress. But she gave him a very good meal and told him other things.

He did not go back to the little old woman who had been so kind to him first, but wandered all day in the wood, waiting for the moontime. Again he waited at the edge of the dell, and when the white moon was high in the heavens, once more he saw the glimmering in the distance, and once more the lovely maiden floated toward him. He knew her name was Princess Daylight, but this time she seemed to him much lovelier than before. She was all in blue like the blue of the sky in summer. (She really was more lovely, you know, because the moon was almost at the full.) All night he watched her, quite forgetting that he ought not to be doing it, until she disappeared on the opposite side of the glade. Then, very tired, he found his way to the little old woman's house, had breakfast with her, and fell fast asleep in the bed she gave him.

The fairy knew well enough by his face that he had seen Daylight, and when he woke up in the evening and started off again, she gave him a strange little flask and told him to use it if ever he needed it.

This night the princess did not appear in the dell until midnight, at the very full of the moon. But when she came, she was so lovely that she took the prince's breath away. Just think! She was dressed in a gown that looked as if it were made of fireflies' wings, embroidered in gold. She danced around and around, singing, swaying, and flitting like a beam of sunlight, until the prince grew quite dazzled.

But while he had been watching her, he had not noticed that the sky was growing dark and the wind was rising. Suddenly there was a clap of thunder. The princess danced on. But another clap came louder, and then a sudden great flash of lightning that lit up the sky from end to end. The prince couldn't help shutting his eyes, but he opened them quickly to see if Daylight was hurt. Alas, she was lying on the ground. The prince ran to her, but she was already up again.

"Who are you?" she said.

"I thought," stammered the prince, "you might be hurt."

"There is nothing the matter. Go away."

The prince went sadly.

"Come back," said the princess. The prince came. "I like you. You do as you are told. Are you good?"

"Not so good as I should like to be," said the prince.

"Then go and grow better," said the princess.

The prince went, more sadly.

"Come back," said the princess. The prince came. "I think you must be a prince," she said.

"Why?" said the prince.

"Because you do as you are told, and you tell the truth. Will you tell me what the sun looks like?"

"Why, everybody knows that," said the prince.

"I am different from everybody," said the princess. "I don't know."

"But," said the prince, "do you not look when you wake up in the morning?"

"That's just it," said the princess, "I never do wake up in the morning. I never can wake up until —" Then the princess remembered that she was talking to a prince, and putting her hands over her face, she walked swiftly away. The prince followed her, but she turned and put up her hand to tell him not to. And like the gentleman prince that he was, he obeyed her at once.

Now, all this time, the wicked swamp fairy had not known a word about what was going on. But now she found out, and she was furious, for fear that little Daylight should be delivered from her spell. So she cast her spells to keep the prince from finding Daylight again. Night after night, the poor prince wandered and wandered and never could find the little dell. And when daytime came, of course, there was no princess to be seen. Finally, at the time that the moon was almost gone, the swamp fairy stopped her spells, because she knew that by this time, Daylight would be so changed and ugly that the prince would never know her if he did see her. She said to herself with a wicked laugh, "No fear of his wanting to kiss her now!"

That night the prince did find the dell, but no princess came. A little after midnight, he passed near the lovely little house where she lived, and there he overheard her waiting-women talking about her.

They seemed in great distress. They were saying that the princess had wandered into the woods and was lost. The prince didn't know, of course, what it meant, but he did understand that the princess was lost somewhere, and he started off to find her. After he had gone a long way without finding her, he came to a big old tree, and there he thought he would light a fire to show her the way if she should happen to see it.

As the blaze flared up, he suddenly saw a little black heap on the other side of the tree. Somebody was lying there. He ran to the spot, his heart beating with hope. But when he lifted the cloak which was huddled about the form, he saw at once that it was not Daylight. A pinched, withered, white, little old woman's face shone out at him. The hood was drawn close down over her forehead, the eyes were closed, and as the prince lifted the cloak, the old woman's lips moaned faintly.

"Oh, poor mother," said the prince, "what is the matter?" The old woman only moaned again. The prince lifted her and carried her over to the warm fire, and rubbed her hands, trying to find out what was the matter. But she only moaned, and her face was so terribly strange and white that the prince's tender heart ached for her. Remembering his little flask, he poured some of his liquid between her lips, and then he thought the best thing he could do was to carry her to the princess's house, where she could be taken care of.

As he lifted the poor little form in his arms, two great tears stole out from the old woman's closed eyes and ran down her wrinkled cheeks.

"Oh, poor, poor mother," said the prince pity-ingly; and he stooped and kissed her withered lips.

As he walked through the forest with the old woman in his arms, it seemed to him that she grew heavier and heavier; he could hardly carry her at all; and then she stirred, and at last he was obliged to set her down, to rest. He meant to lay her on the ground. But the old woman stood upon her feet.

And then the hood fell back from her face. As she looked up at the prince, the first, long, yellow ray of the rising sun struck full upon her. And it was the princess Daylight! Her hair was golden as the sun itself, and her eyes as blue as the flower that grows in the corn.

The prince fell on his knees before her. But she gave him her hand and made him rise.

"You kissed me when I was an old woman," said the princess. "I'll kiss you now that I am a young princess." And she did.

And then she turned her face toward the dawn.

"Dear prince," she said, "is that the sun?"

The Sailor Man[20]

Once upon a time, two children came to the house of a sailor who lived beside the salt sea, and they found the sailor sitting in his doorway knotting ropes.

"How do you do?" asked the sailor.

"We are very well, thank you," said the children, who had learned manners, "and we hope you are the same. We heard that you had a boat, and we thought that perhaps you would take us out in her, and teach us how to sail, for that is what we most wish to know."

"All in good time," said the sailor. "I am busy now, but by and by, when my work is done, I may perhaps take one of you if you are ready to learn. Meantime, here are some ropes that need knotting; you might be doing that, since it has to be done." And he showed them how the knots should be tied, and went away and left them.

[20] From Laura E. Richards's *The Golden Windows*.

When he was gone, the first child ran to the window and looked out.

"There is the sea," he said. "The waves come up on the beach, almost to the door of the house. They run up all white, like prancing horses, and then they go dragging back. Come and look!"

"I cannot," said the second child. "I am tying a knot."

"Oh!" cried the first child. "I see the boat. She is dancing like a lady at a ball; I never saw such a beauty. Come and look!"

"I cannot," said the other. "I am tying a knot."

"I shall have a delightful sail in that boat," said the first child. "I expect that the sailor will take me, because I am the eldest and I know more about it. There was no need of my watching when he showed you the knots, because I knew how already."

Just then the sailor came in.

"Well," he said, "my work is over. What have you been doing in the meantime?"

"I have been looking at the boat," said the first child. "What a beauty she is! I shall have the best time in her that ever I had in my life."

"I have been tying knots," said the second child.

"Come, then," said the sailor and he held out his hand to the second child. "I will take you out in the boat and teach you to sail her."

"But I am the eldest," cried the first child, "and I know a great deal more than she does."

"That may be," said the sailor, "but a person must learn to tie a knot before he can learn to sail a boat."

"But I have learned to tie a knot," cried the child. "I know all about it!"

"How can I tell that?" asked the sailor.

The Story of Jairus's Daughter

Once, while Jesus was journeying about, He passed near a town where a man named Jairus lived. This man was a ruler in the synagogue, and he had just one little daughter, about twelve years of age. At the time that Jesus was there, the little daughter was very sick, and at last she lay dying.

Her father had heard that there was a wonderful Man, Jesus, near the town who was healing sick people whom no one else could help, and in his despair, he ran out into the streets to search for Him. He found Jesus walking in the midst of a crowd of people, and when he saw Him, he fell down at Jesus' feet and besought Him to come into his house, to heal his daughter. And Jesus said yes, He would go with him.

But there were so many people begging to be healed, and so many looking to see what happened, that the crowd thronged them and kept them from moving fast. And before they reached the house, one of the man's servants came to meet them, and said, "Thy daughter is dead; trouble not the Master to come farther."

But instantly Jesus turned to the father and said, "Fear not; only believe, and she shall be made whole." And He went on with Jairus to the house.

When they came to the house, they heard the sound of weeping and lamentation; the household was mourning for the little daughter, who was dead. Jesus sent all the strangers away from the door, and only three of His disciples and the father and mother of the child went in with Him. And when He was within, He said to the mourning people, "Weep not. She is not dead; she is sleeping."

When He had passed, they laughed Him to scorn, for they knew that she was dead.

Then Jesus left them all and went alone into the chamber where the little daughter lay. And when He was there, alone, He went up to the bed where she was, and bent over her and took her by the hand. And He said, "Maiden, arise."

And her spirit came unto her again! And she lived and grew up in her father's house.

Grades 4 and 5

Arthur and the Sword[21]

Once there was a great king in Britain named Uther, and when he died, the other kings and princes disputed over the kingdom, each wanting it for himself. But King Uther had a son named Arthur, the rightful heir to the throne, of whom no one knew, for he had been taken away secretly while he was still a baby by a wise old man called Merlin, who had him brought up in the family of a certain Sir Ector, for fear of the malice of wicked knights. Even the boy himself thought Sir Ector was his father, and he loved Sir Ector's son, Sir Kay, with the love of a brother.

When the kings and princes could not be kept in check any longer, and something had to be done to determine who was to be king, Merlin made the Archbishop of Canterbury send for them all to come to London. It was Christmastime, and in the great cathedral a solemn service was held, and prayer was

---

[21] Adapted from Sir Thomas Malory.

made that some sign should be given, to show who was the rightful king. When the service was over, there appeared a strange stone in the churchyard, against the high altar. It was a great white stone, like marble, with something sunk in it that looked like a steel anvil; and in the anvil was driven a great glistening sword. The sword had letters of gold written on it, which read: "Whoso pulleth out this sword of this stone and anvil is rightwise king born of all England."

All wondered at the strange sword and its strange writing; and when the archbishop himself came out and gave permission, many of the knights tried to pull the sword from the stone, hoping to be king. But no one could move it a hair's breadth.

"He is not here," said the archbishop, "who shall achieve the sword; but doubt not, God will make him known."

Then they set a guard of ten knights to keep the stone, and the archbishop appointed a day when all should come together to try at the stone — kings from far and near.

In the meantime, splendid jousts were held, outside London, and both knights and commons were bidden.

Sir Ector came up to the jousts, with others, and with him rode Kay and Arthur. Kay had been made a knight at Allhallowmas,[22] and when he found there was to be so fine a joust, he wanted a sword, to join it. But he had left his sword behind, where his father and he had slept the night before. So he asked young Arthur to ride for it.

"I will well," said Arthur, and rode back for it. But when he came to the castle, the lady and all her household were at the jousting, and there was none to let him in.

Thereat Arthur said to himself, "My brother Sir Kay shall not be without a sword this day." And he remembered the sword he had seen in the church-yard. "I will to the churchyard," he said, "and take that sword with me." So he rode into the church-yard, tied his horse to the stile, and went up to the stone. The guards were away to the tourney, and the sword was there alone.

Going up to the stone, young Arthur took the great sword by the hilt, and lightly and fiercely he drew it out of the anvil.

Then he rode straight to Sir Kay and gave the sword to him.

Sir Kay knew instantly that it was the sword of the stone, and he rode off at once to his father and said, "Sir, lo, here is the sword of the stone; I must be

[22] All Saints' Day.

king of the land." But Sir Ector asked him where he got the sword. And when Sir Kay said, "From my brother," he asked Arthur how he got it. When Arthur told him, Sir Ector bowed his head before him. "Now I understand you must be king of this land," he said to Arthur.

"Wherefore I?" said Arthur.

"For God will have it so," said Ector. "Never man should have drawn out this sword but he who shall be rightwise king of this land. Now let me see whether you can put the sword as it was in the stone, and pull it out again."

Straightway Arthur put the sword back.

Then Sir Ector tried to pull it out, and after him Sir Kay; but neither could stir it. Then Arthur pulled it out. Thereupon, Sir Ector and Sir Kay kneeled upon the ground before him.

"Alas," said Arthur, "mine own dear father and brother, why kneel ye to me?"

Sir Ector told him, then, all about his royal birth, and how he had been taken privily away by Merlin. But when Arthur found Sir Ector was not truly his father, he was so sad at heart that he cared not greatly to be king. And he begged his father and brother to love him still. Sir Ector asked that Sir Kay might be seneschal when Arthur was king. Arthur promised with all his heart.

Then they went to the archbishop and told him that the sword had found its master. The archbishop appointed a day for the trial to be made in the sight of all men, and on that day the princes and knights came together, and each tried to draw out the sword, as before. But as before, none could so much as stir it.

Then came Arthur and pulled it easily from its place.

The knights and kings were terribly angry that a boy from nowhere in particular had beaten them, and they refused to acknowledge him king. They appointed another day, for another great trial.

Three times they did this, and every time the same thing happened.

At last, at the feast of Pentecost, Arthur again pulled out the sword before all the knights and the commons. And then the commons rose up and cried that he should be king, and that they would slay any who denied him.

So Arthur became king of Britain, and all gave him allegiance.

Tarpeia

There was once a girl named Tarpeia, whose father was guard of the outer gate of the citadel of Rome. It was a time of war; the Sabines were besieging the city. Their camp was close outside the city wall.

Tarpeia used to see the Sabine soldiers when she went to draw water from the public well, for that was outside the gate. And sometimes she stayed about and let the strange men talk with her, because she liked to look at their bright silver ornaments. The Sabine soldiers wore heavy silver rings and bracelets on their left arms; some wore as many as four or five.

The soldiers knew she was the daughter of the keeper of the citadel, and they saw that she had greedy eyes for their ornaments. So day by day, they talked with her, and showed her their silver rings, and tempted her. And at last Tarpeia made a bargain, to betray her city to them. She said she would unlock the great gate and let them in, if *they would give her what they wore on their left arms*.

The night came. When it was perfectly dark and still, Tarpeia stole from her bed, took the great key from its place, and silently unlocked the gate that protected the city. Outside, in the dark, stood the soldiers of the enemy, waiting. As she opened the gate, the long shadowy files pressed forward silently, and the Sabines entered the citadel.

As the first man came inside, Tarpeia stretched forth her hand for her price. The soldier lifted high his left arm. "Take thy reward!" he said, and as he spoke, he hurled upon her that which he wore upon it. Down upon her head crashed, not the silver rings of the soldier, but the great brass shield he carried in battle!

She sank beneath it to the ground.

"Take thy reward," said the next; and his shield rang against the first.

"Thy reward," said the next, and the next, and the next, and the next; every man wore his shield on his left arm.

So Tarpeia lay buried beneath the reward she had claimed, and the Sabines marched past her dead body, into the city she had betrayed.

The Buckwheat

Down by the river were fields of barley and rye and golden oats. Wheat grew there, too, and the heaviest and richest ears bent lowest, in humility. Opposite the corn was a field of buckwheat, but the buckwheat never bent; it held its head proud and stiff on the stem.

The wise old willow tree by the river looked down on the fields, and thought his thoughts.

One day a dreadful storm came. The field flowers folded their leaves together, and bowed their heads. But the buckwheat stood straight and proud.

"Bend your head, as we do," the field flowers called.

"I have no need to," said the buckwheat.

"Bend your head, as we do!" warned the golden wheat ears. "The angel of the storm is coming; he will strike you down."

"I will not bend my head," said the buckwheat.

Then the old willow tree spoke: "Close your flowers and bend your leaves. Do not look at the lightning when the cloud bursts. Even men cannot do that; the sight of heaven would strike them blind. Much less can we who are so inferior to them!"

"Inferior indeed!" said the buckwheat. "Now I will look!" And he looked straight up, while the lightning flashed across the sky.

When the dreadful storm had passed, the flowers and the wheat raised their drooping heads, clean and refreshed in the pure, sweet air. The willow tree shook the gentle drops from its leaves.

But the buckwheat lay like a weed in the field, scorched black by the lightning.

The Judgment of Midas

The Greek god Pan, the god of the open air, was a great musician. He played on a pipe of reeds. And the sound of his reed-pipe was so sweet that he grew proud and believed himself greater than the chief musician of the gods, Apollo, the sun-god. So he challenged great Apollo to make better music than he.

Apollo consented to the test, for he wished to punish Pan's vanity, and they chose the mountain Tmolus for judge, since no one is so old and wise as the hills.

When Pan and Apollo came before Tmolus, to play, their followers came with them to hear, and one of those who came with Pan was a mortal named Midas.

First Pan played; he blew on his reed-pipe, and out came a tune so wild and yet so coaxing that the birds hopped from the trees to get near; the squirrels came running from their holes; and the very trees swayed as if they wanted to dance. The fauns laughed aloud for joy as the melody tickled their furry little ears. And Midas thought it the sweetest music in the world.

Then Apollo rose. His hair shook drops of light from its curls; his robes were like the edge of the sunset cloud; in his hands he held a golden lyre. And when he touched the strings of the lyre, such music stole upon the air as never god nor mortal heard before. The wild creatures of the wood crouched still as stone; the trees kept every leaf from rustling; earth and air were silent as a dream. To hear such music cease was like bidding farewell to father and mother.

When the charm was broken, the hearers fell at Apollo's feet and proclaimed the victory his. All but Midas. He alone would not admit that the music was better than Pan's.

"If thine ears are so dull, mortal," said Apollo, "they shall take the shape that suits them." And he touched the ears of Midas. And straightway the dull ears grew long, pointed, and furry, and they turned this way and that. They were the ears of an ass!

For a long time, Midas managed to hide the telltale ears from everyone; but at last, a servant discovered the secret. He knew he must not tell, yet he could not bear not to; so one day he went into the meadow, scooped a little hollow in the turf, and whispered the secret into the earth. Then he covered it up again, and went away. But, alas, a bed of reeds sprang up from the spot, and whispered the secret to the grass. The grass told it to the treetops, the treetops to the little birds, and they cried it all abroad.

And to this day, when the wind sets the reeds nodding together, they whisper, laughing, "Midas has the ears of an ass! Oh, hush, hush!"

Why the Sea Is Salt

Once there were two brothers. One was rich, and one was poor; the rich one was rather mean. When the poor brother used to come to ask for things, it annoyed him, and finally one day he said, "There, I'll give it to you this time, but the next time you want anything, you can go Below for it!"

Presently the poor brother did want something, and he knew it wasn't any use to go to his brother; he must go Below for it. So he went, and he went, and he went, until he came Below.

It was the queerest place! There were red and yellow fires burning all around, and kettles of boiling oil hanging over them, and an odd sort of men standing around, poking the fires. There was a chief man; he had a long curly tail that curled up behind, and two ugly little horns just over his ears; and one foot was very strange indeed. And as soon as anyone came in the door, these men would catch him up and put him over one of the fires, and turn him on a spit. And then the chief man, who was the worst of all, would come and say, "Eh, how do you feel now? How do you feel now?" And of course the poor people screamed and screeched and said, "Let us out! Let us out!" That was just what the chief man wanted.

When the poor brother came in, they picked him up at once, and put him over one of the hottest fires, and began to turn him around and around like the rest; and of course, the chief man came up to him and said, "Eh, how do you feel now? How do you feel now?" But the poor brother did not say, "Let me out! Let me out!" He said, "Pretty well, thank you."

The chief man grunted and said to the other men, "Make the fire hotter." But the next time he asked the poor brother how he felt, the poor brother smiled and said, "Much better now, thank you." The chief man did not like this at all, because, of course, the whole object in life of the people Below was to make their victims uncomfortable. So he piled on more fuel and made the fire hotter still. But every time he asked the poor brother how he felt, the poor brother would say, "Very much better"; and at last he said, "Perfectly comfortable, thank you; couldn't be better."

You see, when the poor brother was on earth, he had never once had money enough to buy coal enough to keep him warm; so he liked the heat.

At last the chief man could stand it no longer.

"Oh, look here," he said, "you can go home."

"Oh no, thank you," said the poor brother, "I like it here."

"You *must* go home," said the chief man.

"But I won't go home," said the poor brother.

The chief man went away and talked with the other men; but no matter what they did, they could not make the poor brother uncomfortable; so at last the chief man came back and said, "What'll you take to go home?"

"What have you got?" said the poor brother.

"Well," said the chief man, "if you'll go home quietly, I'll give you the little mill that stands behind my door."

"What's the good of it?" said the poor brother.

"It is the most wonderful mill in the world," said the chief man. "Anything at all that you want, you have only to name it, and say, 'Grind this, little mill, and grind quickly,' and the mill will grind that thing until you say the magic word, to stop it."

"That sounds nice," said the poor brother. "I'll take it." And he took the little mill under his arm, and went up, and up, and up, until he came to his own house.

When he was in front of his little old hut, he put the little mill down on the ground and said to it,

"Grind a fine house, little mill, and grind quickly." And the little mill ground, and ground, and ground the finest house that ever was seen. It had fine big chimneys, and gable windows, and broad piazzas; and just as the little mill ground the last step of the last flight of steps, the poor brother said the magic word, and it stopped.

Then he took it around to where the barn was, and said, "Grind cattle, little mill, and grind quickly." And the little mill ground, and ground, and ground, and out came great fat cows, and little woolly lambs, and fine little pigs; and just as the little mill ground the last curl on the tail of the last little pig, the poor brother said the magic word, and it stopped.

He did the same thing with crops for his cattle, pretty clothes for his daughters, and everything else they wanted. At last he had everything he wanted, and so he stood the little mill behind his door.

All this time, the rich brother had been getting more and more jealous, and at last he came to ask the poor brother how he had grown so rich. The poor brother told him all about it. He said, "It all comes from that little mill behind my door. All I have to do when I want anything is to name it to the little mill, and say, 'Grind that, little mill, and grind quickly,' and the little mill will grind that thing until —"

But the rich brother didn't wait to hear any more. "Will you lend me the little mill?" he said.

"Why, yes," said the poor brother, "I will."

So the rich brother took the little mill under his arm and started across the fields to his house. When he got near home, he saw the farmhands coming in from the fields for their luncheon. Now, you remember, he was rather mean. He thought to himself, "It is a waste of good time for them to come into the house; they shall have their porridge where they are." He called all the men to him, and made them bring their porridge bowls. Then he set the little mill down on the ground, and said to it, "Grind oatmeal porridge, little mill, and grind quickly!" The little mill ground, and ground, and ground, and out came delicious oatmeal porridge. Each man held his bowl under the spout. When the last bowl was filled, the porridge ran over onto the ground.

"That's enough, little mill," said the rich brother. "You may stop, and stop quickly."

But this was not the magic word, and the little mill did not stop. It ground, and ground, and ground, and the porridge ran all around and made a little pool. The rich brother said, "No, no, little mill, I said, 'Stop grinding, and stop quickly.' " But the little mill ground and ground, faster than ever; and presently there was a regular pond of porridge, almost up to their knees. The rich brother said, "Stop grinding," in every kind of way; he called the little mill names; but nothing did any good. The little mill ground porridge just the same. At last the men said, "Go and get your brother to stop the little mill, or we shall be drowned in porridge."

So the rich brother started for his brother's house. He had to swim before he got there, and the porridge went up his sleeves, and down his neck, and it was horrid and sticky. His brother laughed when he heard the story, but he went with him, and they took a boat across the lake of porridge to where the little mill was grinding. Then the poor brother whispered the magic word, and the little mill stopped.

But the porridge was a long time soaking into the ground, and nothing would ever grow there afterward except oatmeal.

The rich brother didn't seem to care much about the little mill after this, so the poor brother took it home again and put it behind the door; and there it stayed a long, long while.

Years afterward, a sea captain came there on a visit. He told such big stories that the poor brother said, "Oh, I daresay you have seen wonderful things, but I don't believe you ever saw anything more wonderful than the little mill that stands behind my door."

"What is wonderful about that?" said the sea captain.

"Why," said the poor brother, "anything in the world you want — you have only to name it to the little mill and say, 'Grind that, little mill, and grind quickly,' and it will grind that thing until —"

The sea captain didn't wait to hear another word. "Will you lend me that little mill?" he said eagerly.

The poor brother smiled a little, but he said yes, and the sea captain took the little mill under his arm, and went on board his ship and sailed away.

They had headwinds and storms, and they were so long at sea that some of the food gave out. Worst of all, the salt gave out. It was dreadful, being without salt. But the captain happened to remember the little mill.

"Bring up the salt box!" he said to the cook. "We will have salt enough."

He set the little mill on deck, put the salt box under the spout, and said,

"Grind salt, little mill, and grind quickly!"

And the little mill ground beautiful, white, powdery salt. When they had enough, the captain said, "Now you may stop, little mill, and stop quickly." The little mill kept on grinding; and the salt began to pile up in little heaps on the deck. "I said, 'Stop,'" said the captain. But the little mill ground and ground, faster than ever, and the salt was soon thick on the deck like snow. The captain called the little mill names and told it to stop, in every language he knew, but the little mill went on grinding. The salt covered all the decks and poured down into the hold, and at last the ship began to settle in the water; salt is very heavy. But just before the ship sank to the waterline, the captain had a bright thought: he threw the little mill overboard!

It fell right down to the bottom of the sea. *And it has been grinding salt ever since.*

Billy Beg and His Bull[23]

Once upon a time, there was a king and a queen, and they had one son, whose name was Billy. And Billy had a bull he was very fond of, and the bull was just as fond of him. And when the queen came to die, she put it as her last request to the king that, come what might, come what may, he'd not part Billy and the bull. And the king promised that, come what might, come what may, he would not. Then the good queen died and was buried.

After a time, the king married again, and the new queen could not abide Billy; no more could she stand the bull, seeing him and Billy so thick. So she asked the king to have the bull killed. But the king said he had promised, come what might, come what may, he'd not part Billy Beg and his bull, so he could not.

Then the queen sent for the hen-wife, and asked what she should do. "What will you give me," said the hen-wife, "and I'll very soon part them?"

---

[23] Adapted from Seumas McManus's *In Chimney Corners*.

"Anything at all," said the queen.

"Then take to your bed, very sick with a complaint," said the hen-wife, "and I'll do the rest."

So the queen took to her bed, very sick with a complaint, and the king came to see what could be done for her. "I shall never be better of this," she said, "until I have the medicine the hen-wife ordered."

"What is that?" said the king.

"A mouthful of the blood of Billy Beg's bull."

"I can't give you that," said the king and went away, sorrowful.

Then the queen got sicker and sicker, and each time the king asked what would cure her she said, "A mouthful of the blood of Billy Beg's bull." And at last it looked as if she were going to die.

So the king finally set a day for the bull to be killed. At that, the queen was so happy that she laid plans to get up and see the grand sight. All the people were to be at the killing, and it was to be a great affair.

When Billy Beg heard all this, he was very sorrowful, and the bull noticed his looks. "What are you doitherin' about?" said the bull to him. So Billy told him. "Don't fret yourself about me," said the bull, "it's not I that'll be killed!"

The day came when Billy Beg's bull was to be killed; all the people were there, and the queen, and

Billy. And the bull was led out, to be seen. When he was led past Billy, he bent his head.

"Jump on my back, Billy, my boy," says he, "until I see what kind of a horseman you are!"

Billy jumped on his back, and with that, the bull leaped nine miles high and nine miles broad and came down with Billy sticking between his horns. Then away he rushed, over the head of the queen, killing her dead, where you wouldn't know day by night or night by day, over high hills, low hills, sheep walks and bullock traces, the Cove o' Cork, and old Tom Fox with his bugle horn.

When at last he stopped, he said, "Now, Billy, my boy, you and I must undergo great scenery; there's a mighty great bull of the forest I must fight, here, and he'll be hard to fight, but I'll be able for him. But first we must have dinner. Put your hand in my left ear and pull out the napkin you'll find there, and when you've spread it, it will be covered with eating and drinking fit for a king."

So Billy put his hand in the bull's left ear, and drew out the napkin, and spread it; and, sure enough, it was spread with all kinds of eating and drinking, fit for a king. And Billy Beg ate well.

But just as he finished, he heard a great roar, and out of the forest came a mighty bull, snorting and running.

And the two bulls at it and fought. They knocked the hard ground into soft, the soft into hard, the rocks into spring wells, and the spring wells into rocks. It was a terrible fight. But in the end, Billy Beg's bull was too much for the other bull, and he killed him and drank his blood.

Then Billy jumped on the bull's back, and the bull off and away, where you wouldn't know day from night or night from day, over high hills, low hills, sheep walks and bullock traces, the Cove o' Cork, and old Tom Fox with his bugle horn. And when he stopped, he told Billy to put his hand in his left ear and pull out the napkin, because he had to fight another great bull of the forest. So Billy pulled out the napkin and spread it, and it was covered with all kinds of eating and drinking, fit for a king.

And, sure enough, just as Billy finished eating, there was a frightful roar, and a mighty great bull, greater than the first, rushed out of the forest. And the two bulls at it and fought. It was a terrible fight! They knocked the hard ground into soft, the soft into hard, the rocks into spring wells, and the spring wells into rocks. But in the end, Billy Beg's bull killed the other bull and drank his blood.

Then he off and away, with Billy.

But when he came down, he told Billy Beg that he was to fight another bull, the brother of the other two, and that this time, the other bull would be too much for him, and would kill him and drink his blood.

"When I am dead, Billy, my boy," he said, "put your hand in my left ear and draw out the napkin, and you'll never want for eating or drinking; and put your hand in my right ear, and you'll find a stick there, that will turn into a sword if you wave it three times 'round your head, and give you the strength of a thousand men beside your own. Keep that; then cut a strip of my hide, for a belt, for when you buckle it on, there's nothing can kill you."

Billy Beg was very sad to hear that his friend must die. And very soon he heard a more dreadful roar than ever he heard, and a tremendous bull rushed out of the forest. Then came the worst fight of all. In the end, the other bull was too much for Billy Beg's bull, and he killed him and drank his blood.

Billy Beg sat down and cried for three days and three nights. After that, he was hungry; so he put his hand into the bull's left ear, and drew out the napkin, and ate and drank. Then he put his hand into the right ear and pulled out the stick that was to turn into a sword if waved 'round his head three times, and to give him the strength of a thousand men beside his own. And he cut a strip of the hide for a belt, and started off on his adventures.

Presently he came to a fine place; an old gentle-man lived there. So Billy went up and knocked, and the old gentleman came to the door.

"Are you wanting a boy?" says Billy.

"I am wanting a herd-boy," says the gentleman, "to take my six cows, six horses, six donkeys, and six goats to pasture every morning, and bring them back at night. Maybe you'd do."

"What are the wages?" says Billy.

"Oh, well," says the gentleman, "it's no use to talk of that now; there's three giants live in the wood by the pasture, and every day they drink up all the milk and kill the boy who looks after the cattle; so we'll wait to talk about wages until we see if you come back alive."

"All right," says Billy, and he entered service with the old gentleman.

The first day, he drove the six cows, six horses, six donkeys, and six goats to pasture, and sat down by them. About noon, he heard a kind of roaring from the wood, and out rushed a giant with two heads, spitting fire out of his two mouths.

"O my fine fellow," says the giant to Billy, "you are too big for one swallow and not big enough for two; how would you like to die, then? By a cut with the sword, a blow with the fist, or a swing by the back?"

"That is as may be," says Billy, "but I'll fight you." And he buckled on his hide belt, and swung his stick three times 'round his head, to give him the strength of a thousand men besides his own, and went for the giant. And at the first grapple, Billy Beg lifted the giant up and sunk him in the ground, to his armpits.

"Oh, mercy! Spare my life!" cried the giant.

"I think not," said Billy, and he cut off his heads.

That night, when the cows and the goats were driven home, they gave so much milk that all the dishes in the house were filled, and the milk ran over and made a little brook in the yard.

"This is very queer," said the old gentleman. "They never gave any milk before. Did you see nothing in the pasture?"

"Nothing worse than myself," said Billy. And next morning, he drove the six cows, six horses, six donkeys, and six goats to pasture again.

Just before noon, he heard a terrific roar; and out of the wood came a giant with six heads.

"You killed my brother," he roared, fire coming out of his six mouths, "and I'll very soon have your blood! Will you die by a cut of the sword, or a swing by the back?"

"I'll fight you," said Billy. And buckling on his belt and swinging his stick three times 'round his head, he ran in and grappled the giant. At the first hold, he sunk the giant up to the shoulders in the ground.

"Mercy, mercy, kind gentleman!" cried the giant. "Spare my life!"

"I think not," said Billy and cut off his heads.

That night, the cattle gave so much milk that it ran out of the house and made a stream, and turned a mill wheel that had not been turned for seven years!

"It's certainly very queer," said the old gentleman. "Did you see nothing in the pasture, Billy?"

"Nothing worse than myself," said Billy.

And the next morning, the gentleman said, "Billy, do you know, I heard only one of the giants roaring in the night, and the night before only two. What can ail them, at all?"

"Oh, maybe they are sick or something," says Billy; and with that, he drove the six cows, six horses, six donkeys, and six goats to pasture.

At about ten o'clock, there was a roar like a dozen bulls, and the brother of the two giants came out of the wood, with twelve heads on him, and fire spouting from every one of them.

"I'll have you, my fine boy," cries he. "How will you die, then?"

"We'll see," says Billy. "Come on!"

And swinging his stick 'round his head, he made for the giant, and drove him up to his twelve necks in the ground. All twelve of the heads began begging for mercy, but Billy soon cut them short. Then he drove the beasts home.

And that night, the milk overflowed the millstream and made a lake, nine miles long, nine miles broad, and nine miles deep; and there are salmon and whitefish there to this day.

"You are a fine boy," said the gentleman, "and I'll give you wages."

So Billy was hired.

The next day, his master told him to look after the house while he went up to the king's town, to see a great sight. "What will it be?" said Billy.

"The king's daughter is to be eaten by a fiery dragon," said his master, "unless the champion fighter they've been feeding for six weeks on purpose kills the dragon."

"Oh," said Billy.

After he was left alone, there were people passing on horses and afoot, in coaches and chaises, in carriages and in wheelbarrows, all going to see the great sight. And all asked Billy why he was not on his way. But Billy said he didn't care about going.

When the last passerby was out of sight, Billy ran and dressed himself in his master's best suit of clothes, took the brown mare from the stable, and was off to the king's town.

When he arrived there, Billy saw a big round place with great high seats built up around it, and all the people sitting there. Down in the midst was the champion, walking up and down proudly, with two men behind him to carry his heavy sword. And up in the center of the seats was the princess with her maidens; she was looking very pretty, but nervous.

The fight was about to begin when Billy got there, and the herald was crying out how the champion would fight the dragon for the princess's sake, when suddenly there was heard a fearsome great roaring, and the people shouted, "Here he is now, the dragon!"

The dragon had more heads than the biggest of the giants, and fire and smoke came from every one of them. And when the champion saw the creature, he never waited even to take his sword; he turned and ran, and he never stopped until he came to a deep well, where he jumped in and hid himself, up to the neck.

When the princess saw that her champion was gone, she began wringing her hands, and crying, "Oh, please, kind gentlemen, fight the dragon, some of you, and keep me from being eaten! Will no one fight the dragon for me?" But no one stepped up, at all. And the dragon made to eat the princess.

Just then, out stepped Billy from the crowd, with his fine suit of clothes and his hide belt on him. "I'll fight the beast," he says, and swinging his stick three times 'round his head, to give him the strength of a thousand men besides his own, he walked up to the dragon, with easy gait. The princess and all the people were looking, you may be sure, and the dragon raged at Billy with all his mouths, and they at it and fought. It was a terrible fight, but in the end, Billy Beg had the dragon down, and he cut off his heads with the sword.

There was great shouting, then, and crying that the strange champion must come to the king to be made prince, and to the princess, to be seen. But in the midst of the hullabaloo, Billy Begs slips on the brown mare and is off and away before anyone has seen his face. But, quick as he was, he was not so quick but that the princess caught hold of him as he jumped on his horse, and he got away with one shoe left in her hand. And home he rode, to his master's house, and had his old clothes on and the mare in the stable before his master came back.

When his master came back, he had a great tale for Billy, how the princess's champion had run from the dragon, and a strange knight had come out of

the clouds and killed the dragon and, before anyone
could stop him, had disappeared in the sky. "Wasn't
it wonderful?" said the old gentleman to Billy. "I
should say so," said Billy to him.

Soon there was proclamation made that the man
who had killed the dragon was to be found, and to
be made son of the king and husband of the princess; for that, everyone should come up to the king's
town and try on the shoe that the princess had
pulled off the foot of the strange champion, that he
whom it fitted should be known to be the man. On
the day set, there was passing of coaches and chaises,
of carriages and wheelbarrows, people on horseback
and afoot, and Billy's master was the first to go.

While Billy was watching, at last came along a
raggedy man.

"Will you change clothes with me, and I'll give
you better?" said Billy to him.

"Shame to you to mock a poor raggedy man!" said
the raggedy man to Billy.

"It's no mock," said Billy, and he changed clothes
with the raggedy man, and gave him better.

When Billy came to the king's town, in his dreadful old clothes, no one knew him for the champion
at all, and none would let him come forward to try
the shoe. But after all had tried, Billy spoke up that
he wanted to try. They laughed at him, and pushed

him back, with his rags. But the princess would have it that he should try. "I like his face," said she. "Let him try now."

So up stepped Billy, and put on the shoe, and it fitted him like his own skin.

Then Billy confessed that it was he who had killed the dragon. And that he was a king's son. And they put a velvet suit on him, and hung a gold chain 'round his neck, and everyone said a finer-looking boy they'd never seen.

So Billy married the princess and was the prince of that place.

The Little Hero of Haarlem[24]

A long way off, across the ocean, there is a little country where the ground is lower than the level of the sea, instead of higher, as it is here. Of course, the water would run in and cover the land and houses, if something were not done to keep it out. But something is done. The people build great, thick walls all around the country, and the walls keep the sea out. You see how much depends on those walls: the good crops, the houses, and even the safety of the people. Even the small children in that country know that an accident to one of the walls is a terrible thing. These walls are really great banks, as wide as roads, and they are called dikes.

Once there was a little boy who lived in that country, whose name was Hans. One day, he took his little brother out to play. They went a long way out of the town and came to where there were no houses, but ever so many flowers and green fields. By

[24] Told from memory of the story told me when I was a child.

and by, Hans climbed up on the dike, and sat down; the little brother was playing about at the foot of the bank.

Suddenly the little brother called out, "Oh, what a funny little hole! It bubbles!"

"Hole? Where?" said Hans.

"Here in the bank," said the little brother; "water's in it."

"What!" said Hans, and he slid down as fast as he could to where his brother was playing.

There was the tiniest little hole in the bank. Just an air hole. A drop of water bubbled slowly through.

"It is a hole in the dike!" cried Hans. "What shall we do?"

He looked all around; not a person or a house in sight. He looked at the hole; the little drops oozed steadily through; he knew that the water would soon break a great gap, because that tiny hole gave it a chance. The town was so far away; if they ran for help, it would be too late. What should he do? Once more he looked; the hole was larger now, and the water was trickling.

Suddenly a thought came to Hans. He stuck his little forefinger right into the hole, where it fitted tight; and he said to his little brother, "Run, Dieting! Go to the town and tell the men there's a hole in the dike. Tell them I will keep it stopped until they get here."

The little brother knew by Hans's face that something very serious was the matter, and he started for the town, as fast as his legs could run. Hans, kneeling with his finger in the hole, watched him grow smaller and smaller as he got farther away.

Soon he was as small as a chicken; then he was only a speck; then he was out of sight. Hans was alone, his finger tight in the bank.

He could hear the water, slap, slap, slap, on the stones; and deep down under the slapping was a gurgling, rumbling sound. It seemed very near.

By and by, his hand began to feel numb. He rubbed it with the other hand; but it got colder and more numb, colder and more numb, every minute. He looked to see if the men were coming; the road was bare as far as he could see. Then the cold began creeping, creeping, up his arm; first his wrist, then his arm to the elbow, then his arm to the shoulder; how cold it was! And soon it began to ache. Ugly little cramp-pains streamed up his finger, up his palm, up his arm, until they reached into his shoulder, and down the back of his neck. It seemed hours since the little brother went away. He felt very lonely, and the hurt in his arm grew and grew. He watched the road with all his eyes, but no one came in sight. Then he leaned his head against the dike, to rest his shoulder.

As his ear touched the dike, he heard the voice of the great sea, murmuring. The sound seemed to say, "I am the great sea. No one can stand against me. What are you, a little child, that you try to keep me out? Beware! Beware!"

Hans's heart beat in heavy knocks. Would they never come? He was frightened.

The water went on beating at the wall, and murmuring, "I will come through, I will come through, I will get you, I will get you. Run! Run, before I come through!"

Hans started to pull out his finger; he was so frightened that he felt as if he must run forever. But that minute he remembered how much depended on him; if he pulled out his finger, the water would surely make the hole bigger, and at last break down the dike, and the sea would come in on all the land and houses. He set his teeth, and stuck his finger tighter than ever.

"You shall *not* come through!" he whispered. "I will *not* run!"

At that moment, he heard a far-off shout. Far in the distance he saw a black something on the road, and dust. The men were coming! At last, they were coming. They came nearer, fast, and he could make out his own father, and the neighbors. They had pickaxes and shovels, and they were running. And as they ran, they shouted, "We're coming. Take heart; we're coming!"

The next minute, it seemed, they were there. And when they saw Hans, with his pale face, and his hand tight in the dike, they gave a great cheer — just as people do for soldiers back from war; and they lifted him up and rubbed his aching arm with tender hands, and they told him that he was a real hero and that he had saved the town.

When the men had mended the dike, they marched home like an army, and Hans was carried high on their shoulders, because he was a hero. And to this day, the people of Haarlem tell the story of how a little boy saved the dike.

The Last Lesson

Little Franz didn't want to go to school that morning. He would much rather have played truant. The air was so warm and still; you could hear the blackbird singing at the edge of the wood, and the sound of the Prussians drilling down in the meadow behind the old sawmill. He would so much rather have played truant!

Besides, this was the day for the lesson in the rule of participles; and the rule of participles in French is very, very long, and very hard, and it has more exceptions than rule. Little Franz did not know it at all. He did not want to go to school.

But, somehow, he went. His legs carried him reluctantly into the village and along the street. As he passed the official bulletin-board before the town hall, he noticed a little crowd around it, looking at it. That was the place where the news of lost battles, the requisition for more troops, and the demands for new taxes were posted. Small as he was, little Franz had seen enough to make him think, "What now, I wonder?" But he could not stop to see; he was afraid of being late.

When he came to the schoolyard, his heart beat very fast; he was afraid he *was* late, after all, for the windows were all open, and yet he heard no noise; the schoolroom was perfectly quiet. He had been counting on the noise and confusion before school — the slamming of desk covers, the banging of books, the tapping of the master's cane and his "A little less noise, please," — to let him slip quietly into his seat unnoticed. But no; he had to open the door and walk up the long aisle, in the midst of a silent room, with the master looking straight at him. Oh, how hot his cheeks felt, and how hard his heart beat! But to his great surprise, the master didn't scold at all. All he said was, "Come quickly to your place, my little Franz; we were just going to begin without you!"

Little Franz could hardly believe his ears; that wasn't at all the way the master was accustomed to speak. It was very strange! Somehow, everything was very strange. The room looked queer. Everybody was sitting so still, so straight, as if it were an exhibition day, or something very particular. And the master — he looked strange, too; why, he had on his fine lace jabot and his best coat, that he wore only on holidays, and his gold snuff-box in his hand.

Certainly it was very odd. Little Franz looked all around, wondering. And there in the back of the room was the oddest thing of all. There, on a bench, sat *visitors*. Visitors! He could not make it out; people never came except on great occasions — examination days and such. And it was not a holiday. Yet there were the agent, the old blacksmith, the farmer, sitting quiet and still. It was very, very strange.

Just then the master stood up and opened school. He said, "My children, this is the last time I shall ever teach you. The order has come from Berlin that henceforth nothing but German shall be taught in the schools of Alsace and Lorraine. This is your last lesson in French. I beg you, be very attentive."

His last lesson in French! Little Franz could not believe his ears; his last lesson — ah, *that* was what was on the bulletin board! It flashed across him in an instant. That was it! His last lesson in French — and he scarcely knew how to read and write — why, then, he should never know how! He looked down at his books, all battered and torn at the corners; and suddenly his books seemed quite different to him; they seemed, somehow, like friends. He looked at the master, and he seemed different, too — like a very good friend. Little Franz began to feel strange himself. Just as he was thinking about it, he heard his name called, and he stood up to recite.

It was the rule of participles.

Oh, what wouldn't he have given to be able to say it off from beginning to end, exceptions and all, without a blunder! But he could only stand and hang his head; he did not know a word of it.

Then, through the hot pounding in his ears, he heard the master's voice; it was quite gentle — not at all the scolding voice he expected. And it said, "I'm not going to punish you, little Franz. Perhaps you are punished enough. And you are not alone in your fault. We all do the same thing: we all put off our tasks until tomorrow. And, sometimes, to-morrow never comes. That is what it has been with us. We Alsatians have been always putting off our education until the morrow; and now they have a right, those people down there, to say to us, 'What! You call yourselves French, and you cannot even read and write the French language? Learn German, then!'"

And then the master spoke to them of the French language. He told them how beautiful it was, how clear and musical and reasonable, and he said that no people could be hopelessly conquered so long as it kept its language, for the language was the key to its prison-house. And then he said he was going to tell them a little about that beautiful language, and he explained the rule of participles.

And do you know, it was just as simple as ABC! Little Franz understood every word. It was just the same with the rest of the grammar lesson. I don't know whether little Franz listened harder, or whether the master explained better; but it was all quite clear and simple.

But as they went on with it, and little Franz listened and looked, it seemed to him that the master was trying to put the whole French language into their heads in that one hour. It seemed as if he wanted to teach them all he knew, before he went, to give them all he had, in this last lesson.

From the grammar he went on to the writing lesson. And for this, quite new copies had been prepared. They were written on clean, new slips of paper, and they were:—

France: Alsace. France: Alsace.

All up and down the aisles they hung out from the desks like little banners, waving:

France: Alsace. France: Alsace.

And everybody worked with all his might; not a sound could you hear but the scratching of pens on the "France: Alsace."

Even the little ones bent over their up and down strokes with their tongues stuck out to help them work.

After the writing came the reading lesson, and the little ones sang their *ba, be, bi, bo, bu.*

Right in the midst of it, Franz heard a curious sound, a big deep voice mingling with the children's voices. He turned around, and there, on the bench in the back of the room, the old blacksmith sat with a big ABC book open on his knees. It was his voice Franz had heard. He was saying the sounds with the little children: *ba, be, bi, bo, bu*. His voice sounded so odd, with the little voices — so very odd — it made little Franz feel queer. It seemed so funny that he thought he would laugh; then he thought he wouldn't laugh. He felt — he felt very queer.

So it went on with the lessons; they had them all. And then, suddenly, the town clock struck noon. And at the same time, they heard the tramp of the Prussians' feet, coming back from drill.

It was time to close school.

The master stood up. He was very pale. Little Franz had never seen him look so tall. He said, "My children — my children" — but something choked him; he could not go on. Instead he turned and went to the blackboard and took up a piece of chalk. And then he wrote, high up, in big white letters, *"Vive la France!"*

And he made a little sign to them with his head, "That is all. Go away."

The Story of Christmas

There was once a nation that was very powerful, very fortunate, and very proud. Its lands were fruitful; its armies were victorious in battle; and it had strong kings, wise lawgivers, and great poets. But after a great many years, everything changed. The nation had no more strong kings, no more wise lawgivers; its armies were beaten in battle, and neighboring tribes conquered the country and took the fruitful lands; there were no more poets except a few who made songs of lamentation. The people had become a captive and humiliated people; and the bitterest part of all its sadness was the memory of past greatness.

But in all the years of failure and humiliation, there was one thing that kept this people from despair; one hope lived in their hearts and kept them from utter misery. It was a hope that came from something one of the great poets of the past had said, in prophecy. This prophecy was whispered in the homes of the poor, taught in the churches, repeated from father to son among the rich; it was like a deep, hidden well of comfort in a desert of suffering. The prophecy said that sometime a deliverer should be born for the nation, a new king even stronger than the old ones, mighty enough to conquer its enemies, set it free, and bring back the splendid days of old. This was the hope and expectation all the people looked for; they waited through the years for the prophecy to come true.

In this nation, in a little country town, lived a man and a woman whose names were Joseph and Mary. And it happened, one year, that they had to take a little journey up to the town that was the nearest tax-center, to have their names put on the census list; because that was the custom in that country.

But when they got to the town, so many others were there for the same thing, and it was such a small town, that every place was crowded. There was no room for them at the inn. Finally, the innkeeper said they might sleep in the stable, on the straw. So they went there for the night.

And while they were there, in the stable, their first Child was born to them, a little son. And because there was no cradle to put Him in, the mother made a little warm nest of the hay in the big wooden manger where the oxen had eaten, and wrapped the Baby in swaddling clothes, and laid Him in the manger, for a bed!

That same night, on the hills outside the town, there were shepherds, keeping their flocks through the darkness. They were tired with watching over the sheep, and they stood or sat about, drowsily, talking and watching the stars. And as they watched, behold, an angel of the Lord appeared unto them! And the glory of the Lord shone 'round about them! And they were sore afraid. But the angel said unto them, "Fear not, for behold I bring you good tidings of great joy, which shall be to all people. *For unto you is born, this day, in the city of David, a Savior, which is Christ the Lord.* And this shall be a sign unto you: ye shall find the Babe, wrapped in swaddling clothes, *lying in a manger.*"

And suddenly there was with the angel a multitude of the heavenly host, praising God, and saying, "Glory to God in the highest, and on earth peace, goodwill toward men."

When the angels were gone up from them into heaven, the shepherds said to one another, "Let us go to Bethlehem, and see this thing which is come to pass, which the Lord hath made known unto us."

And they came, with haste, and they found Mary, and Joseph, and the Babe lying in a manger. And when they saw Him in the manger, they knew that the wonderful thing the angel said had really happened, and that the great Deliverer was born at last.

Appendix

The King of the Golden River

by John Ruskin

CHAPTER 1

*How the agricultural system of the Black Brothers
was interfered with by Southwest Wind, Esquire*

In a secluded and mountainous part of Stiria, there was in old time
a valley of the most surprising and luxuriant fertility. It was surrounded on all sides by steep and rocky mountains rising into peaks
that were always covered with snow and from which a number of
torrents descended in constant cataracts. One of these fell west-
ward over the face of a crag so high that when the sun had set to everything else, and all below was darkness, his beams still shone full upon
this waterfall, so that it looked like a shower of gold. It was therefore called by the people of the neighborhood the Golden River.

It was strange that none of these streams fell into the valley itself. They all descended on the other side of the mountains and
wound away through broad plains and by populous cities. But the
clouds were drawn so constantly to the snowy hills, and rested so
softly in the circular hollow, that in time of drought and heat,
when all the country around was burned up, there was still rain in
the little valley; and its crops were so heavy, and its hay so high,
and its apples so red, and its grapes so blue, and its wine so rich,
and its honey so sweet that it was a marvel to everyone who beheld
it and was commonly called the Treasure Valley.

The whole of this little valley belonged to three brothers, called Schwartz, Hans, and Gluck. Schwartz and Hans, the two elder brothers, were very ugly men, with overhanging eyebrows and small, dull eyes that were always half-shut, so that you couldn't see into *them* and always fancied they saw very far into *you*. They lived by farming the Treasure Valley, and very good farmers they were. They killed everything that did not pay for its eating. They shot the blackbirds because they pecked the fruit; they poisoned the crickets for eating the crumbs in the kitchen, and smothered the cicadas which used to sing all summer in the lime trees. They worked their servants without any wages until they would not work anymore, and then quarreled with them and turned them out of doors without paying them.

It would have been very odd if with such a farm and such a system of farming they hadn't gotten very rich; and very rich they *did* get. They generally contrived to keep their corn by them until it was very dear, and then sell it for twice its value; they had heaps of gold lying about on their floors, yet it was never known that they had given so much as a penny or a crust in charity; they never went to church, grumbled perpetually at paying tithes, and were, in a word, of so cruel and grinding a temper as to receive from all those with whom they had any dealings the nickname of the "Black Brothers."

The youngest brother, Gluck, was as completely opposed, in both appearance and character, to his seniors as could possibly be imagined or desired. He was not above twelve years old, fair, blue-eyed, and kind in temper to every living thing. He did not, of course, agree particularly well with his brothers, or, rather, they did not agree with *him*. He was usually appointed to the honorable office of turnspit, when there was anything to roast, which was not often, for, to do the brothers justice, they were hardly less sparing upon themselves than upon other people. At other times, he used to clean the shoes, floors, and sometimes the plates, occasionally getting what was left on them, by way of encouragement, and a wholesome quantity of dry blows by way of education.

Things went on in this manner for a long time. At last came a very wet summer, and everything went wrong in the country around. The hay had hardly been gotten in when the haystacks were floated bodily down to the sea by an inundation; the vines were cut to pieces with the hail; the corn was all killed by a black blight. Only in the Treasure Valley, as usual, was all safe. As it had rain when there was rain nowhere else, so it had sun when there was sun nowhere else. Everybody came to buy corn at the farm and went away pouring maledictions on the Black Brothers. They asked what they liked and got it, except from the poor people, who could only beg, and several of whom were starved at their very door without the slightest regard or notice.

It was drawing toward winter, and very cold weather, when one day the two elder brothers had gone out, with their usual warning to little Gluck, who was left to mind the roast, that he was to let nobody in and give nothing out. Gluck sat down quite close to the fire, for it was raining very hard and the kitchen walls were by no means dry or comfortable-looking. He turned and turned, and the roast got nice and brown.

"What a pity," thought Gluck, "my brothers never ask anybody to dinner. I'm sure, when they've got such a nice piece of mutton as this, and nobody else has got so much as a piece of dry bread, it would do their hearts good to have somebody to eat it with them." Just as he spoke, there came a double knock at the house door, yet heavy and dull, as though the knocker had been tied up — more like a puff than a knock. "It must be the wind," said Gluck. "Nobody else would venture to knock double knocks at our door."

No, it wasn't the wind; there it came again very hard, and, what was particularly astounding, the knocker seemed to be in a hurry and not to be in the least afraid of the consequences. Gluck went to the window, opened it, and put his head out to see who it was.

It was the most extraordinary-looking little gentleman he had ever seen in his life. He had a very large nose, slightly brass-colored; his cheeks were very round and very red, and might have warranted a supposition that he had been blowing a refractory fire for the last eight-and-forty hours; his eyes twinkled merrily through long, silky eyelashes; his mustaches curled twice around like a corkscrew on each side of his mouth; and his hair, of a curious mixed pepper-and-salt color, descended far over his shoulders. He was about four-feet-six in height and wore a conical pointed cap of nearly the same altitude, decorated with a black feather some three feet long. His doublet was prolonged behind into something resembling a violent exaggeration of what is now termed a "swal-lowtail," but was much obscured by the swelling folds of an enor-mous black, glossy-looking cloak, which must have been very much too long in calm weather, as the wind, whistling around the old house, carried it clear out from the wearer's shoulders to about four times his own length.

Gluck was so perfectly paralyzed by the singular appearance of his visitor that he remained fixed without uttering a word, until the old gentleman, having performed another and a more ener-getic concerto on the knocker, turned around to look after his fly-away cloak. In so doing, he caught sight of Gluck's little yellow head jammed in the window, with its mouth and eyes very wide open indeed.

"Hollo!" said the little gentleman. "That's not the way to an-swer the door. I'm wet; let me in."

To do the little gentleman justice, he *was* wet. His feather hung down between his legs like a beaten puppy's tail, dripping like an umbrella, and from the ends of his mustaches the water was run-ning into his waistcoat pockets and out again like a mill stream.

"I beg pardon, sir," said Gluck. "I'm very sorry, but, I really can't."

"Can't what?" said the old gentleman.

"I can't let you in, sir — I can't, indeed. My brothers would beat me to death, sir, if I thought of such a thing. What do you want, sir?"

"Want?" said the old gentleman petulantly. "I want fire and shelter, and there's your great fire there blazing, crackling, and dancing on the walls with nobody to feel it. Let me in, I say. I only want to warm myself."

Gluck had had his head, by this time, so long out of the window that he began to feel it was really unpleasantly cold, and when he turned and saw the beautiful fire rustling and roaring and throwing long, bright tongues up the chimney, as if it were licking its chops at the savory smell of the leg of mutton, his heart melted within him that it should be burning away for nothing.

"He does look very wet," said little Gluck. "I'll just let him in for a quarter of an hour."

Around he went to the door and opened it; and as the little gentleman walked in, there came a gust of wind through the house that made the old chimneys totter.

"That's a good boy," said the little gentleman. "Never mind your brothers. I'll talk to them."

"Pray, sir, don't do any such thing," said Gluck. "I can't let you stay until they come; they'd be the death of me."

"Dear me," said the old gentleman. "I'm very sorry to hear that. How long may I stay?"

"Only until the mutton's done, sir," replied Gluck, "and it's very brown."

Then the old gentleman walked into the kitchen and sat himself down on the hob, with the top of his cap accommodated up the chimney, for it was a great deal too high for the roof.

"You'll soon dry there, sir," said Gluck, and sat down again to turn the mutton. But the old gentleman did *not* dry there, but went on drip, drip, dripping among the cinders, and the fire fizzed and sputtered and began to look very black and uncomfortable. Never was such a cloak; every fold in it ran like a gutter.

"I beg pardon, sir," said Gluck at length, after watching the water spreading in long, quicksilver-like streams over the floor for a quarter of an hour. "Mayn't I take your cloak?"

"No, thank you," said the old gentleman.

"Your cap, sir?"

"I am all right, thank you," said the old gentleman rather gruffly.

"But — sir — I'm very sorry," said Gluck hesitatingly, "but — really, sir — you're — putting the fire out."

"It'll take longer to do the mutton, then," replied his visitor dryly. Gluck was very much puzzled by the behavior of his guest; it was such a strange mixture of coolness and humility. He turned away at the string meditatively for another five minutes.

"That mutton looks very nice," said the old gentleman at length. "Can't you give me a little bit?"

"Impossible, sir," said Gluck.

"I'm very hungry," continued the old gentleman. "I've had nothing to eat yesterday or today. They surely couldn't miss a bit from the knuckle!" He spoke in so very melancholy a tone that it quite melted Gluck's heart.

"They promised me one slice today, sir," said he. "I can give you that, but not a bit more."

"That's a good boy," said the old gentleman again.

Then Gluck warmed a plate and sharpened a knife.

"I don't care if I do get beaten for it," thought he. Just as he had cut a large slice out of the mutton, there came a tremendous rap at the door. The old gentleman jumped off the hob as if it had suddenly become inconveniently warm. Gluck fitted the slice into the mutton again, with desperate efforts at exactitude, and ran to open the door.

"What did you keep us waiting in the rain for?" said Schwartz, as he walked in, throwing his umbrella in Gluck's face.

"Aye! what for, indeed, you little vagabond?" said Hans, administering an educational box on the ear as he followed his brother into the kitchen.

"Bless my soul!" said Schwartz when he opened the door.

"Amen," said the little gentleman, who had taken his cap off and was standing in the middle of the kitchen, bowing with the utmost possible velocity.

"Who's that?" said Schwartz, catching up a rolling-pin and turning to Gluck with a fierce frown.

"I don't know, indeed, brother," said Gluck in great terror.

"How did he get in?" roared Schwartz.

"My dear brother," said Gluck deprecatingly, "he was so *very* wet!"

The rolling-pin was descending on Gluck's head, but, at the instant, the old gentleman interposed his conical cap, on which it crashed with a shock that shook the water out of it all over the room. What was very odd, the rolling-pin no sooner touched the cap than it flew out of Schwartz's hand, spinning like a straw in a high wind, and fell into the corner at the further end of the room.

"Who are you, sir?" demanded Schwartz, turning upon him.

"What's your business?" snarled Hans.

"I'm a poor old man, sir," the little gentleman began very modestly, "and I saw your fire through the window and begged shelter for a quarter of an hour."

"Have the goodness to walk out again, then," said Schwartz. "We've quite enough water in our kitchen without making it a drying house."

"It is a cold day to turn an old man out in, sir; look at my gray hairs."

They hung down to his shoulders, as I told you before.

"Aye!" said Hans. "There are enough of them to keep you warm. Walk!"

"I'm very, very hungry, sir; couldn't you spare me a bit of bread before I go?"

"Bread, indeed!" said Schwartz. "Do you suppose we've nothing to do with our bread but to give it to such red-nosed fellows as you?"

"Why don't you sell your feather?" said Hans sneeringly. "Out with you!"

"A little bit," said the old gentleman.

"Be off!" said Schwartz.

"Pray, gentlemen."

"Off, and be hanged!" cried Hans, seizing him by the collar. But he had no sooner touched the old gentleman's collar than away he went after the rolling-pin, spinning around and around until he fell into the corner on the top of it.

Then Schwartz was very angry and ran at the old gentleman to turn him out; but he also had hardly touched him when away he went after Hans and the rolling-pin, and hit his head against the wall as he tumbled into the corner. And so there they lay, all three. Then the old gentleman spun himself around with velocity in the opposite direction, continued to spin until his long cloak was all wound neatly about him, clapped his cap on his head, very much on one side (for it could not stand upright without going through the ceiling), gave an additional twist to his corkscrew mustaches, and replied with perfect coolness, "Gentlemen, I wish you a very good morning. At twelve o'clock tonight I'll call again; after such a refusal of hospitality as I have just experienced, you will not be surprised if that visit is the last I ever pay you."

"If ever I catch you here again," muttered Schwartz, coming, half-frightened, out of the corner — but before he could finish his sentence, the old gentleman had shut the house door behind him with a great bang, and there drove past the window at the same instant a wreath of ragged cloud that whirled and rolled away down the valley in all manner of shapes, turning over and over in the air and melting away at last in a gush of rain.

"A very pretty business, indeed, Mr. Gluck!" said Schwartz. "Dish the mutton, sir. If ever I catch you at such a trick again — bless me, why, the mutton's been cut!"

"You promised me one slice, brother, you know," said Gluck.

"Oh! And you were cutting it hot, I suppose, and going to catch all the gravy. It'll be long before I promise you such a thing again. Leave the room, sir; and have the kindness to wait in the coal cellar until I call you." Gluck left the room melancholy enough. The brothers ate as much mutton as they could, locked the rest in the cupboard, and proceeded to drink a lot of wine after dinner.

Such a night as it was! Howling wind and rushing rain, without intermission. The brothers had just sense enough left to put up all the shutters and double-bar the door before they went to bed. They usually slept in the same room. As the clock struck twelve, they were both awakened by a tremendous crash. Their door burst open with a violence that shook the house from top to bottom.

"What's that?" cried Schwartz, starting up in his bed.

"Only I," said the little gentleman.

The two brothers sat up on their bolster and stared into the darkness. The room was full of water, and by a misty moonbeam, which found its way through a hole in the shutter, they could see in the midst of it an enormous foam globe, spinning around and bobbing up and down like a cork, on which, as on a most luxurious cushion, reclined the little old gentleman, cap and all. There was plenty of room for it now, for the roof was off.

"Sorry to incommode you," said their visitor ironically. "I'm afraid your beds are dampish. Perhaps you had better go to your brother's room; I've left the ceiling on there."

They required no second admonition, but rushed into Gluck's room, wet through and in an agony of terror.

"You'll find my card on the kitchen table," the old gentleman called after them. "Remember, the *last* visit."

"Pray Heaven it may!" said Schwartz, shuddering. And the foam globe disappeared.

Dawn came at last, and the two brothers looked out of Gluck's little window in the morning. The Treasure Valley was one mass of ruin and desolation. The inundation had swept away trees, crops, and cattle, and left in their stead a waste of red sand and gray mud.

The two brothers crept shivering and horror-struck into the kitchen. The water had gutted the whole first floor; corn, money, almost every movable thing, had been swept away, and there was left only a small white card on the kitchen table. On it, in large, breezy, long-legged letters, were engraved the words: *Southwest Wind, Esquire*.

CHAPTER 2

Of the proceedings of the three brothers after the visit
of Southwest Wind, Esquire; and how little Gluck
had an interview with the King of the Golden River

Southwest Wind, Esquire, was as good as his word. After the momentous visit already related, he entered the Treasure Valley no more; and, what was worse, he had so much influence with his relations, the West Winds in general, and used it so effectually, that they all adopted a similar line of conduct. So no rain fell in the valley from one year's end to another.

Although everything remained green and flourishing in the plains below, the inheritance of the three brothers was a desert. What had once been the richest soil in the kingdom became a shifting heap of red sand, and the brothers, unable to contend with the adverse skies any longer, abandoned their valueless patrimony in despair, to seek some means of gaining a livelihood among the cities and people of the plains. All their money was gone, and they had nothing left but some curious old-fashioned pieces of gold plate, the last remnants of their ill-gotten wealth.

"Suppose we turn goldsmiths," said Schwartz to Hans as they entered the large city. "It is a good knave's trade; we can put a great deal of copper into the gold without anyone's finding it out." The thought was agreed to be a very good one; they hired a furnace and turned goldsmiths.

But two slight circumstances affected their trade: the first, that people did not approve of the coppered gold; the second, that the two elder brothers, whenever they had sold anything, used to leave little Gluck to mind the furnace, and go and drink out the money in the alehouse next door. So they melted all their gold without making money enough to buy more and were at last reduced to one large drinking mug, which an uncle of his had given to little Gluck, and which he was very fond of and would not have parted with for the world, although he never drank anything out of it but milk and water.

The mug was a very odd mug to look at. The handle was formed of two wreaths of flowing golden hair, so finely spun that it looked more like silk than metal, and these wreaths descended into and mixed with a beard and whiskers of the same exquisite workmanship, which surrounded and decorated a very fierce little face, of the reddest gold imaginable, right in the front of the mug, with a pair of eyes in it that seemed to command its whole circumference. It was impossible to drink out of the mug without being subjected to an intense gaze out of the side of these eyes, and Schwartz positively averred that once, after emptying it, full of wine, seventeen times, he had seen them wink!

When it came to the mug's turn to be made into spoons, it half-broke poor little Gluck's heart; but the brothers only laughed at him, tossed the mug into the melting pot, and staggered out to the alehouse, leaving him, as usual, to pour the gold into bars when it was all ready. When they were gone, Gluck took a farewell look at his old friend in the melting pot. The flowing hair was all gone; nothing remained but the red nose and the sparkling eyes, which looked more malicious than ever. "And no wonder," thought Gluck, "after being treated in that way."

He sauntered disconsolately to the window and sat himself down to catch the fresh evening air and escape the hot breath of the furnace. Now, this window commanded a direct view of the range of mountains that, as I told you before, overhung the Treasure Valley, and more especially of the peak from which fell the Golden River. It was just at the close of the day, and when Gluck sat down at the window, he saw the rocks of the mountaintops, all crimson and purple with the sunset; and there were bright tongues of fiery cloud burning and quivering about them; and the river, brighter than all, fell, in a waving column of pure gold, from precipice to precipice, with the double arch of a broad purple rainbow stretched across it, flushing and fading alternately in the wreaths of spray.

"Ah!" said Gluck aloud, after he had looked at it for a little while, "if that river were really all gold, what a nice thing it would be."

"No, it wouldn't, Gluck," said a clear, metallic voice close at his ear.

"Bless me, what's that?" exclaimed Gluck, jumping up. There was nobody there. He looked around the room and under the table and a great many times behind him, but there was certainly nobody there, and he sat down again at the window. This time he didn't speak, but he couldn't help thinking again that it would be very convenient if the river were really all gold.

"Not at all, my boy," said the same voice, louder than before.

"Bless me!" said Gluck again. "What is that?" He looked again into all the corners and cupboards, and then began turning around and around as fast as he could, in the middle of the room, thinking there was somebody behind him, when the same voice struck again on his ear. It was singing now, very merrily, "Lala-lira-la" — no words, only a soft, running, effervescent melody, something like that of a kettle on the boil. Gluck looked out the window; no, it was certainly in the house. Upstairs and downstairs; no, it was certainly in that very room, coming in quicker time and clearer notes every moment: "Lala-lira-la."

All at once, it struck Gluck that it sounded louder near the furnace. He ran to the opening and looked in. Yes, he saw right; it seemed to be coming not only out of the furnace but out of the pot. He uncovered it, and ran back in a great fright, for the pot was certainly singing! He stood in the farthest corner of the room, with his hands up and his mouth open, for a minute or two, when the singing stopped and the voice became clear and pronunciative.

"Hollo!" said the voice. Gluck made no answer.

"Hollo, Gluck, my boy," said the pot again.

Gluck summoned all his energies, walked straight up to the crucible, drew it out of the furnace, and looked in. The gold was all melted, and its surface as smooth and polished as a river, but instead of reflecting little Gluck's head, as he looked in he saw, meeting his glance from beneath the gold, the red nose and sharp eyes of his old friend of the mug, a thousand times redder and sharper than ever he had seen them in his life.

"Come, Gluck, my boy," said the voice out of the pot again. "I'm all right; pour me out." But Gluck was too much astonished to do anything of the kind.

"Pour me out, I say," said the voice rather gruffly. Still Gluck couldn't move.

"WILL you pour me out?" said the voice passionately. "I am too hot."

By a violent effort, Gluck recovered the use of his limbs, took hold of the crucible, and sloped it, so as to pour out the gold. But instead of a liquid stream, there came out, first a pair of pretty little yellow legs, then some coattails, then a pair of arms stuck akimbo, and finally the well-known head of his friend the mug; all these articles, uniting as they rolled out, stood up energetically on the floor in the shape of a little golden dwarf about a foot and a half high.

"That's right!" said the dwarf, stretching out first his legs and then his arms, and then shaking his head up and down and as far around as it would go, for five minutes without stopping, apparently with the view of ascertaining if he were quite correctly put together, while Gluck stood contemplating him in speechless amazement.

He was dressed in a slashed doublet of spun gold, so fine in its texture that the prismatic colors gleamed over it as if on a surface of mother-of-pearl; and over this brilliant doublet his hair and beard fell full halfway to the ground in waving curls, so exquisitely delicate that Gluck could hardly tell where they ended; they seemed to melt into air. The features of the face, however, were by no means finished with the same delicacy; they were rather coarse, slightly inclining to coppery in complexion, and indicative, in expression, of a very pertinacious and intractable disposition in their small proprietor.

When the dwarf had finished his self-examination, he turned his small, sharp eyes full on Gluck and stared at him deliberately for a minute or two.

"No, it wouldn't, Gluck, my boy," said the little man.

This was certainly rather an abrupt and unconnected mode of commencing conversation. It might indeed be supposed to refer to the course of Gluck's thoughts, which had first produced the dwarf's observations out of the pot; but whatever it referred to, Gluck had no inclination to dispute the dictum.

"Wouldn't it, sir?" said Gluck very mildly and submissively indeed.

"No," said the dwarf, conclusively. "No, it wouldn't."

And with that, the dwarf pulled his cap hard over his brows and took two turns, of three feet long, up and down the room, lifting his legs up very high and setting them down very hard. This pause gave time for Gluck to collect his thoughts a little, and, seeing no great reason to view his diminutive visitor with dread, and feeling his curiosity overcome his amazement, he ventured on a question of peculiar delicacy.

"Pray, sir," said Gluck, rather hesitatingly, "were you my mug?"

At this, the little man turned sharply around, walked straight up to Gluck, and drew himself up to his full height.

"I," said the little man, "am the King of the Golden River." Whereupon he turned about again and took two more turns, some six feet long, in order to allow time for the consternation that this announcement produced in his auditor to evaporate. After this, he again walked up to Gluck and stood still, as if expecting some comment on his communication. Gluck determined to say something at all events.

"I hope your Majesty is very well," said Gluck.

"Listen!" said the little man, deigning no reply to this polite inquiry. "I am the king of what you mortals call the Golden River. The shape you saw me in was owing to the malice of a stronger king, from whose enchantments you have this instant freed me. What I have seen of you and your conduct to your wicked brothers renders me willing to serve you; therefore, attend to what I tell you. Whoever shall climb to the top of that mountain from which you see the Golden River issue, and shall cast into the stream at its source three drops of holy water, for him and for him only the river shall turn to gold. But no one failing in his first attempt can succeed in a second one, and if anyone shall cast unholy water into the river, it will overwhelm him and he will become a black stone."

So saying, the King of the Golden River turned away and deliberately walked into the center of the hottest flame of the furnace. His figure became red, white, transparent, dazzling — a blaze of intense light — rose, trembled, and disappeared. The King of the Golden River had evaporated.

"Oh!" cried poor Gluck, running to look up the chimney after him. "O dear, dear, dear me! My mug! My mug! My mug!"

CHAPTER 3

How Mr. Hans set off on an expedition to the
Golden River, and how he prospered therein

The King of the Golden River had hardly made the extraordinary exit before Hans and Schwartz came roaring into the house. At the discovery of the total loss of their last piece of plate, they beat Gluck very steadily for a quarter of an hour; at the expiration of which period they dropped into a couple of chairs and requested to know what he had to say for himself.

Gluck told them his story, of which, of course, they did not believe a word. They beat him again, until their arms were tired, and staggered to bed. In the morning, however, the steadiness with which he adhered to his story obtained him some degree of credence; the immediate consequence of which was that the two brothers, after wrangling a long time on the knotty question, which of them should try his fortune first, drew their swords and began fighting. The noise of the fray alarmed the neighbors, who, finding they could not pacify the combatants, sent for the constable. Hans, on hearing this, contrived to escape, and hid himself; but Schwartz was taken before the magistrate, fined for breaking the peace, and, having drunk out his last penny the evening before, was thrown into prison until he should pay. When Hans heard this, he was much delighted, and determined to set out immediately for the Golden River.

How to get the holy water was the question. He went to the priest, but the priest could not give any holy water to so abandoned a character. So Hans went to vespers in the evening for the first time in his life and, under pretense of crossing himself, stole a cupful and returned home in triumph.

Next morning, he got up before the sun rose, put the holy water into a strong flask, and two bottles of wine and some meat into a basket, slung them over his back, took his alpine staff in his hand, and set off for the mountains. On his way out of the town, he had to pass the prison, and as he looked in at the windows, whom should he see but Schwartz himself peeping out of the bars and looking very disconsolate.

"Good morning, brother," said Hans. "Have you any message for the King of the Golden River?"

Schwartz gnashed his teeth with rage and shook the bars with all his strength, but Hans only laughed at him and, advising him to make himself comfortable until he came back again, shouldered his basket, shook the bottle of holy water in Schwartz's face until it frothed again, and marched off in the highest spirits in the world.

It was indeed a morning that might have made anyone happy, even with no Golden River to seek for. Level lines of dewy mist lay stretched along the valley, out of which rose the massy mountains, their lower cliffs in pale gray shadow, hardly distinguishable from the floating vapor but gradually ascending until they caught the sunlight, which ran in sharp touches of ruddy color along the angular crags, and pierced, in long, level rays, through their fringes of spearlike pine. Far above shot up red, splintered masses of castellated rock, jagged and shivered into myriads of fantastic forms, with here and there a streak of sunlit snow traced down their chasms like a line of forked lightning; and far beyond and far above all these, fainter than the morning cloud but purer and changeless, slept, in the blue sky, the utmost peaks of the eternal snow. The Golden River, which sprang from one of the lower and snowless elevations, was now nearly in shadow — all but the uppermost jets of spray, which rose like slow smoke above the undulating line of the cataract and floated away in feeble wreaths upon the morning wind.

On this object, and on this alone, Hans's eyes and thoughts were fixed. Forgetting the distance he had to traverse, he set off at an imprudent rate of walking, which greatly exhausted him before he had scaled the first range of the green and low hills.

He was, moreover, surprised, on surmounting them, to find that a large glacier, of whose existence, notwithstanding his previous knowledge of the mountains, he had been absolutely ignorant, lay between him and the source of the Golden River. He entered on it with the boldness of a practiced mountaineer, yet he thought he had never traversed so strange or so dangerous a glacier in his life. The ice was excessively slippery, and out of all its chasms came wild sounds of gushing water — not monotonous or low, but changeful and loud, rising occasionally into drifting passages of wild melody, then breaking off into short, melancholy tones or sudden shrieks resembling those of human voices in distress or pain. The ice was broken into thousands of confused shapes, but none, Hans thought, like the ordinary forms of splintered ice. There seemed a curious *expression* about all their outlines — a perpetual resemblance to living features, distorted and scornful. Myriads of deceitful shadows and lurid lights played and floated about and through the pale blue pinnacles, dazzling and confusing the sight of the traveler, while his ears grew dull and his head giddy with the constant gush and roar of the concealed waters.

These painful circumstances increased upon him as he advanced; the ice crashed and yawned into fresh chasms at his feet; tottering spires nodded around him and fell thundering across his path; and although he had repeatedly faced these dangers on the most terrific glaciers and in the wildest weather, it was with a new and oppressive feeling of panic terror that he leaped the last chasm and flung himself, exhausted and shuddering, onto the firm turf of the mountain.

He had been compelled to abandon his basket of food, which became a perilous encumbrance on the glacier, and had now no means of refreshing himself but by breaking off and eating some of the pieces of ice. This, however, relieved his thirst. An hour's repose recruited his hardy frame, and with the indomitable spirit of avarice, he resumed his laborious journey.

His way now lay straight up a ridge of bare red rocks, without a blade of grass to ease the foot or a projecting angle to afford an inch of shade from the south sun. It was past noon, and the rays beat intensely upon the steep path, while the whole atmosphere was motionless and penetrated with heat. Intense thirst was soon added to the bodily fatigue with which Hans was now afflicted; glance after glance he cast on the flask of water that hung at his belt.

"Three drops are enough," at last thought he. "I may, at least, cool my lips with it." He opened the flask and was raising it to his lips when his eye fell on an object lying on the rock beside him; he thought it moved. It was a small dog, apparently in the last agony of death from thirst. Its tongue was out, its jaws dry, its limbs extended lifelessly, and a swarm of black ants was crawling about its lips and throat.

Its eye moved to the bottle that Hans held in his hand. He raised it, drank, spurned the animal with his foot, and passed on. And he did not know how it was, but he thought that a strange shadow had suddenly come across the blue sky.

The path became steeper and more rugged every moment, and the high hill air, instead of refreshing him, seemed to throw his blood into a fever. The noise of the hill cataracts sounded like mockery in his ears; they were all distant, and his thirst increased every moment. Another hour passed, and he again looked down to the flask at his side; it was half empty, but there was much more than three drops in it. He stopped to open it, and again, as he did so, something moved in the path above him.

It was a fair child, stretched nearly lifeless on the rock, his breast heaving with thirst, his eyes closed, and his lips parched and burning. Hans eyed him deliberately, drank, and passed on. And a dark gray cloud came over the sun, and long, snakelike shadows crept up along the mountainsides.

Hans struggled on. The sun was sinking, but its descent seemed to bring no coolness; the leaden height of the dead air pressed upon his brow and heart, but the goal was near. He saw the cataract of the Golden River springing from the hillside scarcely five hundred feet above him. He paused for a moment to breathe, and sprang on to complete his task.

At this instant, a faint cry fell on his ear. Hans turned and saw a gray-haired old man extended on the rocks. His eyes were sunk, his features deadly pale and gathered into an expression of despair.

"Water!" He stretched his arms to Hans, and cried feebly, "Water! I am dying."

"I have none," replied Hans. "Thou hast had thy share of life."

He strode over the prostrate body and darted on. And a flash of blue lightning rose out of the East, shaped like a sword; it shook thrice over the whole heaven and left it dark with one heavy, impenetrable shade.

The sun was setting; it plunged toward the horizon like a red-hot ball. The roar of the Golden River rose on Hans's ear. He stood at the brink of the chasm through which it ran. Its waves were filled with the red glory of the sunset; they shook their crests like tongues of fire, and flashes of bloody light gleamed along their foam. Their sound came mightier and mightier on his senses; his brain grew giddy with the prolonged thunder.

Shuddering, he drew the flask from his girdle and hurled it into the center of the torrent. As he did so, an icy chill shot through his limbs; he staggered, shrieked, and fell. The waters closed over his cry, and the moaning of the river rose wildly into the night as it gushed over

the black stone.

CHAPTER 4

How Mr. Schwartz set off on an expedition to
the Golden River, and how he prospered therein

Poor little Gluck waited very anxiously, alone in the house, for Hans's return. Finding he did not come back, he was terribly frightened and went and told Schwartz in the prison all that had happened.

Then Schwartz was very much pleased and said that Hans must certainly have been turned into a black stone and he should have all the gold to himself. But Gluck was very sorry and cried all night.

When he got up in the morning, there was no bread in the house, nor any money; so Gluck went and hired himself to another goldsmith, and he worked so hard and so neatly and so long every day that he soon got money enough together to pay his brother's fine, and he went and gave it all to Schwartz, and Schwartz got out of prison. Then Schwartz was quite pleased and said he should have some of the gold of the river. But Gluck only begged he would go and see what had become of Hans.

Now, when Schwartz had heard that Hans had stolen the holy water, he thought to himself that such a proceeding might not be considered altogether correct by the King of the Golden River, and determined to manage matters better. So he took some more of Gluck's money and went to a bad priest, who gave him some holy water very readily for it. Then Schwartz was sure it was all quite right.

So Schwartz got up early in the morning before the sun rose, and took some bread and wine in a basket, and put his holy water in a flask, and set off for the mountains.

Like his brother, he was much surprised at the sight of the glacier and had great difficulty in crossing it, even after leaving his basket behind him.

The day was cloudless but not bright; there was a heavy purple haze hanging over the sky, and the hills looked lowering and gloomy. And as Schwartz climbed the steep rock path, the thirst came upon him, as it had upon his brother, until he lifted his flask to his lips to drink. Then he saw the fair child lying near him on the rocks, and the child cried to him and moaned for water.

"Water, indeed," said Schwartz. "I haven't half enough for myself," and he passed on.

And as he went, he thought the sunbeams grew more dim, and he saw a low bank of black cloud rising out of the west; and when he had climbed for another hour, the thirst overcame him again and he would have drunk. Then he saw the old man lying before him on the path, and heard him cry out for water.

"Water, indeed," said Schwartz. "I haven't half enough for myself," and on he went.

Then again the light seemed to fade from before his eyes, and he looked up, and, behold, a mist, of the color of blood, had come over the sun; and the bank of black cloud had risen very high, and its edges were tossing and tumbling like the waves of the angry sea, and they cast long shadows that flickered over Schwartz's path.

Then Schwartz climbed for another hour, and again his thirst returned; and as he lifted his flask to his lips, he thought he saw his brother Hans lying exhausted on the path before him, and as he gazed, the figure stretched its arms to him and cried for water.

"Ha, ha!" laughed Schwartz. "Are you there? Remember the prison bars, my boy. Water, indeed! Do you suppose I carried it all the way up here for you?" And he strode over the figure; yet, as he passed, he thought he saw a strange expression of mockery about its lips. And when he had gone a few yards farther, he looked back, but the figure was not there.

And a sudden horror came over Schwartz, he knew not why; but the thirst for gold prevailed over his fear, and he rushed on. And the bank of black cloud rose to the zenith, and out of it came bursts of spiry lightning, and waves of darkness seemed to heave and float, between their flashes, over the whole heavens. And the sky where the sun was setting was all level and like a lake of blood; and a strong wind came out of that sky, tearing its crimson clouds into fragments and scattering them far into the darkness

And when Schwartz stood by the brink of the Golden River, its waves were black like thunderclouds, but their foam was like fire; and the roar of the waters below and the thunder above met as he cast the flask into the stream. And as he did so, the lightning glared in his eyes, and the earth gave way beneath him, and the waters closed over his cry. And the moaning of the river rose wildly into the night as it gushed over

the two black stones.

CHAPTER 5

How little Gluck set off on an expedition to the Golden River,
and how he prospered therein, with other matters of interest

When Gluck found that Schwartz did not come back, he was very sorry and did not know what to do. He had no money and was obliged to go and hire himself again to the goldsmith, who worked him very hard and gave him very little money. So, after a month or two, Gluck grew tired and made up his mind to go and try his fortune with the Golden River.

"The little king looked very kind," thought he. "I don't think he will turn me into a black stone." So he went to the priest, and the priest gave him some holy water as soon as he asked for it. Then Gluck took some bread in his basket, and the bottle of water, and set off very early for the mountains.

If the glacier had occasioned a great deal of fatigue in his brothers, it was twenty times worse for him, who was neither so strong nor so practiced on the mountains. He had several very bad falls, lost his basket and bread, and was very much frightened at the strange noises under the ice. He lay a long time to rest on the grass, after he had gotten over, and began to climb the hill just in the hottest part of the day. When he had climbed for an hour, he got dreadfully thirsty and was going to drink, like his brothers, when he saw an old man coming down the path above him, looking very feeble and leaning on a staff.

"Why son," said the old man, "I am faint with thirst; give me some of that water."

Then Gluck looked at him, and when he saw that he was pale and weary, he gave him the water. "Only, pray, don't drink it all," said Gluck.

But the old man drank a great deal and gave him back the bottle two-thirds empty. Then he bade him good speed, and Gluck went on again merrily. And the path became easier to his feet, and two or three blades of grass appeared upon it, and some grasshoppers began singing on the bank beside it, and Gluck thought he had never heard such merry singing.

Then he went on for another hour, and the thirst increased on him so that he thought he should be forced to drink. But as he raised the flask, he saw a little child lying panting by the roadside, and he cried out piteously for water. Then Gluck struggled with himself and determined to bear the thirst a little longer; and he put the bottle to the child's lips, and the child drank all but a few drops. Then he smiled on Gluck and got up and ran down the hill; and Gluck looked after him until he became as small as a little star, and then turned and began climbing again.

And then there were all kinds of sweet flowers growing on the rocks: bright green moss with pale pink, starry flowers, and soft belled gentians, bluer than the sky at its deepest, and pure-white transparent lilies. And crimson and purple butterflies darted hither and thither, and the sky sent down such pure light that Gluck had never felt so happy in his life.

Yet, when he had climbed for another hour, his thirst became intolerable again; and when he looked at his bottle, he saw that there were only five or six drops left in it, and he could not venture to drink. And as he was hanging the flask to his belt again, he saw a little dog lying on the rocks, gasping for breath — just as Hans had seen it on the day of his ascent. And Gluck stopped and looked at it, and then at the Golden River, not five hundred yards above him; and he thought of the dwarf's words, that no one could succeed except in his first attempt; and he tried to pass the dog, but it whined piteously, and Gluck stopped again.

"Poor beastie," said Gluck. "It will be dead when I come down again, if I don't help it." Then he looked closer and closer at it, and its eye turned on him so mournfully that he could not stand it.

"Confound the king and his gold, too," said Gluck, and he opened the flask and poured all the water into the dog's mouth. The dog sprang up and stood on its hind legs. Its tail disappeared; its ears became long, longer, silky, golden; its nose became very red; its eyes became very twinkling. In three seconds, the dog was gone, and before Gluck stood his old acquaintance, the King of the Golden River.

"Thank you," said the monarch. "But don't be frightened; it's all right" — for Gluck showed manifest symptoms of consternation at this unlooked-for reply to his last observation.

"Why didn't you come before," continued the dwarf, "instead of sending me those rascally brothers of yours, for me to have the trouble of turning into stones? Very hard stones they make, too."

"Oh, dear me!" said Gluck. "Have you really been so cruel?"

"Cruel!" said the dwarf. "They poured unholy water into my stream. Do you suppose I'm going to allow that?"

"Why," said Gluck, "I am sure, sir — your Majesty, I mean — they got the water out of the church font."

"Very probably," replied the dwarf, "but" — and his countenance grew stern as he spoke — "the water that has been refused to the cry of the weary and dying is unholy, even though it had been blessed by every saint in Heaven; and the water that is found in the vessel of mercy is holy, even though it had been defiled with corpses."

So saying, the dwarf stooped and plucked a lily that grew at his feet. On its white leaves there hung three drops of clear dew. And the dwarf shook them into the flask that Gluck held in his hand.

"Cast these into the river," he said, "and descend on the other side of the mountains into the Treasure Valley. And so good speed." As he spoke, the figure of the dwarf became indistinct. The playing colors of his robe formed themselves into a prismatic mist of dewy light; he stood for an instant veiled with them as with the belt of a broad rainbow. The colors grew faint; the mist rose into the air; the monarch had evaporated.

And Gluck climbed to the brink of the Golden River, and its waves were as clear as crystal and as brilliant as the sun. And when he had cast the three drops of dew into the stream, there opened where they fell a small, circular whirlpool, into which the waters descended with a musical noise. Gluck stood watching it for some time, very much disappointed, because not only had the river not turned into gold, but its waters seemed much diminished in quantity.

Yet he obeyed his friend the dwarf and descended the other side of the mountains toward the Treasure Valley; and as he went, he thought he heard the noise of water working its way under the ground. And when he came in sight of the Treasure Valley, behold, a river, like the Golden River, was springing from a new cleft of the rocks above it and was flowing in innumerable streams among the dry heaps of red sand. And as Gluck gazed, fresh grass sprang beside the new streams, and creeping plants grew and climbed among the moistening soil. Young flowers opened suddenly along the riversides, as stars leap out when twilight is deepening, and thickets of myrtle and tendrils of vine cast lengthening shadows over the valley as they grew. And thus the Treasure Valley became a garden again, and the inheritance that had been lost by cruelty was regained by love.

And Gluck went and dwelt in the valley, and the poor were never driven from his door, so that his barns became full of corn and his house of treasure.

And for him the river had, according to the dwarf's promise, become a river of gold. And to this day, the inhabitants of the valley point out the place where the three drops of holy dew were cast into the stream, and trace the course of the Golden River under the ground until it emerges in the Treasure Valley. And at the top of the cataract of the Golden River are still to be seen two black stones, around which the waters howl mournfully every day at sunset; and these stones are still called by the people of the valley the Black Brothers.

The Nurnberg Stove

by Louisa de la Rame (Ouida)

August lived in a little town called Hall. Hall is a favorite name for
several towns in Austria and in Germany; but this one especial little Hall, in the Upper Innthal, is one of the most charming Old
World places that I know, and August, for his part, did not know
any other. It has the green meadows and the great mountains all
about it, and the gray-green glacier-fed water rushes by it. It has
paved streets and enchanting little shops that have all latticed
panes and iron gratings to them; it has a very grand old Gothic
church that has the noblest blendings of light and shadow, and
marble tombs of dead knights, and a look of infinite strength and
repose as a church should have.

Then there is the Muntze Tower, black and white, rising out of
greenery and looking down on a long wooden bridge and the
broad rapid river; and there is an old schloss that has been made
into a guard-house, with battlements and frescos and heraldic devices in gold and colors, and a man-at-arms carved in stone standing life-size in his niche and bearing his date, 1530.

A little farther on, but close at hand, is a cloister with beautiful
marble columns and tombs, and a colossal wood-carved Calvary,
and beside that a small and very rich chapel: indeed, so full is the
little town of the undisturbed past, that to walk in it is like opening a missal of the Middle Ages, all emblazoned and illuminated

with saints and warriors, and it is so clean, and so still, and so noble, by reason of its monuments and its historical color, that I marvel much no one has ever cared to sing its praises. The old pious
heroic life of an age at once more restful and more brave than ours
still leaves its spirit there, and then there is the girdle of the mountains all around, and that alone means strength, peace, majesty.

In this little town a few years ago, August Strehla lived with his
people in the stone-paved irregular square where the grand church
stands. He was a small boy of nine years at that time — a chubby-
faced little man with rosy cheeks, big hazel eyes, and clusters of
curls the brown of ripe nuts. His mother was dead, his father was
poor, and there were many mouths at home to feed.

In this country, the winters are long and very cold, the whole
land lies wrapped in snow for many months, and this night that he
was trotting home, with a jug of beer in his numb red hands, was
terribly cold and dreary. The good burghers of Hall had shut their
double shutters, and the few lamps there were flickered dully behind their quaint, old-fashioned iron casings. The mountains indeed were beautiful, all snow-white under the stars that are so big
in frost. Hardly anyone was astir; a few good souls wending home
from vespers, a tired post-boy who blew a shrill blast from his tas-
seled horn as he pulled up his sledge before a hostelry, and little
August hugging his jug of beer to his ragged sheepskin coat were
all who were abroad, for the snow fell heavily and the good folks of
Hall go early to their beds.

August could not have run, or he would have spilled the beer;
he was half-frozen and a little frightened, but he kept up his courage by saying over and over again to himself, "I shall soon be at
home with dear Hirschvogel." He went on through the streets,
past the stone man-at-arms of the guardhouse, and so into the place
where the great church was, and where, near it, stood the house of
his father, Karl Strehla, with a sculptured Bethlehem over the

doorway, and the pilgrimage of the Three Kings painted on its wall. He had been sent on a long errand outside the gates in the afternoon, over the frozen fields and the broad white snow, and had been belated, and had thought he had heard the wolves behind him at every step, and had reached the town in a great state of terror, thankful with all his little panting heart to see the oil-lamp burning under the first house-shrine. But he had not forgotten to call for the beer, and he carried it carefully now, even though his hands were so numb that he was afraid they would let the jug down at every moment.

The snow outlined with white every gable and cornice of the beautiful old wooden houses; the moonlight shone on the gilded signs, the lambs, the grapes, the eagles, and all the quaint devices that hung before the doors; covered lamps burned before the Nativities and Crucifixions painted on the walls or let into the woodwork; here and there, where a shutter had not been closed, a ruddy firelight lit up a homely interior, with the noisy band of children clustering around the house-mother and a big brown loaf, or some gossips spinning and listening to the cobbler's or the barber's story of a neighbor, while the oil-wicks glimmered, and the hearth-logs blazed, and the chestnuts sputtered in their iron roasting-pot.

Little August saw all these things, as he saw everything with his two big bright eyes that had such curious lights and shadows in them; but he went heedfully on his way for the sake of the beer, which a single slip of the foot would make him spill. At his knock and call, the solid oak door, four centuries old if one, flew open, and the boy darted in with his beer and shouted, with all the force of mirthful lungs, "Oh, dear Hirschvogel, but for the thought of you I should have died!"

It was a large barren room into which he rushed with so much pleasure, and the bricks were bare and uneven. It had a walnut-wood press, handsome and very old, a broad deal table, and several wooden stools for all its furniture; but at the top of the chamber, sending out warmth and color together as the lamp shed its rays upon it, was a tower of porcelain, burnished with all the hues of a king's peacock and a queen's jewels, and surmounted with armed figures, and shields, and flowers of heraldry, and a great golden crown upon the highest summit of all.

It was a stove of 1532, and on it were the letters H.R.H., for it was in every portion the handwork of the great potter of Nurnberg, Augustin Hirschvogel, who put his mark thus, as all the world knows. The stove no doubt had stood in palaces and been made for princes, had warmed the crimson stockings of cardinals and the gold-broidered shoes of archduchesses, had glowed in presence-chambers and lent its carbon to help kindle sharp brains in anxious councils of state; no one knew what it had seen or done or been fashioned for; but it was a right royal thing. Yet perhaps it had never been more useful than it was now in this poor desolate room, sending down heat and comfort into the troop of children tumbled together on a wolfskin at its feet, who received frozen August among them with loud shouts of joy.

"Oh, dear Hirschvogel, I am so cold, so cold!" said August, kissing its gilded lion's claws. "Is Father not in, Dorothea?"

"No, dear. He is late."

Dorothea was a girl of seventeen, dark-haired and serious, and with a sweet, sad face, for she had had many cares laid on her shoulders, even while still a mere baby. She was the eldest of the Strehla family, and there were ten of them in all. Next to her there came Jan and Karl and Otho, big lads, gaining a little for their own living; and then came August, who went up in the summer to the high Alps with the farmers' cattle, but in winter could do nothing to fill his own little platter and pot; and then all the little ones, who could only open their mouths to be fed like young birds: Albrecht and Hilda, and Waldo and Christof, and last of all, little three-year-old Ermengilda, with eyes like forget-me-nots, whose birth had cost them the life of their mother.

They were of that mixed race, half-Austrian, half-Italian, so common in the Tyrol. Some of the children were white and golden as lilies; others were brown and brilliant as fresh-fallen chestnuts.

The father was a good man, but weak and weary with so many to find for and so little to do it with. He worked at the salt-furnaces, and by that gained a few florins; people said he would have worked better and kept his family more easily if he had not loved his pipe and a draft of ale too well; but this had been said of him only after his wife's death, when trouble and perplexity had begun to dull a brain never too vigorous, and to enfeeble further a character already too yielding.

As it was, the wolf often bayed at the door of the Strehla household, without a wolf from the mountains coming down. Dorothea was one of those maidens who almost work miracles, so far can their industry and care and intelligence make a home sweet and wholesome and a single loaf seem to swell into twenty. The children were always clean and happy, and the table was seldom without its big pot of soup once a day. Still, very poor they were, and Dorothea's heart ached with shame, for she knew that their father's debts were many for flour and meat and clothing. Of fuel to feed the big stove they had always enough without cost, for their mother's father was alive, and sold wood and fircones and coke, and never grudged them to his grandchildren, although he grumbled at Strehla's improvidence and hapless, dreamy ways.

"Father says we are never to wait for him: we will have supper, now you have come home, dear," said Dorothea, who, however she might fret her soul in secret as she knitted their hose and mended their shirts, never let her anxieties cast a gloom on the children; only to August she did speak a little sometimes, because he was so thoughtful and so tender of her always, and knew as well as she did that there were troubles about money — although these troubles were vague to them both, and the debtors were patient and kindly, being neighbors all in the old twisting streets between the guardhouse and the river. Supper was a huge bowl of soup, with big slices of brown bread swimming in it and some onions bobbing up and down. The bowl was soon emptied by ten wooden spoons, and then the three eldest boys slipped off to bed, being tired with their rough bodily labor in the snow all day, and Dorothea drew her spinning-wheel by the stove and set it whirring, and the little ones got August down upon the old worn wolfskin and clamored to him for a picture or a story.

For August was the artist of the family. He had a piece of planed wood that his father had given him, and some sticks of charcoal, and he would draw a hundred things he had seen in the day, sweeping each out with his elbow when the children had seen enough of it and sketching another in its stead: faces and dogs' heads, and men in sledges, and old women in their furs, and pine trees, and cocks and hens, and all sorts of animals, and now and then — very reverently — a Madonna and Child. It was all very rough, for there was no one to teach him anything. But it was all life-like, and kept the whole troop of children shrieking with laughter, or watching breathless, with wide-open, wondering, awed eyes.

They were all so happy: what did they care for the snow outside? Their little bodies were warm, and their hearts merry. Even Dorothea, troubled about the bread for the morrow, laughed as she spun; and August, with all his soul in his work, and little rosy Ermengilda's cheek on his shoulder, glowing after his frozen afternoon, cried out loud, smiling, as he looked up at the stove that was shedding its heat down on them all.

"Oh, dear Hirschvogel! You are almost as great and good as the sun! No, you are greater and better, I think, because he goes away nobody knows where all these long, dark, cold hours, and does not care how people die for want of him. But you — you are always ready: just a little bit of wood to feed you, and you will make a summer for us all the winter through!"

The grand old stove seemed to smile through all its iridescent surface at the praises of the child. No doubt the stove, although it had known three centuries and more, had known but very little gratitude. It was one of those magnificent stoves in enameled faience which so excited the jealousy of the other potters of Nurnberg that in a body they demanded of the magistracy that Augustin Hirschvogel should be forbidden to make any more of them — the magistracy, happily, proving of a broader mind, and having no sympathy with the wish of the artisans to cripple their greater fellow.

It was of great height and breadth, with all the majolica luster that Hirschvogel learned to give to his enamels when he was courting the young Venetian girl whom he afterward married. There was the statue of a king at each corner, modeled with as much force and splendor as his friend Albrecht Duerer could have given to them on copperplate or canvas. The body of the stove itself was divided into panels, which had the Ages of Man painted on them in polychrome; the borders of the panels had roses and holly and laurel and other foliage, and German mottoes in black letter of odd Old-World moralizing, such as the old Teutons, and the Dutch after them, love to have on their chimney-places and their drinking-cups, their dishes and flagons. The whole was burnished with gilding in many parts, and was radiant everywhere with that brilliant coloring of which the Hirschvogel family, painters on glass and great in chemistry as they were, were all masters.

The stove was a very grand thing, as I say. Possibly Hirschvogel had made it for some mighty lord of the Tyrol at that time when he was an imperial guest at Innsbruck and fashioned so many things for the Schloss Amras and beautiful Philippine Welser, the burgher's daughter, who gained an archduke's heart by her beauty and the right to wear his honors by her wit.

Nothing was known of the stove at this latter day in Hall. The grandfather Strehla, who had been a master-mason, had dug it up out of some ruins where he was building, and, finding it without a flaw, had taken it home, and only thought it worth finding because it was such a good one to burn. That was now sixty years past, and ever since then, the stove had stood in the big desolate empty room, warming three generations of the Strehla family, and having seen nothing prettier perhaps in all its many years than the children tumbled now in a cluster like gathered flowers at its feet. For the Strehla children, born to nothing else, were all born with beauty: white or brown, they were equally lovely to look upon, and when they went into the church to Mass, with their curling locks and their clasped hands, they stood under the grim statues like cherubs flown down off some fresco.

⌒

"Tell us a story, August," they cried, in chorus, when they had seen charcoal pictures until they were tired; and August did as he did every night pretty nearly: looked up at the stove and told them what he imagined of the many adventures and joys and sorrows of the human being who figured on the panels from his cradle to his grave.

To the children, the stove was a household god. In summer, they laid a mat of fresh moss all around it and dressed it up with green boughs and the numberless beautiful wildflowers of the Tyrol country. In winter, all their joys centered in it, and scampering home from school over the ice and snow, they were happy, knowing that they would soon be cracking nuts or roasting chestnuts in the broad ardent glow of its noble tower, which rose eight feet high above them with all its spires and pinnacles and crowns.

Once a traveling peddler had told them that the letters on it meant Augustin Hirschvogel, and that Hirschvogel had been a great German potter and painter, like his father before him, in the art-sanctified city of Nurnberg, and had made many such stoves that were all miracles of beauty and of workmanship, putting all his heart and his soul and his faith into his labors, as the men of those earlier ages did, and thinking but little of gold or praise.

An old trader, too, who sold curiosities not far from the church had told August a little more about the brave family of Hirsch-vogel, whose houses can be seen in Nurnberg to this day; of old Veit, the first of them, who painted the Gothic windows of St. Sebald with the marriage of the Margravine; of his sons and of his grandsons, potters, painters, engravers all, and chief of them great Augustin, the Luca della Robbia of the North.

And August's imagination, always quick, had made a living personage out of these few records, and saw Hirschvogel as though he were in the flesh walking up and down the Maximilian-Strass in his visit to Innsbruck, and maturing beautiful things in his brain as he stood on the bridge and gazed on the emerald-green flood of the Inn. So the stove had got to be called Hirschvogel in the fam-ily, as if it were a living creature, and little August was very proud because he had been named after that famous old dead German who had had the genius to make so glorious a thing.

All the children loved the stove, but with August the love of it was a passion; and in his secret heart, he used to say to himself, "When I am a man, I will make just such things too, and then I will set Hirschvogel in a beautiful room in a house that I will build my-self in Innsbruck, just outside the gates, where the chestnuts are, by the river. That is what I will do when I am a man."

For August, a salt-baker's son and a little cow-keeper when he was anything, was a dreamer of dreams, and when he was upon the high Alps with his cattle, with the stillness and the sky around him, was quite certain that he would live for greater things than driving the herds up when the spring-tide came among the blue sea of gentians, or toiling down in the town with wood and with timber as his father and grandfather did every day of their lives. He was a strong and healthy little fellow, fed on the free mountain air, and he was very happy, and loved his family devotedly, and was as active as a squirrel and as playful as a hare. But he kept his thoughts to himself, and some of them went a very long way for a little boy who was only one among many, and to whom nobody had ever paid any attention except to teach him his letters and tell him to fear God.

August in winter was only a little, hungry schoolboy, trotting to be catechized by the priest, or to bring the loaves from the bake-house, or to carry his father's boots to the cobbler; and in summer, he was only one of hundreds of cow-herds, who drove the poor, half-blind, blinking, stumbling cattle, ringing their throat-bells, out into the sweet intoxication of the sudden sunlight, and lived up with them in the heights among the Alpine roses, with only the clouds and the snow-summits near.

But he was always thinking, thinking, thinking, for all that; and under his little sheepskin winter coat and his rough hempen summer shirt, his heart had as much courage in it as Hofer's ever had — great Hofer, who is a household word in all the Innthal, and whom August always reverently remembered when he went to the city of Innsbruck and ran out by the foaming water-mill and under the wooded height of Berg Isel.

August lay now in the warmth of the stove and told the children stories, his own little brown face growing red with excitement as his imagination glowed to fever-heat. That human being on the panels, who was drawn there as a baby in a cradle, as a boy playing among flowers, as a lover sighing under a casement, as a soldier in the midst of strife, as a father with children around him, as a weary, old, blind man on crutches, and, lastly, as a ransomed soul raised up by angels, had always had the most intense interest for August, and he had made, not one history for him, but a thousand; he seldom told them the same tale twice. He had never seen a storybook in his life; his primer and his Mass-book were all the volumes he had. But nature had given him Fancy, and she is a good fairy that makes up for the want of very many things! Only, alas, her wings are so very soon broken, poor thing, and then she is of no use at all.

"It is time for you all to go to bed, children," said Dorothea, looking up from her spinning. "Father is very late tonight; you must not sit up for him."

"Oh, five minutes more, dear Dorothea!" they pleaded; and little rosy and golden Ermengilda climbed up into her lap. "Hirsch-vogel is so warm, the beds are never so warm as he. Can't you tell us another tale, August?"

"No," cried August, whose face had lost its light, now that his story had come to an end, and who sat serious, with his hands clasped on his knees, gazing onto the luminous arabesques of the stove. "It is only a week to Christmas," he said suddenly.

"Grandmother's big cakes!" chuckled little Christof, who was five years old and thought Christmas meant a big cake and nothing else.

"What will Santa Claus find for 'Gilda if she be good?" murmured Dorothea over the child's sunny head; for, however hard poverty might pinch, it could never pinch so tightly that Dorothea would not find some wooden toy and some rosy apples to put in her little sister's socks.

"Father Max has promised me a big goose, because I saved the calf's life in June," said August. It was the twentieth time he had told them so that month, he was so proud of it.

How to Tell Stories to Children

"And Aunt Maila will be sure to send us wine and honey and a barrel of flour; she always does," said Albrecht. Their aunt Maila had a chalet and a little farm over on the green slopes toward Dorp Ampas.

"I shall go up into the woods and get Hirschvogel's crown," said August; they always crowned Hirschvogel for Christmas with pine boughs and ivy and mountain-berries. The heat soon withered the crown; but it was part of the religion of the day to them, as much so as it was to cross themselves in church and raise their voices in the *O Salutaris Hostia*. And they fell chatting of all they would do on the Christ-night, and one little voice piped loud against another's, and they were as happy as though their stockings would be full of golden purses and jeweled toys, and the big goose in the soup-pot seemed to them such a meal as kings would envy.

In the midst of their chatter and laughter, a blast of frozen air and a spray of driven snow struck like ice through the room, and reached them even in the warmth of the old wolfskins and the great stove. It was the door that had opened and let in the cold; it was their father who had come home.

The younger children ran joyously to meet him. Dorothea pushed the one wooden armchair of the room to the stove, and August flew to set the jug of beer on a little round table, and fill a long clay pipe; for their father was good to them all, and seldom raised his voice in anger, and they had been trained by the mother they had loved to dutifulness and obedience and a watchful affection.

Tonight Karl Strehla responded very wearily to the young ones' welcome, and came to the wooden chair with a tired step and sat down heavily, not noticing either pipe or beer.

"Are you not well, dear Father?" his daughter asked him.

"I am well enough," he answered, dully, and sat there with his head bent, letting the lighted pipe grow cold. He was a fair, tall man, gray before his time, and bowed with labor. "Take the children to bed," he said suddenly, at last, and Dorothea obeyed.

August stayed behind, curled before the stove; at nine years old, and when one earns money in the summer from the farmers, one is not altogether a child anymore, at least in one's own estimation. August did not heed his father's silence: he was used to it. Karl Strehla was a man of few words and, being of weakly health, was usually too tired at the end of the day to do more than drink his beer and sleep.

August lay on the wolfskin, dreamy and comfortable, looking up through his drooping eyelids at the golden coronets on the crest of the great stove, and wondering for the millionth time whom it had been made for, and what grand places and scenes it had known. Dorothea came down from putting the little ones in their beds; the cuckoo-clock in the corner struck eight; she looked to her father and the untouched pipe, then sat down to her spinning, saying nothing. She thought he had been drinking in some tavern; it had been often so with him of late.

There was a long silence; the cuckoo called the quarter twice. August dropped asleep, his curls falling over his face. Dorothea's wheel hummed like a cat. Suddenly Karl Strehla struck his hand on the table, sending the pipe on the ground.

"I have sold Hirschvogel," he said, and his voice was husky and ashamed in his throat. The spinning-wheel stopped. August sprang erect out of his sleep. "Sold Hirschvogel!" If their father had dashed the holy crucifix on the floor at their feet and spat on it, they could not have shuddered under the horror of a greater blasphemy. "I have sold Hirschvogel!" said Karl Strehla, in the same husky, dogged voice. "I have sold it to a traveling trader in such things for two hundred florins. What would you? — I owe double that. He saw it this morning when you were all out. He will pack it and take it to Munich tomorrow."

Dorothea gave a low shrill cry: "Oh, Father! The children — in mid-winter!" She turned white as the snow without; her words died away in her throat.

August stood, half-blind with sleep, staring with dazed eyes as his cattle stared at the sun when they came out from their winter's prison. "It is not true! It is not true!" he muttered. "You are jesting, Father?"

Strehla broke into a dreary laugh. "It is true. Would you like to know what is true too? That the bread you eat, and the meat you put in this pot, and the roof you have over your heads, are none of them paid for, have been none of them paid for months and months. If it had not been for your grandfather, I should have been in prison all summer and autumn, and he is out of patience and will do no more now. There is no work to be had; the masters go to younger men: they say I work ill; it may be so. Who can keep his head above water with ten hungry children dragging him down? When your mother lived, it was different. Boy, you stare at me as if I were a mad dog! You have made a god of yon china thing. Well — it goes. Goes tomorrow. Two hundred florins: that is something. It will keep me out of prison for a little, and with the spring things may turn —"

August stood like a creature paralyzed. His eyes were wide open, fastened on his father's with terror and incredulous horror; his face had grown as white as his sister's; his chest heaved with tearless sobs. "It is not true! It is not true!" he echoed, stupidly. It seemed to him that the very skies must fall, and the earth perish, if they could take away Hirschvogel. They might as soon talk of tearing down God's sun out of the heavens.

"You will find it true," said his father, doggedly, and angered because he was in his own soul bitterly ashamed to have bartered away the heirloom and treasure of his race and the comfort and health-giver of his young children. "You will find it true. The dealer has paid me half the money tonight and will pay me the other half tomorrow when he packs it up and takes it away to Munich. No doubt it is worth a great deal more — at least I suppose so, as he gives that — but beggars cannot be choosers. The little black stove in the kitchen will warm you all just as well. Who would keep a gilded, painted thing in a poor house like this, when one can make two hundred florins by it? Dorothea, you never sobbed more when your mother died. What is it, when all is said? A bit of hardware much too grand-looking for such a room as this. If all the Strehlas had not been born fools, it would have been sold a century ago, when it was dug up out of the ground. 'It is a stove for a museum,' the trader said when he saw it. To a museum let it go."

August gave a shrill shriek like a hare's when it is caught for its death, and threw himself on his knees at his father's feet.

"Oh, Father, Father!" he cried, convulsively, his hands closing on Strehla's knees, and his uplifted face blanched and distorted with terror. "Oh, Father, dear Father, you cannot mean what you say? Send *it* away — our life, our sun, our joy, our comfort? We shall all die in the dark and cold. Sell *me* rather. Sell me to any trade or any pain you like; I will not mind. But Hirschvogel! It is like selling the very cross off the altar! You must be in jest. You could not do such a thing! You could not — you who have always been gentle and good, and who have sat in the warmth here year after year with our mother. It is not a piece of hardware, as you say; it is a living thing, for a great man's thoughts and fancies have put life into it, and it loves us even though we are only poor little children, and we love it with all our hearts and souls, and up in Heaven I am sure the dead Hirschvogel knows! Oh, listen; I will go and try to get work tomorrow! I will ask them to let me cut ice or make the paths through the snow. There must be something I could do, and I will beg the people we owe money to to wait. They are all neighbors; they will be patient. But sell Hirschvogel! Oh, never! never! never! Give the florins back to the vile man. Tell him it would be like selling the shroud out of mother's coffin, or the golden curls off Ermengilda's head! Oh, Father, dear Father! Do hear me, for pity's sake!"

Strehla was moved by the boy's anguish. He loved his children, even though he was often weary of them, and their pain was pain to him. But besides emotion, and stronger than emotion, was the anger that August roused in him. He hated and despised himself for the barter of the heirloom of his race, and every word of the child stung him with a stinging sense of shame. And he spoke in his wrath rather than in his sorrow.

"You are a little fool," he said, harshly, as they had never heard him speak. "You rave like a play-actor. Get up and go to bed. The stove is sold. There is no more to be said. Children like you have nothing to do with such matters. The stove is sold and goes to Munich tomorrow. What is it to you? Be thankful I can get bread for you. Get on your legs, I say, and go to bed."

Strehla took up the jug of ale as he paused, and drained it slowly as a man who had no cares. August sprang to his feet and threw his hair back off his face; the blood rushed into his cheeks, making them scarlet; his great soft eyes flamed alight with furious passion.

"You *dare* not!" he cried, aloud. "You dare not sell it, I say! It is not yours alone; it is ours —"

Strehla flung the emptied jug on the bricks with a force that shivered it to atoms and, rising to his feet, struck his son a blow that felled him to the floor. It was the first time in all his life that he had ever raised his hand against any one of his children. Then he took the oil-lamp that stood at his elbow and stumbled off to his own chamber with a cloud before his eyes.

"What has happened?" said August, a little while later, as he opened his eyes and saw Dorothea weeping above him on the wolfskin before the stove. He had been struck backward, and his head had fallen on the hard bricks where the wolfskin did not reach. He sat up a moment, with his face bent upon his hands.

"I remember now," he said, very low, under his breath. Dorothea showered kisses on him, while her tears fell like rain.

"But, oh, dear, how could you speak so to Father?" she murmured. "It was very wrong."

"No, I was right," said August, and his little mouth, that hitherto had only curled in laughter, curved downward with a fixed and bitter seriousness. "How dare he? How dare he?" he muttered, with his head sunk in his hands. "It is not his alone. It belongs to us all. It is as much yours and mine as it is his."

Dorothea could only sob in answer. She was too frightened to speak. The authority of their parents in the house had never in her remembrance been questioned.

"Are you hurt by the fall, dear August?" she murmured, at length, for he looked to her so pale and strange.

"Yes — no. I do not know. What does it matter?" He sat up upon the wolfskin with passionate pain upon his face; all his soul was in rebellion, and he was only a child and was powerless. "It is a sin; it is a theft; it is an infamy," he said slowly, his eyes fastened on the gilded feet of Hirschvogel.

"Oh, August, do not say such things of Father!" sobbed his sister. "Whatever he does, we ought to think it right."

August laughed aloud. "Is it right that he should spend his money in drink? That he should let orders lie unexecuted? That he should do his work so ill that no one cares to employ him? That he should live on grandfather's charity, and then dare sell a thing that is ours every whit as much as it is his? To sell Hirschvogel! I would sooner sell my soul!"

"August!" cried Dorothea, with piteous entreaty. He terrified her; she could not recognize her little, gay, gentle brother in those fierce and blasphemous words.

August laughed aloud again; then all at once his laughter broke down into bitterest weeping. He threw himself forward on the stove, covering it with kisses, and sobbing as though his heart would burst from his bosom. What could he do? Nothing, nothing, nothing!

"August, dear August," whispered Dorothea, piteously, and trembling all over — for she was a very gentle girl, and fierce feeling terrified her — "August, do not lie there. Come to bed. It is quite late. In the morning you will be calmer. It is horrible indeed, and we shall die of cold, at least the little ones; but if it be Father's will —"

"Let me alone," said August, through his teeth, striving to still the storm of sobs that shook him from head to foot. "Let me alone. In the morning! How can you speak of the morning?"

"Come to bed, dear," sighed his sister. "Oh, August, do not lie and look like that! You frighten me. Do come to bed."

"I shall stay here."

"Here! All night!"

"They might take it in the night. Besides, to leave it *now*!"

"But it is cold! The fire is out."

"It will never be warm anymore, nor shall we."

All his childhood had gone out of him, all his gleeful, careless, sunny temper had gone with it; he spoke sullenly and wearily, choking down the great sobs in his chest. To him it was as if the end of the world had come. His sister lingered by him while striving to persuade him to go to his place in the little crowded bedchamber with Albrecht and Waldo and Christof. But it was in vain.

"I shall stay here," was all he answered her. And he stayed — all the night long.

The lamps went out; the rats came and ran across the floor; as the hours crept on through midnight and past, the cold intensified and the air of the room grew like ice. August did not move; he lay with his face downward on the golden and rainbow-hued pedestal of the household treasure, which henceforth was to be cold forevermore, an exiled thing in a foreign city in a far-off land. While yet it was dark, his three elder brothers came down the stairs and let themselves out, each bearing his lantern and going to his work in stoneyard and timberyard and at the salt-works. They did not notice him; they did not know what had happened. A little later, his sister came down with a light in her hand to make ready the house ere morning should break. She stole up to him and laid her hand on his shoulder timidly.

"Dear August, you must be frozen. August, do look up! Do speak!"

August raised his eyes with a wild, feverish, sullen look in them that she had never seen there. His face was ashen white; his lips were like fire. He had not slept all night; but his passionate sobs had given way to delirious waking dreams and numb senseless trances, which had alternated one on another all through the freezing, lonely, horrible hours.

"It will never be warm again," he muttered, "never again!"

Dorothea clasped him with trembling hands. "August! Do you not know me?" she cried, in an agony. "I am Dorothea. Wake up, dear! Wake up! It is morning, only so dark!"

August shuddered all over. "The morning!" he echoed. He slowly rose up onto his feet. "I will go to grandfather," he said, very low. "He is always good: perhaps he could save it."

Loud blows with the heavy iron knocker of the house-door drowned his words. A strange voice called aloud through the keyhole: "Let me in! Quick! There is no time to lose! More snow like this, and the roads will all be blocked. Let me in! Do you hear? I am come to take the great stove."

August sprang erect, his fists doubled, his eyes blazing. "You shall never touch it!" he screamed. "You shall never touch it!"

"Who shall prevent us?" laughed a big man, who was a Bavarian, amused at the fierce little figure fronting him.

"I!" said August. "You shall never have it! You shall kill me first!"

"Strehla," said the big man, as August's father entered the room, "you have got a little mad dog here. Muzzle him."

One way or another, they did muzzle him. He fought like a little demon, and hit out right and left, and one of his blows gave the Bavarian a black eye. But he was soon mastered by four grown men, and his father flung him with no light hand out the door of the back entrance, and the buyers of the stately and beautiful stove set to work to pack it heedfully and carry it away.

When Dorothea stole out to look for August, he was nowhere in sight. She went back to little 'Gilda, who was ailing, and sobbed over the child, while the others stood looking on, dimly understanding that with Hirschvogel was going all the warmth of their bodies, all the light of their hearth.

Even their father now was sorry and ashamed; but two hundred florins seemed a big sum to him, and, after all, he thought the children could warm themselves quite as well at the black iron stove in the kitchen. Besides, whether he regretted it now or not, the work of the Nurnberg potter was sold irrevocably, and he had to stand still and see the men from Munich wrap it in manifold wrappings and bear it out into the snowy air to where an ox-cart stood waiting for it.

In another moment Hirschvogel was gone — gone forever and aye. August had stood still for a time, leaning, sick and faint from the violence that had been used to him, against the back wall of the house. The wall looked on a court where a well was, and the backs of other houses, and beyond them the spire of the Muntze Tower and the peaks of the mountains. Into the court an old neighbor hobbled for water, and, seeing the boy, said to him, "Child, is it true your father is selling the big painted stove?"

August nodded his head, then burst into a passion of tears.

"Well, for sure he is a fool," said the neighbor. "Heaven forgive me for calling him so before his own child! But the stove was worth a mint of money. I do remember in my young days, in old Anton's time (that was your great-grandfather, my lad), a stranger from Vienna saw it, and said that it was worth its weight in gold."

August's sobs went on their broken, impetuous course. "I loved it! I loved it!" he moaned. "I do not care what its value was. I loved it! *I loved it!*"

"You little simpleton!" said the old man, kindly. "But you are wiser than your father, when all's said. If sell it he must, he should have taken it to good Herr Steiner over at Spruez, who would have given him honest value. But no doubt they took him over his beer, ay, ay! But if I were you, I would do better than cry. I would go after it."

August raised his head, the tears raining down his cheeks.

"Go after it when you are bigger," said the neighbor, with a good-natured wish to cheer him up a little. "The world is a small thing, after all. I was a traveling clockmaker once upon a time, and I know that your stove will be safe enough whoever gets it; anything that can be sold for a round sum is always wrapped up in cotton wool by everybody. Ay, ay, don't cry so much; you will see your stove again someday."

Then the old man hobbled away to draw his brazen pail full of water at the well. August remained leaning against the wall; his head was buzzing and his heart fluttering with the new idea that had presented itself to his mind.

"Go after it," had said the old man. He thought, "Why not go with it?" He loved it better than anyone, even better than Dorothea; and he shrank from the thought of meeting his father again, his father who had sold Hirschvogel. He was by this time in that state of exaltation in which the impossible looks quite natural and commonplace.

His tears were still wet on his pale cheeks, but they had ceased to fall. He ran out of the courtyard by a little gate, and across to the huge Gothic porch of the church. From there he could watch unseen his father's house-door, at which were always hanging some blue-and-gray pitchers, such as are common and so picturesque in Austria, for a part of the house was let to a man who dealt in pottery. He hid himself in the grand portico, which he had so often passed through to go to Mass or Compline within, and presently his heart gave a great leap, for he saw the straw-enwrapped stove brought out and laid with infinite care on the bullock-dray. Two of the Bavarian men mounted beside it, and the sleigh-wagon slowly crept over the snow of the place — snow crisp and hard as stone. The noble old minster looked its grandest and most solemn, with its dark-gray stone and its vast archways, and its porch that was itself as big as many a church, and its strange gargoyles and lamp-irons black against the snow on its roof and on the pavement; but for once, August had no eyes for it: he watched only for his old friend.

Then he, a little unnoticeable figure enough, like a score of other boys in Hall, crept, unseen by any of his brothers or sisters, out of the porch and over the shelving uneven square, and followed in the wake of the dray. Its course lay toward the station of the railway, which is close to the salt-works, whose smoke at times sullies this part of clean little Hall, although it does not do very much damage. From Hall the iron road runs northward through glorious country to Salzburg, Vienna, Prague, Buda, and southward over the Brenner into Italy. Was Hirschvogel going north or south? This at least he would soon know.

⁓

August had often hung about the little station, watching the trains come and go and dive into the heart of the hills and vanish. No one said anything to him for idling about; people are kind-hearted and easy of temper in this pleasant land, and children and dogs are both happy there. He heard the Bavarians arguing and vociferating a great deal, and learned that they meant to go, too, and wanted to go with the great stove itself. But this they could not do, for neither could the stove go by a passenger-train nor they themselves go in a goods-train. So at length they insured their precious burden for a large sum, and consented to send it by a luggage-train that was to pass through Hall in half an hour.

The swift trains seldom deign to notice the existence of Hall at all. August heard, and a desperate resolve made itself up in his little mind. Where Hirschvogel went, he would go. He gave one terrible thought to Dorothea — poor, gentle Dorothea! — sitting in the cold at home, then set to work to execute his project.

How he managed it he never knew very clearly himself, but certain it is that when the goods-train from the north, that had come all the way from Linz on the Danube, moved out of Hall, August was hidden behind the stove in the great covered truck, and wedged, unseen and undreamed of by any human creature, amid the cases of wood-carving, of clocks and clock-work, of Vienna toys, of Turkish carpets, of Russian skins, of Hungarian wines, which shared the same abode as did his swathed and bound Hirschvogel. No doubt he was very naughty, but it never oc-curred to him that he was so. His whole mind and soul were ab-sorbed in the one entrancing idea: to follow his beloved friend and fire-king.

It was very dark in the closed truck, which had only a little window above the door; and it was crowded and had a strong smell in it from the Russian hides and the hams that were in it. But August was not frightened; he was close to Hirschvogel, and presently he meant to be closer still; for he meant to do nothing less than get inside Hirschvogel itself. Being a shrewd little boy, and having had by great luck two silver groschen in his breeches-pocket, which he had earned the day before by chopping wood, he had bought some bread and sausage at the station of a woman there who knew him, and who thought he was going out to his Uncle Joachim's chalet above Jenbach. This he had with him, and this he ate in the darkness and the lumbering, pounding, thundering noise which made him giddy, as never had he been in a train of any kind before. Still he ate, having had no breakfast, and being a child, and half a German, and not knowing at all how or when he ever would eat again.

When he had eaten, not as much as he wanted, but as much as he thought was prudent (for who could say when he would be able to buy anything more?), he set to work like a little mouse to make a hole in the withes of straw and hay that enveloped the stove. If it had been put in a packing-case, he would have been defeated at the onset. As it was, he gnawed, and nibbled, and pulled, and pushed, just as a mouse would have done, making his hole where he guessed that the opening of the stove was — the opening through which he had so often thrust the big oak logs to feed it. No one disturbed him; the heavy train went lumbering on and on, and he saw nothing at all of the beautiful mountains, and shining waters, and great forests through which he was being carried.

He was hard at work getting through the straw and hay and twisted ropes; and get through them at last he did, and found the door of the stove, which he knew so well, and which was quite large enough for a child of his age to slip through, and it was this that he had counted upon doing. Slip through he did, as he had often done at home for fun, and curled himself up there to see if he could anyhow remain during many hours. He found that he could; air came in through the brass fret-work of the stove; and with admirable caution in such a little fellow, he leaned out, drew the hay and straw together, and rearranged the ropes, so that no one could ever have dreamed a little mouse had been at them. Then he curled himself up again, this time more like a dormouse than anything else; and, being safe inside his dear Hirschvogel and intensely cold, he went fast asleep as if he were in his own bed at home with Albrecht and Christof on either side of him.

The train lumbered on, stopping often and long, as the habit of goods-trains is, sweeping the snow away with its cow-switcher, and rumbling through the deep heart of the mountains, with its lamps aglow like the eyes of a dog in a night of frost. The train rolled on in its heavy, slow fashion, and the child slept soundly for a long while. When he did awaken, it was quite dark outside in the land; he could not see, and of course he was in absolute darkness; and for a while he was sorely frightened, and trembled terribly, and sobbed in a quiet heart-broken fashion, thinking of them all at home. Poor Dorothea! How anxious she would be! How she would run over the town and walk up to grandfather's at Dorf Ampas, and perhaps even send over to Jenbach, thinking he had taken refuge with Uncle Joachim!

His conscience smote him for the sorrow he must be even then causing to his gentle sister; but it never occurred to him to try to go back. If he once were to lose sight of Hirschvogel, how could he ever hope to find it again? How could he ever know whither it had gone — north, south, east, or west? The old neighbor had said that the world was small; but August knew at least that it must have a great many places in it; he had seen that himself on the maps on his schoolhouse walls.

Almost any other little boy would, I think, have been frightened out of his wits at the position in which he found himself; but August was brave, and he had a firm belief that God and Hirschvogel would take care of him. The master-potter of Nurnberg was always present to his mind, a kindly, benign, and gracious spirit, dwelling manifestly in that porcelain tower whereof he had been the maker. A droll fancy, you say? But every child with a soul in him has quite as quaint fancies as this one was of August's. So he got over his terror and his sobbing both, although he was so utterly in the dark. He did not feel cramped at all, because the stove was so large, and air he had in plenty, as it came through the fret-work running 'round the top.

He was hungry again, and again nibbled with prudence at his loaf and his sausage. He could not at all tell the hour. Every time the train stopped and he heard the banging, stamping, shouting, and jangling of chains that went on, his heart seemed to jump up into his mouth. If they should find him out! Sometimes porters came and took away this case and the other, a sack here, a bale there, now a big bag, now a dead chamois. Every time the men trampled near him, and swore at each other, and banged this and that to and fro, he was so frightened that his very breath seemed to stop. When they came to lift the stove out, would they find him? And if they did find him, would they kill him? That was what he kept thinking of all the way, all through the dark hours, which seemed without end.

The goods-trains are usually very slow, and are many days doing what a quick train does in a few hours. This one was quicker than most, because it was bearing goods to the King of Bavaria; still, it took all the short winter's day and the long winter's night and half another day to go over ground that the mail-trains cover in a forenoon. It passed great armored Kuffstein standing across the beautiful and solemn gorge, denying the right of way to all the foes of Austria. It passed twelve hours later, after lying by in out-of-the-way stations, pretty Rosenheim, that marks the border of Bavaria.

And here the Nurnberg stove, with August inside it, was lifted out heedfully and set under a covered way. When it was lifted out, the boy had hard work to keep in his screams; he was tossed to and fro as the men lifted the huge thing, and the earthenware walls of his beloved fire-king were not cushions of down. However, although they swore and grumbled at the weight of it, they never suspected that a living child was inside it, and they carried it out onto the platform and set it down under the roof of the goods-shed. There it passed the rest of the night and all the next morning, and August was all the while within it.

The winds of early winter sweep bitterly over Rosenheim, and all the vast Bavarian plain was one white sheet of snow. If there had not been whole armies of men at work always clearing the iron rails of the snow, no trains could ever have run at all. Happily for August, the thick wrappings in which the stove was enveloped and the stoutness of its own make screened him from the cold, of which, else, he must have died — frozen.

He had still some of his loaf, and a little — a very little — of his sausage. What he did begin to suffer from was thirst; and this frightened him almost more than anything else, for Dorothea had read aloud to them one night a story of the tortures some wrecked men had endured because they could not find any water but the salt sea. It was many hours since he had last taken a drink from the wooden spout of their old pump, which brought them the sparkling, ice-cold water of the hills.

But, fortunately for him, the stove, having been marked and registered as "fragile and valuable," was not treated quite like a mere bale of goods, and the Rosenheim station-master, who knew its consignees, resolved to send it on by a passenger-train that would leave there at daybreak. And when this train went out, in it, among piles of luggage belonging to other travelers, to Vienna, Prague, Buda-Pesth, and Salzburg, was August, still undiscovered, still doubled up like a mole in the winter under the grass.

Those words "fragile and valuable" had made the men lift Hirschvogel gently and with care. He had begun to get used to his prison, and a little used to the incessant pounding and jumbling and rattling and shaking with which modern travel is always accompanied, although modern invention does deem itself so mightily clever.

All in the dark he was, and he was terribly thirsty; but he kept feeling the earthenware sides of the Nurnberg giant and saying softly, "Take care of me; oh, take care of me, dear Hirschvogel!" He did not say, "Take me back," for now that he was fairly out in the world, he wished to see a little of it.

He began to think that they must have been all over the world in all this time that the rolling and roaring and hissing and jangling had been about his ears; shut up in the dark, he began to remember all the tales that had been told in Yule around the fire at his grandfather's good house at Dorf, of gnomes and elves and subterranean terrors, and the Erl King riding on the black horse of night, and — and — and he began to sob and to tremble again, and this time did scream outright. But the steam was screaming itself so loudly that no one, had there been anyone nigh, would have heard him; and in another minute or so, the train stopped with a jar and a jerk, and he in his cage could hear men crying aloud, "Muenchen! Muenchen!"

Then he knew enough of geography to know that he was in the heart of Bavaria. He had had an uncle killed in the Bayerischenwald by the Bavarian forest guards, when in the excitement of hunting a black bear he had overpassed the limits of the Tyrol frontier. That fate of his kinsman, a gallant young chamois-hunter who had taught him to handle a trigger and load a muzzle, made the very name of Bavaria a terror to August.

"It is Bavaria! It is Bavaria!" he sobbed to the stove; but the stove said nothing to him; it had no fire in it. A stove can no more speak without fire than a man can see without light. Give it fire, and it will sing to you, tell tales to you, offer you in return all the sympathy you ask.

"It is Bavaria!" sobbed August, for it is always a name of dread augury to the Tyroleans, by reason of those bitter struggles and midnight shots and untimely deaths which come from those meetings of jaeger and hunter in the Bayerischenwald.

But the train stopped. Munich was reached, and August, hot and cold by turns, and shaking like a little aspen-leaf, felt himself once more carried out on the shoulders of men, rolled along on a truck, and finally set down, where he knew not; only he knew he was thirsty — so thirsty! If only he could have reached his hand out and scooped up a little snow!

He thought he had been moved on this truck many miles, but in truth, the stove had been taken only from the railway-station to a shop in the Marienplatz.

Fortunately, the stove was always set upright on its four gilded feet, an injunction to that effect having been affixed to its written label, and on its gilded feet it stood now in the small dark curiosity-shop of one Hans Rhilfer.

"I shall not unpack it until Anton comes," he heard a man's voice say; and then he heard a key grate in a lock, and by the unbroken stillness that ensued, he concluded he was alone, and ventured to peep through the straw and hay.

What he saw was a small square room filled with pots and pans, pictures, carvings, old blue jugs, old steel armor, shields, daggers,

Chinese idols, Vienna china, Turkish rugs, and all the art lumber and fabricated rubbish of a *bric-a-brac* dealer's.

It seemed a wonderful place to him; but, oh! was there one drop of water in it all? That was his single thought; for his tongue was parching, and his throat felt on fire, and his chest began to be dry and choked as with dust. There was not a drop of water, but there was a lattice window grated, and beyond the window was a wide stone ledge covered with snow. August cast one look at the locked door, darted out of his hiding-place, ran and opened the window, crammed the snow into his mouth again and again, and then flew back into the stove, drew the hay and straw over the place he had entered by, tied the cords, and shut the brass door down on himself. He had brought some big icicles in with him, and by them his thirst was finally, if only temporarily, quenched. Then he sat still in the bottom of the stove, listening intently, wide awake, and once more recovering his natural boldness.

The thought of Dorothea kept nipping his heart and his con-science with a hard squeeze now and then; but he thought to him-self, "If I can take her back Hirschvogel, then how pleased she will be, and how little 'Gilda will clap her hands!"

He was not at all selfish in his love for Hirschvogel: he wanted it for them all at home quite as much as for himself. There was at the bottom of his mind a kind of ache of shame that his father — his own father — should have stripped their hearth and sold their honor thus.

A robin had been perched upon a stone griffin sculptured on a house-eave near. August had felt for the crumbs of his loaf in his pocket, and had thrown them to the little bird sitting so easily on the frozen snow. In the darkness where he was, he now heard a lit-tle song, made faint by the stove-wall and the window-glass that was between him and it, but still distinct and exquisitely sweet. It was the robin, singing after feeding on the crumbs.

August, as he heard, burst into tears. He thought of Dorothea, who every morning threw out some grain or some bread on the snow before the church. "What use is it going *there*," she said, "if we forget the sweetest creatures God has made?" Poor Dorothea! Poor, good, tender, much-burdened little soul! He thought of her until his tears ran like rain. Yet it never once occurred to him to dream of going home. Hirschvogel was here.

⌒

Presently the key turned in the lock of the door, and he heard heavy footsteps and the voice of the man who had said to his father, "You have a little mad dog. Muzzle him!" The voice said, "Ay, ay, you have called me a fool many times. Now you shall see what I have gotten for two hundred dirty florins. *Potztausend!* Never did *you* do such a stroke of work."

Then the other voice grumbled and swore, and the steps of the two men approached more closely, and the heart of the child went *pit-a-pat, pit-a-pat*, as a mouse's does when it is on the top of a cheese and hears a housemaid's broom sweeping near. They began to strip the stove of its wrappings; that he could tell by the noise they made with the hay and the straw. Soon they had stripped it wholly; that, too, he knew by the oaths and exclamations of wonder and surprise and rapture that broke from the man who had not seen it before.

"A right royal thing! A wonderful and never-to-be-rivaled thing! Grander than the great stove of Hohen-Salzburg! Sublime! Magnificent! Matchless!"

So the epithets ran on in thick guttural voices, diffusing a smell of lager-beer so strong as they spoke that it reached August crouching in his stronghold. If they should open the door of the stove! That was his frantic fear. If they should open it, it would be all over with him. They would drag him out; most likely they would kill him, he thought, as his mother's young brother had been killed in the Wald.

The perspiration rolled off his forehead in his agony; but he had control enough over himself to keep quiet, and after standing by the Nurnberg master's work for nigh an hour, praising, marveling, and expatiating in the lengthy German tongue, the men moved to a little distance and began talking of sums of money and divided profits, of which discourse he could make out no meaning. All he could make out was that the name of the king — the king — the king came over very often in their arguments. He fancied at times they quarreled, for they swore lustily and their voices rose hoarse and high.

But after a while, they seemed to pacify each other and agree to something, and were in great glee, and so in these merry spirits came and slapped the luminous sides of stately Hirschvogel, and shouted to it, "Old Mumchance, you have brought us rare good luck! To think you were smoking in a silly fool of a salt-baker's kitchen all these years!"

Then inside the stove August jumped up, with flaming cheeks and clinching hands, and was almost on the point of shouting out to them that they were the thieves and should say no evil of his father, when he remembered, just in time, that to breathe a word or make a sound was to bring ruin on himself and sever him forever from Hirschvogel. So he kept still, and the men barred the shutters of the little lattice and went out by the door, double-locking it after them.

He had made out from their talk that they were going to show Hirschvogel to some great person; therefore, he kept quite still and dared not move. Muffled sounds came to him through the shutters from the streets below: the rolling of wheels, the clanging of church-bells, and bursts of that military music which is so seldom silent in the streets of Munich.

An hour perhaps passed by; sounds of steps on the stairs kept him in perpetual apprehension. In the intensity of his anxiety, he forgot that he was hungry and many miles away from cheerful, Old World little Hall, lying by the clear gray river-water, with the ramparts of the mountains all around.

Presently the door opened again sharply. He could hear the two dealers' voices murmuring unctuous words, in which *honor, gratitude*, and many fine long noble titles played the chief parts. The voice of another person, more clear and refined than theirs, answered them curtly, and then, close by the Nurnberg stove and the boy's ear, ejaculated a single *"Wunderschoen!"*

August almost lost his terror for himself in his thrill of pride at his beloved Hirschvogel being thus admired in the great city. He thought the master-potter must be glad too.

"Wunderschoen!" exclaimed the stranger a second time, and then examined the stove in all its parts, read all its mottoes, gazed long on all its devices. "It must have been made for the Emperor Maximilian," he said at last; and the poor little boy, meanwhile, within, was "hugged up into nothing," as you children say, dreading that every moment he would open the stove. And open it truly he did, and examined the brass-work of the door; but inside it was so dark that crouching August passed unnoticed, screwed up into a ball like a hedgehog as he was.

The gentleman shut the door at length, without having seen anything strange inside it; and then he talked long and low with the tradesmen, and, as his accent was different from that which August was used to, the child could distinguish little that he said, except the name of the king and the word *gulden* again and again.

After a while, he went away, one of the dealers accompanying him, one of them lingering behind to bar up the shutters. Then this one also withdrew again, double-locking the door.

The poor little hedgehog uncurled itself and dared to breathe aloud. What time was it? Late in the day, he thought, for to accompany the stranger they had lighted a lamp; he had heard the scratch of the match, and through the brass fret-work had seen the lines of light. He would have to pass the night here; that was certain. He and Hirschvogel were locked in, but at least they were together.

If only he could have had something to eat! He thought with a pang of how, at this hour at home, they ate the sweet soup, sometimes with apples in it from Aunt Maila's farm orchard, and sang together, and listened to Dorothea's reading of little tales, and basked in the glow and delight that had beamed on them from the great Nurnberg fire-king.

"Oh, poor, poor little 'Gilda! What is she doing without the dear Hirschvogel?" he thought. Poor little 'Gilda! She had only now the black iron stove of the ugly little kitchen.

Oh, how cruel of Father! August could not bear to hear the dealers blame or laugh at his father, but he did feel that it had been so, so cruel to sell Hirschvogel. The mere memory of all those long winter evenings, when they had all closed around it, and roasted chestnuts or crab-apples in it, and listened to the howling of the wind and the deep sound of the church-bells, and tried very much to make each other believe that the wolves still came down from the mountains into the streets of Hall, and were that very minute growling at the house-door — all this memory coming on him with the sound of the city bells, and the knowledge that night drew near upon him so completely, being added to his hunger and his fear, so overcame him that he burst out crying for the fiftieth time since he had been inside the stove, and felt that he would starve to death, and wondered dreamily if Hirschvogel would care.

Yes, he was sure Hirschvogel would care. Had he not decked it all summer long with Alpine roses and edelweiss and heaths and made it sweet with thyme and honeysuckle and great garden-lilies? Had he ever forgotten when Santa Claus came to make it its crown of holly and ivy and wreathe it all around?

"Oh, shelter me; save me; take care of me!" he prayed to the old fire-king, and forgot, poor little man, that he had come on this wild-goose chase northward to save and take care of Hirschvogel!

After a time, he dropped asleep, as children can do when they weep, and little robust hill-born boys most surely do, be they where they may. It was not very cold in this lumber-room; it was tightly shut up, and very full of things, and at the back of it were the hot pipes of an adjacent house, where a great deal of fuel was burned. Moreover, August's clothes were warm ones, and his blood was young. So he was not cold, even though Munich is terribly cold in the nights of December; and he slept on and on — which was a comfort to him, for he forgot his woes, and his perils, and his hunger, for a time.

Midnight was once more chiming from all the brazen tongues of the city when he awoke, and, all being still around him, he ventured to put his head out of the brass door of the stove to see why such a strange bright light was around him. It was a very strange and brilliant light indeed; and yet, what is perhaps still stranger, it did not frighten or amaze him, nor did what he saw alarm him either, and yet I think it would have done you or me. For what he saw was nothing less than all the *bric-a-brac* in motion.

A big jug, an Apostel-Krug, of Kruessen, was solemnly dancing a minuet with a plump Faenza jar; a tall Dutch clock was going through a gavotte with a spindle-legged ancient chair; a very droll porcelain figure of Littenhausen was bowing to a very stiff soldier in *terre cuite* of Ulm; an old violin of Cremona was playing itself, and an odd little shrill plaintive music that thought itself merry came from a painted spinet covered with faded roses; some gilt Spanish leather had got up on the wall and laughed; a Dresden mirror was tripping about, crowned with flowers, and a Japanese bonze was riding along on a griffin; a slim Venetian rapier had come to blows with a stout Ferrara sabre, all about a little pale-faced chit of a damsel in white Nymphenburg china; and a portly Franconian pitcher in *grès gris* was calling aloud, "Oh, these Italians! Always at feud!" But nobody listened to him at all.

A great number of little Dresden cups and saucers were all skipping and waltzing; the teapots, with their broad round faces, were spinning their own lids like teetotums; the high-backed gilded chairs were having a game of cards together; and a little Saxe poodle, with a blue ribbon at its throat, was running from one to another, while a yellow cat of Cornelis Lachtleven's rode about on a Delft horse in blue pottery of 1489.

Meanwhile the brilliant light shed on the scene came from three silver candelabra, even though they had no candles set up in them; and, what is the greatest miracle of all, August looked on at these mad freaks and felt no sensation of wonder! He only, as he heard the violin and the spinet playing, felt an irresistible desire to dance too.

No doubt his face said what he wished; for a lovely little lady, all in pink and gold and white, with powdered hair, and high-heeled shoes, and all made of the very finest and fairest Meissen china, tripped up to him, and smiled, and gave him her hand, and led him out to a minuet. And he danced it perfectly — poor little August in his thick, clumsy shoes, and his thick, clumsy sheepskin jacket, and his rough homespun linen, and his broad Tyrolean hat! He must have danced it perfectly, this dance of kings and queens in days when crowns were duly honored, for the lovely lady always smiled benignly and never scolded him at all, and danced so divinely herself to the stately measures the spinet was playing that

August could not take his eyes off her until, their minuet ended, she sat down on her own white-and-gold bracket.

"I am the Princess of Saxe-Royale," she said to him, with a benignant smile. "And you have got through that minuet very fairly."

Then he ventured to say to her, "Madame my princess, could you tell me kindly why some of the figures and furniture dance and speak, and some lie up in a corner like lumber? It does make me curious. Is it rude to ask?" For it greatly puzzled him why, when some of the *bric-a-brac* was all full of life and motion, some was quite still and had not a single thrill in it.

"My dear child," said the powdered lady, "is it possible that you do not know the reason? Why, those silent, dull things are *imitation!*" This she said with so much decision that she evidently considered it a condensed but complete answer.

"Imitation?" repeated August, timidly, not understanding.

"Of course! Lies, falsehoods, fabrications!" said the princess in pink shoes, very vivaciously. "They only *pretend* to be what we *are!* They never wake up; how can they? No imitation ever had any soul in it yet."

"Oh!" said August, humbly, not even sure that he understood entirely yet. He looked at Hirschvogel. Surely it had a royal soul within it. Would it not wake up and speak? Oh dear! How he longed to hear the voice of his fire-king! And he began to forget that he stood by a lady who sat upon a pedestal of gold-and-white china, with the year 1746 cut on it, and the Meissen mark.

"What will you be when you are a man?" said the little lady, sharply, for her black eyes were quick although her red lips were smiling. "Will you work for the *Koenigliche Porcellan-Manufactur,* like my great dead Kandler?"

"I have never thought," said August, stammering. "At least — that is — I do wish — I do hope to be a painter, as was Master Augustin Hirschvogel at Nurnberg."

"Bravo!" said all the real *bric-a-brac* in one breath, and the two Italian rapiers left off fighting to cry, *"Benone!"* For there is not a bit of true *bric-a-brac* in all Europe that does not know the names of the mighty masters. August felt quite pleased to have won so much applause, and grew as red as the lady's shoes with bashful contentment.

"I knew all the Hirschvogels, from old Veit downward," said a fat *grès de Flandre* beer-jug. "I myself was made at Nurnberg." And he bowed to the great stove very politely, taking off his own silver hat — I mean lid — with a courtly sweep that he could scarcely have learned from burgomasters.

The stove, however, was silent, and a sickening suspicion (for what is such heart-break as a suspicion of what we love?) came through the mind of August: *Was Hirschvogel only imitation?*

"No, no, no, no!" he said to himself, stoutly. Even though Hirschvogel never stirred, never spoke, yet would he keep all faith in it! After all their happy years together, after all the nights of warmth and joy he owed it, should he doubt his own friend and hero, whose gilt lion's feet he had kissed in his babyhood? "No, no, no, no!" he said, again, with so much emphasis that the Lady of Meissen looked sharply again at him.

"No," she said, with pretty disdain. "No, believe me, they may 'pretend' forever. They can never look like us! They imitate even our marks, but never can they look like the real thing, never can they *chassent de race.*"

"How should they?" said a bronze statuette of Vischer's. "They daub themselves green with verdigris, or sit out in the rain to get rusted; but green and rust are not *patina;* only the ages can give that!"

"And *my* imitations are all in primary colors, staring colors, hot as the colors of a hostelry's sign-board!" said the Lady of Meissen, with a shiver.

"Well, there is a *grès de Flandre* over there, who pretends to be a Hans Kraut, as I am," said the jug with the silver hat, pointing with his handle to a jug that lay prone on its side in a corner. "He has copied me as exactly as it is given to moderns to copy us. Almost he might be mistaken for me. But yet what a difference there is! How crude are his blues! How evidently done over the glaze are his black letters! He has tried to give himself my very twist; but what a lamentable exaggeration of that playful deviation in my lines which in his becomes actual deformity!"

"And look at that," said the gilt Cordovan leather, with a contemptuous glance at a broad piece of gilded leather spread out on a table. "They will sell him cheek by jowl with me, and give him my name. But look! *I* am overlaid with pure gold beaten thin as a film and laid on me in absolute honesty by worthy Diego de las Gorgias, worker in leather of lovely Cordova in the blessed reign of Ferdinand the Most Christian. *His* gilding is one part gold to eleven other parts of brass and rubbish, and it has been laid on him with a brush — a brush! — *pah!* Of course, he will be as black as a crock in a few years' time, while I am as bright as when I first was made, and, unless I am burned, as my Cordova burned its heretics, I shall shine on forever."

"They carve pear-wood because it is so soft, and dye it brown, and call it *me!*" said an old oak cabinet, with a chuckle. "That is not so painful; it does not vulgarize you so much as the cups they paint today and christen after *me!*" said a Carl Theodor cup subdued in hue, yet gorgeous as a jewel.

"Nothing can be so annoying as to see common gimcracks aping *me!*" interposed the princess in the pink shoes.

"They even steal my motto, although it is Scripture," said a *Trauerkrug* of Regensburg in black and white.

"And my own dots they put on plain English china creatures!" sighed the little white maid of Nymphenburg.

"And they sell hundreds and thousands of common china plates, calling them after me, and baking my saints and my legends in a muffle of today; it is blasphemy!" said a stout plate of Gubbio, which in its year of birth had seen the face of Maestro Giorgio.

"That is what is so terrible in these *bric-a-brac* places," said the princess of Meissen. "It brings one in contact with such low, imitative creatures; one really is safe nowhere nowadays unless under glass at the Louvre or South Kensington."

"And they get even there," sighed the *grès de Flandre*. "A terrible thing happened to a dear friend of mine, a *terre cuite* of Blasius (you know the *terres cuites* of Blasius date from 1560). Well, he was put under glass in a museum that shall be nameless, and he found himself set next to his own imitation, born and baked yesterday at Frankfort, and what think you the miserable creature said to him, with a grin? 'Old Pipe-clay' — that is what he called my friend — 'the fellow who bought *me* got just as much commission on me as the fellow who bought *you*, and that was all that *he* thought about. You know it is only the public money that goes!' And the horrid creature grinned again until he actually cracked himself. There is a Providence above all things, even museums."

"Providence might have interfered before, and saved the public money," said the little Meissen lady with the pink shoes.

"After all, does it matter?" said a Dutch jar of Haarlem. "All the shamming in the world will not *make* them us!"

"One does not like to be vulgarized," said the Lady of Meissen, angrily.

"My maker, the Krabbetje,[25] did not trouble his head about that," said the Haarlem jar, proudly. "The Krabbetje made me for the kitchen, the bright, clean, snow-white Dutch kitchen, well-nigh

---

[25] Jan Asselyn (1610-1652), called Krabbetje, "the Little Crab," master-potter of Delft and Haarlem.

three centuries ago, and now I am thought worthy the palace; yet I wish I were at home; yes, I wish I could see the good Dutch vrouw, and the shining canals, and the great green meadows dotted with the kine."

"Ah! if we could all go back to our makers!" sighed the Gubbio plate, thinking of Giorgio Andreoli and the glad and gracious days of the Renaissance: and somehow the words touched the frolic-some souls of the dancing jars, the spinning teapots, the chairs that were playing cards; and the violin stopped its merry music with a sob, and the spinet sighed — thinking of dead hands. Even the little Saxe poodle howled for a master forever lost; and only the swords went on quarreling, and made such a clattering noise that the Japanese bonze rode at them on his monster and knocked them both right over, and they lay straight and still, looking fool-ish, and the little Nymphenburg maid, although she was crying, smiled and almost laughed.

Then from where the great stove stood there came a solemn voice. All eyes turned upon Hirschvogel, and the heart of its little human comrade gave a great jump of joy.

"My friends," said that clear voice from the turret of Nurnberg faience, "I have listened to all you have said. There is too much talking among the Mortalities whom one of themselves has called the Windbags. Let us not be like them. I hear among men so much vain speech, so much precious breath and precious time wasted in empty boasts, foolish anger, useless reiteration, blatant argument, ignoble mouthings, that I have learned to deem speech a curse, laid on man to weaken and envenom all his undertakings. For over two hundred years I have never spoken myself: you, I hear, are not so reticent. I only speak now because one of you said a beautiful thing that touched me. If we all might but go back to our makers! Ah, yes! If we might! We were made in days when even men were true creatures, and so we, the work of their hands, were true too.

How to Tell Stories to Children

We, the begotten of ancient days, derive all the value in us from the fact that our makers wrought at us with zeal, with piety, with integrity, with faith — not to win fortunes or to glut a market, but to do nobly an honest thing and create for the honor of the Arts and God. I see amid you a little human thing who loves me, and in his own ignorant childish way loves Art. Now, I want him forever to remember this night and these words; to remember that we are what we are, and precious in the eyes of the world, because centuries ago those who were of single mind and of pure hand so created us, scorning sham and haste and counterfeit.

"Well do I recollect my master, Augustin Hirschvogel. He led a wise and blameless life, and wrought in loyalty and love, and made his time beautiful thereby, like one of his own rich, many-colored church casements, that told holy tales as the sun streamed through them. Ah, yes, my friends, to go back to our masters! That would be the best that could befall us. But they are gone, and even the perishable labors of their lives outlive them.

"For many, many years, I, once honored of emperors, dwelt in a humble house and warmed in successive winters three generations of little, cold, hungry children. When I warmed them, they forgot that they were hungry; they laughed and told tales, and slept at last about my feet. Then I knew that, humble as it had become, my lot was one that my master would have wished for me, and I was content. Sometimes a tired woman would creep up to me, and smile because she was near me, and point out my golden crown or my ruddy fruit to a baby in her arms. That was better than to stand in a great hall of a great city, cold and empty, even though wise men came to gaze and throngs of fools gaped, passing with flattering words.

"Where I go now I know not; but since I go from that humble house where they loved me, I shall be sad and alone. They pass so soon — those fleeting mortal lives! Only we endure — we, the things that the human brain creates. We can but bless them a little as they glide by. If we have done that, we have done what our masters wished. So, in us, our masters, being dead, yet may speak and live."

Then the voice sank away in silence, and a strange golden light that had shone on the great stove faded away; so also the light died down in the silver candelabra. A soft, pathetic melody stole gently through the room. It came from the old, old spinet that was covered with the faded roses. Then that sad, sighing music of a bygone day died too; the clocks of the city struck six of the morning; day was rising over the Bayerischenwald.

August awoke with a great start and found himself lying on the bare bricks of the floor of the chamber, and all the *bric-a-brac* was lying quite still all around. The pretty Lady of Meissen was motionless on her porcelain bracket, and the little Saxe poodle was quiet at her side. He rose slowly to his feet. He was very cold, but he was not sensible of it or of the hunger that was gnawing his little empty entrails. He was absorbed in the wondrous sight, in the wondrous sounds, that he had seen and heard.

All was dark around him. Was it still midnight, or had morning come? Morning, surely; for against the barred shutters he heard the tiny song of the robin. *Tramp, tramp,* too, came a heavy step up the stair. He had but a moment in which to scramble back into the interior of the great stove, when the door opened and the two dealers entered, bringing burning candles with them to see their way. August was scarcely conscious of danger more than he was of cold or hunger. A marvelous sense of courage, of security, of happiness was about him, like strong and gentle arms enfolding him and lifting him upward, upward, upward! Hirschvogel would defend him.

The dealers undid the shutters, scaring the red-breast away, and then tramped about in their heavy boots and chattered in contented voices, and began to wrap up the stove once more in all its straw and hay and cordage. It never once occurred to them to glance inside. Why should they look inside a stove that they had bought and were about to sell again for all its glorious beauty of exterior?

The child still did not feel afraid. A great exaltation had come to him; he was like one lifted up by his angels. Presently the two traders called up their porters, and the stove, heedfully swathed and wrapped and tended as though it were some sick prince going on a journey, was borne on the shoulders of six stout Bavarians down the stairs and out the door into the Marienplatz.

Even behind all those wrappings, August felt the icy bite of the intense cold of the outer air at dawn of a winter's day in Munich. The men moved the stove with exceeding gentleness and care, so that he had often been far more roughly shaken in his big brothers' arms than he was in his journey now; and although both hunger and thirst made themselves felt, being foes that will take no denial, he was still in that state of nervous exaltation which deadens all physical suffering and is at once a cordial and an opiate. He had heard Hirschvogel speak; that was enough.

The stout carriers tramped through the city, six of them, with the Nurnberg fire-castle on their brawny shoulders, and went right across Munich to the railway station, and August in the dark recognized all the ugly, jangling, pounding, roaring, hissing railway noises, and thought, despite his courage and excitement, "Will it be a *very* long journey?" For his stomach had at times an odd sinking sensation, and his head sadly often felt light and swimming. If it was a very, very long journey, he felt half-afraid that he would be dead or something bad before the end, and Hirschvogel would be so lonely. That was what he thought most about; not much about himself, and not much about Dorothea and the house at home. He was "high strung to high emprise," and could not look behind him.

Whether for a long or a short journey, whether for weal or woe, the stove with August still within it was once more hoisted up into a great van; but this time, it was not all alone, and the two dealers as well as the six porters were all with it. August in his darkness knew that; for he heard their voices.

The train glided away over the Bavarian plain southward; and he heard the men say something of Berg and the Wurm-See, but their German was strange to him, and he could not make out what these names meant. The train rolled on, with all its fume and fuss, and roar of steam, and stench of oil and burning coal. It had to go quietly and slowly on account of the snow that was falling and had fallen all night.

"He might have waited until he came to the city," grumbled one man to another. "What weather to stay on at Berg!" But who he was that stayed on at Berg, August could not make out at all. Although the men grumbled about the state of the roads and the season, they were hilarious and well content, for they laughed often and, when they swore, did so good-humoredly, and promised their porters fine presents at New Year; and August, like a shrewd little boy as he was, who even in the secluded Innthal had learned that money is the chief mover of men's mirth, thought to himself, with a terrible pang, "They have sold Hirschvogel for some great sum. They have sold him already!"

Then his heart grew faint and sick within him, for he knew very well that he must soon die, shut up without food and water thus; and what new owner of the great fire-palace would ever permit him to dwell in it? "Never mind; I *will* die," thought he, "and Hirschvogel will know it." Perhaps you think him a very foolish little fellow; but I do not. It is always good to be loyal and ready to endure to the end.

It is but an hour and a quarter that the train usually takes to pass from Munich to the Wurm-See or Lake of Starnberg; but this morning the journey was much slower, because the way was encumbered by snow. When it did reach Possenhofen and stop, and the Nurnberg stove was lifted out once more, August could see through the fret-work of the brass door, as the stove stood upright facing the lake, that this Wurm-See was a calm and noble piece of water, of great width, with low wooded banks and distant mountains, a peaceful, serene place, full of rest. It was now near ten o'clock. The sun had come forth; there was a clear gray sky hereabouts; the snow was not falling, although it lay white and smooth everywhere, down to the edge of the water, which before long would itself be ice.

Before he had time to get more than a glimpse of the green gliding surface, the stove was again lifted up and placed on a large boat that was in waiting — one of those very long and huge boats that the women in these parts use as laundries, and the men as timber-rafts. The stove, with much labor and much expenditure of time and care, was hoisted into this, and August would have grown sick and giddy with the heaving and falling if his big brothers had not long gotten him used to such tossing about, so that he was as much at ease head, as feet, downward.

The stove once in it safely with its guardians, the big boat moved across the lake to Leoni. How a little hamlet on a Bavarian lake got that Tuscan-sounding name I cannot tell; but Leoni it is. The big boat was a long time crossing: the lake here is about three miles broad, and these heavy barges are unwieldy and heavy to move, even though they are towed and tugged at from the shore.

"If we should be too late!" the two dealers muttered to each other, in agitation and alarm. "He said eleven o'clock."

"Who was he?" thought August. "The buyer, of course, of Hirschvogel."

The slow passage across the Wurm-See was accomplished at length. The lake was placid; there was a sweet calm in the air and on the water; there was a great deal of snow in the sky, although the sun was shining and gave a solemn hush to the atmosphere. Boats and one little steamer were going up and down. In the clear frosty light, the distant mountains of Zillerthal and the Algau Alps were visible. Market-people, cloaked and furred, went by on the water or on the banks. The deep woods of the shores were black and gray and brown.

Poor August could see nothing of a scene that would have delighted him; as the stove was now set, he could see only the old worm-eaten wood of the huge barge.

Presently they touched the pier at Leoni.

"Now, men, for a stout mile and half! You shall drink your reward at Christmastime," said one of the dealers to his porters, who, stout, strong men as they were, showed a disposition to grumble at their task. Encouraged by large promises, they shouldered sullenly the Nurnberg stove, grumbling again at its preposterous weight, but little dreaming that they carried within it a small, panting, trembling boy; for August began to tremble now that he was about to see the future owner of Hirschvogel.

"If he look a good, kind man," he thought, "I will beg him to let me stay with it."

The porters began their toilsome journey and moved off from the village pier. August could see nothing, for the brass door was over his head, and all that gleamed through it was the clear gray sky. He had been tilted onto his back, and if he had not been a little mountaineer, used to hanging head-downward over crevasses, and, moreover, seasoned to rough treatment by the hunters and guides of the hills and the salt-workers in the town, he would have been made ill and sick by the bruising and shaking and many changes of position to which he had been subjected.

The way the men took was a mile and a half in length, but the road was heavy with snow, and the burden they bore was heavier still. The dealers cheered them on, swore at them, and praised them in one breath; besought them and reiterated their splendid promises, for a clock was striking eleven, and they had been ordered to reach their destination at that hour, and, although the air was so cold, the heat-drops rolled off their foreheads as they walked, they were so frightened at being late.

But the porters would not budge a foot quicker than they chose, and as they were not poor four-footed carriers, their employers dared not thrash them, although most willingly would they have done so. The road seemed terribly long to the anxious tradesmen, to the plodding porters, and to the poor little man inside the stove, as he kept sinking and rising, sinking and rising, with each of their steps. Where they were going he had no idea, only after a very long time, he lost the sense of the fresh icy wind blowing on his face through the brass-work above, and felt by their movements beneath him that they were mounting steps or stairs.

Then he heard a great many different voices, but he could not understand what was being said. He felt that his bearers paused some time, then moved on and on again. Their feet went so softly he thought they must be moving on carpet, and as he felt a warm air come to him he concluded that he was in some heated chambers, for he was a clever little fellow, and could put two and two together, although he was so hungry and so thirsty and his empty stomach felt so strange.

They must have gone, he thought, through some very great number of rooms, for they walked so long on and on, on and on. At last the stove was set down again, and, happily for him, set so that his feet were downward. What he fancied was that he was in some museum, like that which he had seen in the city of Innsbruck. The voices he heard were very hushed, and the steps seemed to go away, far away, leaving him alone with Hirschvogel. He dared not look out, but he peeped through the brass work, and all he could see was a big carved lion's head in ivory, with a gold crown atop. It belonged to a velvet fauteuil, but he could not see the chair, only the ivory lion. There was a delicious fragrance in the air — a fragrance as of flowers.

"Only how can it be flowers?" thought August. "It is December!"

From afar off, as it seemed, there came a dreamy, exquisite music, as sweet as the spinet's had been, but so much fuller, so much richer, seeming as though a chorus of angels were singing all together. August ceased to think of the museum; he thought of Heaven.

"Are we gone to the Master?" he thought, remembering the words of Hirschvogel. All was so still around him; there was no sound anywhere except the sound of the far-off choral music. He did not know it, but he was in the royal castle of Berg, and the music he heard was the music of Wagner, who was playing in a distant room some of the motives of "Parsival."

Presently he heard a fresh step near him, and he heard a low voice say, close behind him, "So!" An exclamation no doubt, he thought, of admiration and wonder at the beauty of Hirschvogel. Then the same voice said, after a long pause, during which no doubt, as August thought, this newcomer was examining all the details of the wondrous fire-tower, "It was well bought; it is exceedingly beautiful! It is most undoubtedly the work of Augustin Hirschvogel."

Then the hand of the speaker turned the round handle of the brass door, and the fainting soul of the poor little prisoner within grew sick with fear. The handle turned, the door was slowly drawn open, someone bent down and looked in, and the same voice that he had heard in praise of its beauty called aloud, in surprise, "What is this in it? A live child!"

Then August, terrified beyond all self-control, and dominated by one master-passion, sprang out of the body of the stove and fell at the feet of the speaker. "Oh, let me stay! Pray, *meinherr*, let me stay!" he sobbed. "I have come all the way with Hirschvogel!"

Some gentlemen's hands seized him, not gently by any means, and their lips angrily muttered in his ear, "Little knave, peace! Be quiet! Hold your tongue! It is the king!"

They were about to drag him out of the august atmosphere as if he had been some venomous, dangerous beast come there to slay, but the voice he had heard speak of the stove said, in kind accents, "Poor little child! He is very young. Let him go. Let him speak to me."

The word of a king is law to his courtiers, so, sorely against their wish, the angry and astonished chamberlains let August slide out of their grasp, and he stood there in his little rough sheepskin coat and his thick, mud-covered boots, with his curling hair all in a tangle, in the midst of the most beautiful chamber he had ever dreamed of, and in the presence of a young man with a beautiful dark face, and eyes full of dreams and fire; and the young man said to him, "My child, how came you here, hidden in this stove? Be not afraid. Tell me the truth. I am the king."

August, in an instinct of homage, cast his great battered black hat with the tarnished gold tassels down on the floor of the room, and folded his little brown hands in supplication. He was too intensely in earnest to be in any way abashed; he was too lifted out of himself by his love for Hirschvogel to be conscious of any awe before any earthly majesty. He was only so glad — so glad it was the king. Kings were always kind; so the Tyrolese think, who love their lords.

"Oh, dear king," he said, with trembling entreaty in his faint little voice, "Hirschvogel was ours, and we have loved it all our lives; and father sold it. And when I saw that it did really go from us, then I said to myself I would go with it; and I have come all the way inside it. And last night, it spoke and said beautiful things. And I do pray you to let me live with it, and I will go out every morning and cut wood for it and you, if only you will let me stay beside it. No one ever has fed it with fuel but me since I grew big enough, and it loves me — it does indeed; it said so last night, and it said that it had been happier with us than if it were in any palace —"

And then his breath failed him, and as he lifted his little, eager, pale face to the young king's, great tears were falling down his cheeks.

Now, the king liked all poetic and uncommon things, and there was that in the child's face which pleased and touched him. He motioned to his gentlemen to leave the little boy alone.

"What is your name?" he asked him.

"I am August Strehla. My father is Karl Strehla. We live in Hall, in the Innthal; and Hirschvogel has been ours so long — so long!" His lips quivered with a broken sob.

"And have you truly traveled inside this stove all the way from Tyrol?"

"Yes," said August. "No one thought to look inside until you did."

The king laughed; then another view of the matter occurred to him. "Who bought the stove of your father?" he inquired.

"Traders of Munich," said August, who did not know that he ought not to have spoken to the king as to a simple citizen, and whose little brain was whirling and spinning dizzily around its one central idea.

"What sum did they pay your father, do you know?" asked the sovereign. "Two hundred florins," said August, with a great sigh of shame. "It was so much money, and he is so poor, and there are so many of us." The king turned to his gentlemen-in-waiting. "Did these dealers of Munich come with the stove?" He was answered in the affirmative. He desired them to be sought for and brought before him. As one of his chamberlains hastened on the errand, the monarch looked at August with compassion.

"You are very pale, little fellow. When did you eat last?"

"I had some bread and sausage with me. Yesterday afternoon I finished it."

"You would like to eat now?"

"If I might have a little water, I would be glad. My throat is very dry."

The king had water and wine brought for him, and cake also; but August, although he drank eagerly, could not swallow anything. His mind was in too great a tumult.

"May I stay with Hirschvogel? May I stay?" he said, with feverish agitation. "Wait a little," said the king and asked abruptly, "What do you wish to be when you are a man?"

"A painter. I wish to be what Hirschvogel was — I mean the master that made *my* Hirschvogel."

"I understand," said the king. Then the two dealers were brought into their sovereign's presence. They were so terribly alarmed, not being either so innocent or so ignorant as August was, that they were trembling as though they were being led to the slaughter, and they were so utterly astonished, too, at a child's having come all the way from Tyrol in the stove, as a gentleman of the court had just told them this child had done, that they could not tell what to say or where to look, and presented a very foolish aspect indeed.

"Did you buy this Nurnberg stove of this little boy's father for two hundred florins?" the king asked them; and his voice was no longer soft and kind as it had been when addressing the child, but very stern.

"Yes, your majesty," murmured the trembling traders.

"And how much did the gentleman who purchased it for me give to you?" "Two thousand ducats, your majesty," muttered the dealers, frightened out of their wits, and telling the truth in their fright. The gentleman was not present: he was a trusted counselor in art matters of the king's, and often made purchases for him. The king smiled a little, and said nothing. The gentleman had made out the price to him as eleven thousand ducats.

"You will give at once to this boy's father the two thousand gold ducats that you received, less the two hundred Austrian florins that you paid him," said the king to his humiliated and abject subjects. "You are great rogues. Be thankful you are not more greatly punished."

He dismissed them by a sign to his courtiers, and to one of these gave the mission of making the dealers of the Marienplatz disgorge their ill-gotten gains. August heard, and felt dazzled yet miserable. Two thousand gold Bavarian ducats for his father! Why, his father would never need to go anymore to the salt-baking! And yet, whether for ducats or for florins, Hirschvogel was sold just the same, and would the king let him stay with it? Would he?

"Oh, do! Oh, please do!" he murmured, joining his little brown weather-stained hands, and kneeling before the young monarch, who himself stood absorbed in painful thought, for the deception so basely practiced for the greedy sake of gain on him by a trusted counselor was bitter to him. He looked down on the child and, as he did so, smiled once more.

"Rise up, my little man," he said, in a kind voice. "Kneel only to your God. Will I let you stay with your Hirschvogel? Yes, I will; you shall stay at my court, and you shall be taught to be a painter — in oils or on porcelain as you will, and you must grow up worthily, and win all the laurels at our Schools of Art, and if, when you are twenty-one years old, you have done well and bravely, then I will give you your Nurnberg stove, or, if I am no more living, then those who reign after me shall do so. And now go away with this gentleman, and be not afraid, and you shall light a fire every morning in Hirschvogel, but you will not need to go out and cut the wood."

Then he smiled and stretched out his hand; the courtiers tried to make August understand that he ought to bow and touch it with his lips, but August could not understand that anyhow; he was too happy. He threw his two arms about the king's knees, and kissed his feet passionately.

Then he lost all sense of where he was, and fainted away from hunger, and tiredness, and emotion, and wondrous joy. As the darkness of his swoon closed in on him, he heard in his fancy the voice from Hirschvogel saying, "Let us be worthy of our maker!"

He is only a scholar yet, but he is a happy scholar, and promises to be a great man. Sometimes he goes back for a few days to Hall, where the gold ducats have made his father prosperous. In the old house-room, there is a large white porcelain stove of Munich, the king's gift to Dorothea and 'Gilda. And August never goes home without going into the great church and saying his thanks to God, who blessed his strange winter's journey in the Nurnberg stove.

As for his dream in the dealers' room that night, he will never admit that he did dream it; he still declares that he saw it all, and heard the voice of Hirschvogel. And who shall say that he did not? For what is the gift of the poet and the artist except to see the sights that others cannot see and to hear the sounds that others cannot hear?

Sophia Institute Press®

Sophia Institute® is a nonprofit institution that seeks to restore man's knowledge of eternal truth, including man's knowledge of his own nature, his relation to other persons, and his relation to God. Sophia Institute Press® serves this end in numerous ways: it publishes translations of foreign works to make them accessible for the first time to English-speaking readers; it brings out-of-print books back into print; and it publishes important new books that fulfill the ideals of Sophia Institute®. These books afford readers a rich source of the enduring wisdom of mankind.

Sophia Institute Press® makes these high-quality books available to the general public by using advanced technology and by soliciting donations to subsidize its general publishing costs. Your generosity can help Sophia Institute Press® to provide the public with editions of works containing the enduring wisdom of the ages. Please send your tax-deductible contribution to the address below. We welcome your questions, comments, and suggestions.

For your free catalog, call:
Toll-free: 1-800-888-9344

Sophia Institute Press®
Box 5284
Manchester, NH 03108
www.sophiainstitute.com